RELIGION IN EXILE
A Spiritual Homecoming

D0064008

RELIGION IN EXILE
A Spiritual Homecoming

Diarmuid O Murchu MSC

A CROSSROAD BOOK
THE CROSSROAD PUBLISHING COMPANY
NEW YORK

The Crossroad Publishing Company
370 Lexington Avenue
New York
NY 10017

Copyright © 2000 Diarmuid Ó Murchú

Printed in Malaysia

Library of Congress Catalog Card Number: 99–069474
ISBN: 8–8245–1841–1

1 2 3 4 5 6 7 8 9 10   04   03   02   01   00

Contents

Introduction

The institutionalized understanding of religion has led many Western academics to sterile conclusions about the function and role of religion within society.

Anna S. King

THIS IS A BOOK for those who like to befriend questions rather than for those who search for secure answers. It is aimed at seekers and explorers, for those who want to dig deeply; who, like contemporary scientists, want to know the mind of God; but, unlike them, do not wish to control it.

I am attempting a fresh appraisal of religion and its relevance in the world of our time. With as much honesty and integrity as I can muster, I try to confront the critical questions of our time, including the rather basic one: 'Do we need religion at all?'

Some people believe that religion is as old as humanity itself. Others believe that it was handed down to us by the Gods and therefore should never be tampered with. Religionists themselves tend to view it as a special endowment to be nurtured and preserved for posterity, while believers follow one or other religion because it helps them to live their lives with greater meaning and purpose.

People who are interested in religion, or follow one themselves, do not like mixing religions. You should stick to your own and not meddle around. If you do experiment you are likely to be labelled anything from a liberal, to a syncretist, to a relativist, maybe even an agnostic. And if you are into religion, the chances are that you will consider yours to be the more authentic version; or, like Christians, Jews and Muslims, the *only* true faith to follow.

And beyond all that, are those who don't follow any particular religion – estimated to be over half of humanity's six billion people. These include those who are simply not interested and see no reason why they should be, to those who feel quite indifferent (some of whom may have been quite religious once upon a time), to those who are vociferously opposed and make no secret about that fact.

All in all, it makes an interesting conglomerate, but also quite a confusing one. And many scholarly works on the subject offer little to clear up the muddle. Why? Because the scholars themselves tend to belong to one or other of the above categories and have their own vested interests. More significantly, they think, speak and write out of a dominant paradigm, which tends to view religion and all that relates to it as a specialised field of research in which non-religious specialists must not dabble. This is the great delusion, an ideology of imperialism, that characterises many fields of research in our world today.

To suggest that one is trying to undermine a delusion, particu-larly one with centuries of affirmation and research underpinning it, sounds like an arrogant, even a convoluted, claim. I doubt if any one human being, myself included, is adequately resourced for such a task. What one can offer is a critique of the underlying assumptions, approached from a fresh perspective.

Returning from exile

The central contention of this book is that we are a species living in exile, or in the language of Brueggemann (1993) a species that has largely forgotten its own story; that religion itself has contributed significantly to our alienated state; and, moreover, that religion thrives on perpetuating that state of exile and alienation.

In Chapter 4 I will offer a brief outline on how the theme of exile surfaces in all the major religions. I will suggest that it is more pronounced in the monotheistic religions than in the other great world faiths, that it is associated with the patriarchal understanding of God rather than with other notions of what divinity entails.

Part Two outlines my proposed solution to our human and religious predicament. As a people now living in exile, how do we come home to who we really are? What does the homecoming entail? And what are the skills we need – personal and cultural – to achieve that goal?

What I seek to reclaim, more than anything else, is our cosmic and planetary identity as a human species, an identity that situates us in an evolving world and grounds us in planetary earthiness – something that was happening for millions of years before religion ever evolved, and will continue to happen long after religion has outlived its usefulness.

The home-coming requires us to rediscover who we really are. We need to reconnect with (*re-member*) the great story itself – our emergence as a human species some five to ten million years ago. We need to reconnect with the power of the sacred at work in that ancient unfolding. It is precisely that ability to *re-connect* (which is what the word *religare* actually means) that is fundamental to all true religion, while it is the disconnections, distinctions and separations often created in the name of religion that reap so much bigotry and division in the world today.

Because of the encrustations of time and culture, we are not just about *reforming* religion; people have been attempting that for centuries, and with not much success. We are dealing with *revolution* – turning the whole thing on its head, getting back to basics, unearthing the deep questions and the soul-searching aspirations which have characterised us, humans, over many millennia, and now haunt us in our state of religious exile.

The purpose of this book is to help us come home to ourselves, in the wholeness of our being as personal-planetary-cosmic creatures, endowed with a deep hunger for meaning and love, for purpose and hope. The home-coming involves the painful process of shedding the baggage of centuries past, especially those religious traditions that offered *certainty* in the name of *place* or *word*. The *place* has become too congested and the *word* echoes ever more loudly as empty rhetoric.

The new angle I wish to offer is, in fact, a very old one. I will take the story of evolution itself, with the contemporary insights and understandings on how life has been unfolding before our eyes – for many millennia, and for several billennia before we humans evolved. When we explore that story, with the aid of a *multi-disciplinary hermeneutic* we begin to glimpse a very different landscape, a place we recognise as being strangely familiar, a place from which we have been exiled, a place many now wish to reclaim as their true spiritual home.

More than anything else, you need to bring an open heart and a questioning mind to the reading of this book. It is all about the *big* picture, not the punctuated developments that have cropped up here and there in the past 5,000 years – during which the formal religions came into being. Religion one time had the tools to keep us in creative balance; more accurately it provided the crucial cement for the societal bonding required by patriarchal power. It is the imminent collapse of the patriarchal system that is forcing us to re-think the whole meaning of religion and its spiritual significance in our lives.

Today, our pilgrimage is different. The wisdom that led us into the desert places, one-time home to heroic spiritual asceticism, today is a barren bosom no longer capable of nourishing or sustaining us. The journey back home requires a whole new set of skills and learnings. That is what we are about to explore in this book.

Part One

Deported Into Exile

— 1 —

Faith That No Longer Sustains

A book is the only place in which you can examine a fragile thought
without breaking it, or explore a dangerous idea without fearing it will
go off in your face. It is one of the few sources left where information
is served up without the silent black noise of a headline or the
hullabaloo of a commercial. It is one of the few havens remaining
where a person's mind can get both provocation and privacy.

Edward Morgan

IN WRITING MY FIRST BOOK, some twenty years ago, I came
across the above quote in an edition of *Reader's Digest*. Now, as
then, it speaks to my ongoing search, my questions and my hopes.
My pursuit then was the Religious Life into which I had made a
lifelong commitment. My concern today is *religion* itself and its
significance for the world of our time.

In noting this parallel, I am excitedly and painfully aware of the
huge gulf that now exists between those two realities. It was my
religion that brought me into the vowed life in the first place, and
sustained me within it for many years. Gradually that balance
shifted, not because of subversive forces from without, but primarily
from within that exploration into God that has characterised the
vowed life across all the religions and for much longer than history
can actually record.

That the commitment to the vowed life, itself based on religion,
could lead one into such a radical questioning of religion is largely
incomprehensible – to believers and non-believers alike. To some
it is shocking; to others, heretical or even blasphemous; and to
fellow-seekers after truth it is both a consolation and an affirmation
of their own deep yearnings.

My own faith journey includes many transitions in which new
ways of understanding superseded those which previously seemed
unalterable or, according to official teaching, could never change

and therefore should never be abandoned. I share some of those experiences to 'flesh out' the notions of *exile* and *home-coming*, the key concepts in the reflections and deliberations of subsequent chapters.

Fraying at the edges

Being the product of a strict Catholic upbringing, I inherited a faith based on fear of a judgemental God and unquestioned allegiance to a rather legalistic Church. The seams of that tapestry began to fray in my early twenties through a number of quite-by-chance incidents. I recall vividly the first time I read Louis Evely's *A Religion for Our Time* (1968), describing a God who could (and experientially did) enter into my human struggles and realities. That was a cherished moment of *home-coming*; *incarnation* meant something quite special from there on.

I next found myself enthralled by the writings of the then Jesuit priest, Ladislaus Boros, who in the 1960s and 1970s was one of several scholars pursuing a 'Christian anthropology'. The sacredness of God and the sacredness of my humanity, estranged because of my dualistic conditioning, now challenged me into what turned out to be a long, and at times arduous, process of personal and spiritual integration.

Then came something of a quantum leap! Much of my early formation in Religious Life was about abandoning and fleeing 'the world' in order to give myself more fully to God. Somehow or other that never made sense, and despite all my efforts to be a loyal and obedient 'child of God', I could not (and fortunately did not) let go of that deep suspicion that God also had a great deal to do with 'the world', that the world was not an exilic place of imperfection and temptation, but in some as-yet undiscovered way, was primary evidence to the grandeur and creativity of God.

I began reading the works of Teilhard de Chardin – despite the admonition from one of my theology lecturers that it was 'unsuitable reading material for a theology student' and could be 'misleading and dangerous'. Not only did Teilhard enable me to reclaim my sense of God's abundant and abiding presence in the whole of creation; it proved to be the catalyst whereby I consciously chose to abandon the rigidity and dogmatism of so much I had imbibed from my faith tradition.

Leaving behind a faith that does not nourish is one thing; reclaiming one that will is a much more difficult task, because the prevailing culture, especially within formal Church or religion, tends to protect the old values and can be quite harsh in its treatment of those whose spiritual growth leads them in other directions. Small but significant anecdotes proved important on my 'home-coming', two of which I cherish to this day.

The first was a train journey in Great Britain in which I had a long conversation with two British soldiers, both in their late teens. They were on their way to do service in Northern Ireland; two days later one of them was shot dead by *my* fellow-countrymen. The impact of that experience threw me into personal and religious confusion; almost like a Damascus Road insight I began to feel a sense of revulsion at my own deeply rooted prejudices and sectarian beliefs. It was like a violent expulsion from the womb – of the insular religiosity that had fuelled my spiritual values for over twenty years of my life. It was a painful moment of exilic estrangement!

Another outstanding 'conversion' happened a few months later when I joined an ecumenical group on a pilgrimage to Taizé in Southern France. I had been ordained a priest the previous year and was still full of that clerical fervour and zeal to do everything according to approved norms. It was a Sunday as we drove through central France; we stopped at the roadside and the group leader, an Anglican priest, invited me (and another clergyman) to concelebrate Eucharist with him. Everything in my training had told me that it would be an abomination to have participated, so I promptly declined. In fact, I felt quite resentful that he didn't know better and had the indiscretion to ask a Roman Catholic priest to do an outrageous thing like that!

It was probably the most restless religious experience I have ever had in my life. In my confusion and internal turmoil, I threw caution to the wind and received Communion at that same 'ecumenical' Eucharist, embarking subsequently on a guilt trip that lasted nearly a whole week, one made none the easier by the young lady in the group who asked me why I – a Catholic – received Holy Communion at a Protestant service. She seemed as baffled and confused as I was.

That episode proved to be a major turning-point in my life. On the one hand, it alerted me to the sensitivity and pain that accompanies so much ecumenical dialogue; but more significantly in my own faith journey, it alerted me to the ritualistic reductionism that has bedevilled so much religious dialogue and sacramental practice. Surely the Jesus who shared table-fellowship with tax-collectors, prostitutes, the sick, the blind and the lame, with all those excluded by the respectability of the day, never intended Eucharist to be reduced to a legalistic ritual, reserved for those belonging to one or other Christian denomination?

I quickly realised that a great deal of ecumenical dialogue – genuinely and sincerely motivated – was preoccupied with ecclesiastical niceties that meant little or nothing to the vast majority of believers. It fed the culture of exile rather than that of home-coming. I am even more convinced now that the so-called ecumenical movement thrives on an ideological diatribe that has little or no relevance to genuine faith and belief.

Multi-faith and beyond

It was largely my disillusionment with ecumenism that led me to explore multi-faith dialogue. This seemed to be a movement with more substance to it and and a wider global interconnectedness. I was quite impressed by Hans Kung's remark (made at a public lecture in London) that dialogue among the major religions would serve as a model for other forms of dialogue across many political, racial and ethnic divides.

It quickly became clear that this was yet another Christian initiative, pushing something that didn't, and still doesn't, have much appeal to the other religions. It also highlighted the salient imperialism I had long suspected in my own Christian tradition. While the slogan 'outside the Church there's no salvation' was no longer imposed on all and sundry, multi-faith dialogue sought to safeguard the superior nature of Christianity among the world religions. I had no problem claiming the uniqueness of Christianity for me as a Christian, but expecting Hindus, Buddhists or Muslims to appropriate something of the special revelation of God in Jesus Christ smacked more of Western imperialism than of theological integrity.

My journey in multi-faith dialogue took quite a different direction. Earlier studies in anthropology had opened me up to the thousands of years in which we humans had been grappling with religious questions. In fact, we had been doing it for some

70,000 years before the formal religions ever emerged. So why all the fuss about the formal religions? They are of very recent origin and from a spiritual point of view have not necessarily produced anything more wholesome or coherent than the spiritual development of previous millennia. In fact, there is substantial evidence to show that the religions contribute significantly to conflict, warfare and division, while validating gross exploitation of planet Earth in the name of the patriarchal conquering God. Religion, far from being a sacred reality meriting the highest respect and admiration, became a questionable entity, culminating in the disturbing suspicion that religion might be more of a *human* than a *divine* invention.

It was at this juncture that the distinction between religion and spirituality became crucially important for me, and has remained so ever since. I had now met so many people, from various cultures and social classes, who did not follow a particular religion, but whose hearts were clearly touched by a sense of the divine which impacted to varying degrees upon their daily lives, I could no longer ignore the work of God in the lives of 'non-believers'. As a psychologist, I had long been aware of the spiritual hunger which imbues the human psyche and manifests primarily in a persistent search for *meaning* in life.[1] Whereas religion was an inherited cultural wisdom, *spirituality* was an innate endowment.

We are born into the world as spiritual people, and ironically it seems that the existence of religion is largely responsible for inhibiting or even preventing people from taking a more direct ownership and responsibility for their spiritual selves. This is precisely the dilemma which I explore under the rubric of *exile* throughout the course of this book. We have so confused religion and spirituality that the former has seriously eroded the power of the latter and, as I shall argue in later chapters, that is precisely the spiritual alienation of our time, and the ultimate explanation for the culture of exile within which we are engulfed.

How that imbalance arose – historically and culturally – is an issue that continues to engage me experientially and intellectually. As outlined in a previous work, I believe the rise of patriarchy about 10,000 years ago is a major consideration. We are now unearthing significant anthropological and archaeological evidence indicating a widespread sense of belief – and an accompanying ethical system – in a divine *energy* which endowed the whole of creation and evolved co-creatively with the unfolding universe itself.

For many years now, I have been fascinated by Ice Age art, those various images, statues and inscriptions found in the caves of Southern France and Northern Spain about 150 years ago, and since then right across what was the populated world of paleolithic times (c. 40000 to 10000 BCE), stretching from Africa to Tasmania. For people in those ancient cultures, these were highly creative artifacts that proved, and still do, that our ancient ancestors were not just 'noble savages' but people endowed with creative potential proportionately every bit as real and expressive as we witness in the modern world.

I have followed with immense interest the debates about the religious significance of these ancient drawings, and particularly the suggestion that people for much of that ancient epoch may have worshipped God as a woman, later named as the Great Earth Mother Goddess. I experience a deep personal and spiritual resonance with this notion.

I am well aware of the controversy surrounding this view and the tendency of many (most?) scholars to dismiss the notion of Goddess as a lot of 'unfounded drivel'. In Appendix 1 I outline the current state of research. However one interprets that evidence, and that will vary for many years to come, I am in little doubt that the notion of the Goddess will continue to engage theology and spirituality well into the next millennium. It characterises a re-awakening in our time that speaks deeply to many people's experience.

A people deprived of our spiritual heritage

In more recent years, these discoveries have impregnated the spiritual landscape of my heart and mind. I don't believe anybody can engage with these realities without themselves being profoundly changed. Much of that change, while exciting and energising, has often left me feeling isolated and vulnerable – a person in *exile*!

One yearns to share this new story, but often there are no kindred spirits around (or, at least, so it seems); one feels a reckless sense of joy that wishes to abandon totally the ritualism and legalism of so much formal religion; one is haunted at times by a sense of rage and anger at those responsible for my education and formation into such a narrow academic understanding of life and faith; it is frightening to think how much energy, time and resources go into shielding us from the wonder of our universe and from engaging with the co-creative God who works so wonderfully within it!

Somewhere along the way, we humans have got it drastically wrong! We have virtually destroyed the mystery behind it all, which, in fact, is a mystery right in front of our eyes, if we could only trust the intuitions of our hearts and the probings of the imagination. And while not wishing to be dogmatic myself, I can't avoid the conclusion that it is during the very time that we describe as the *age of civilisation* (the past 3,000–5,000 years), that we have made the most serious mistakes.

I have always had a sense of revulsion about the theological claim that the revelation of the Christian faith is superior to any other form of wisdom humans have ever known; common sense alone indicates the warped ideology that underlies such a conviction. I have found it even more disturbing to see and hear people trying to persuade me and others that everything we humans did prior to 5,000 years ago was primitive, barbaric, illiterate and unenlightened. It is particularly sad to see theologians endorse these views, more or less suggesting that God was up to nothing good for the long aeons of divine creation!

All of which gives me the credentials to be a well-rounded heretic, by the standards of most, if not all, the great religions! What disturbs a lot of people is the awesomeness of my sense of God, and to many that feels very impersonal. Many people seem to have a need for a rather infantile image of God: 'little Jesus, meek and mild', or the carved image that ornates many a Hindu or Muslim home. We don't feel at home with an adult sense of God, very much the image suggested by the Covenantal relationship of the Jewish Scriptures or the New Reign of God (Basileia) proposed by Jesus.

Much more serious is the apparently compulsive need in all the religions to reduce God to an anthropocentric artifact (albeit a personal one) of the past few thousand years. The God whom contemporary cosmologists encounter (and often try to avoid), the God who has been co-creating for billennia right down to our own time, and presumably for billennia yet to come, gets little recognition in the formal religious systems of humankind. Even God ends up in exile!

That quality (and quantity) of religiosity that seeks to dampen our intellectual and spiritual curiosity – shielding us from our spiritual heritage – began to crumble when I started studying theology in the 1970s. Although the context was strictly Catholic, and the Church's official teaching was pursued consistently, the larger reality of life evoked deeper questions and pursued me into relating my theology with the experience of everyday life. At times this, too, was a confusing and frustrating task; but, aided by the few friends who did understand, and that quality of affirmation that comes from being touched by a deeper truth, theology eventually enabled me to break through the boundaries that limit, to the horizons that open us all to the creative mystery of life.

As I seek to unearth the deeper meaning of religion and its impact on our lives, theology continues to be a primary resource for questioning and exploration. Many times I return to St Anselm's simple but profound description that theology is about *faith seeking understanding*. Why, then, did we Christians try to restrict theology to the exclusive domain of Christian apologetics? Why does the truth on which theology works have to be exclusively reserved to the Christian Scriptures? The mystery within which we are all held, the mystery that awakens our theological hunger in the first place, belongs to the whole of life and, to me at least, it seems blasphemous that we should ever try to restrict it to human boundaries.

I draw hope and courage from the inspiring words of Walter Brueggemann (1993, p. 1):

> It is now clear to many of us . . . that we are in a quite new inter-pretative situation that constitutes something of an emergency. That emergency in interpretation is the result of a radical shift of categories of culture, for which interpreters of faith in the West have not been well prepared.

Now, more than ever, I believe theology is uniquely placed to grapple with the great questions of our age. To do that, however, theologians – and there is something of a theologian in each one of us (see Appendix 2) – have to drink from many wells, and the deeper they are, the better! Theology is very much about exploring the meaning of mystery from within the wisdom of our inherited tradition (cf. Kaufman, 1993). And this becomes one of the perennial theological and spiritual questions of our time: What do we mean by *tradition*?

Reclaiming our sacred tradition

I one time heard a preacher describe the birth of Jesus as 'the most important event in the history of humankind'. What 'history' was he alluding to? It is reasonable to assume that he was operating out of a widespread Christian belief that what really matters is what happened *after* the time of Jesus, and tragically that often means that we are largely ignorant about what happened throughout the many aeons prior to the Christian revelation.

Orthodox theology reinforces that same ideological ignorance in claiming that the fullness of revelation is in Jesus and that revelation ceases with the death of the last apostle. Nowadays, theologians strive to be more inclusive of the religious insights of the other great faiths and, subconsciously at least, extend their understanding of tradition back to (at least) 3000 BCE, when Hinduism first began to unfold.

This puts the theologian in quite a precarious space, with the great danger of being lured into a collusion with the patriarchal wisdom of our age which dates the rise of civilisation to about 5000 BCE. On everything that happened since then, we (humans) can exert a good measure of dominance and control, but back beyond that time we are unable to establish enough facts to know where exactly we stand with things. So, let's hold to what we can be certain about, what we can verify and prove and test out in laboratory conditions (whether scientific or ecclesiastical). And lest some maverick might like to stray into pre-civilisation times, let's deter him/her by highlighting the primitive, pre-logical, savage, pagan nature of that ancient reality. Thus, we close the door on our ancient past and leave its story to the ruminations of those marginalised scholars called anthropologists, ethnologists and cultural historians – whose research we won't take seriously because we already claim to have 'the fullness of truth'.

It is not just the theologian who has become stuck in this cultural and intellectual bottle-neck. In fact, theology, precisely because it cannot escape the global ambience of mystery, can wriggle its way out of this congested quagmire. It takes some courage and risk to do so (as many have discovered to their cost) but the pursuit of truth requires this of us. Not to do so condemns us and the theological enterprise to stillbirth.

The challenge to reclaim tradition is at the heart of the new paradigm shift taking place in the world today. Major cultural shifts in every age mobilise the resources and wisdom of the past to energise the quantum leap forward. The inherent wisdom of life itself – the planetary propensity for self-renewal (*autopoiesis*) – guarantees this process. We humans – especially throughout the patriarchal epoch – often try to hinder nature's propensity to evolve, but always to our own detriment. We can neither subvert nor arrest the will-to-life that God awakens within the co-creative process.

More than anything else, the new insights into cosmology – particularly those emerging in the last quarter of the twentieth century – provide pivotal information on what we need to incorporate into our understanding of tradition. We live in a universe in which our co-creative God has been overtly at work for at least fifteen billion years. We share in the creative expedition of our unfolding species for at least four million years; in fact, Mithen (1996, p. 17) dates the evolution of mind back to six million years ago. A tradition which fails to acknowledge and incorporate these 'timeless' unfoldings betrays the elegance and creativity of God and leaves us with a stilted and stultified vision of life, the root cause of our exile and alienation. And any theology which seeks to build merely on such foundations of recent millennia, from the very start, stands condemned as a form of atheism.

Theology and the Christian tradition

Once upon a time . . . it was easy to be a theologian! Easy, in the sense that you inherited a body of sacred wisdom, called the Scriptures, and you made yourself familiar with the long Christian tradition of scriptural exposition. After that, it was a case of regurgitating what you yourself had assimilated, opening up the deeper meanings of the inherited wisdom. Your task was to develop rather than question or interpret. After all, you are dealing primarily with God's own Word, divinely inspired and divinely bestowed. You take it at its face value, unpack its deeper meaning and unearth its application to daily living.

Once upon a time . . . in fact, right up to about 1960, the study of theology was exclusively *Christian* – even to this day the concept is not used in the other great religions; reserved to *male clerics* – since they alone were considered holy, wise and powerful enough to engage in 'divine' discourse; and engaging solely with *religious questions* – since all things outside religion belonged to the 'world' of ungodly secularism.

A gross exaggeration? Those among us familiar with religious and ecclesiastical matters prior to 1960 can identify with these realities. But being products of our time and culture, those of us educated prior to 1960 find it both emotionally and intellectually difficult to criticise that which we were expected to treat with unquestioned loyalty and the all too obvious threat of severe punishment if we chose to follow the questions that arose in our hearts.

1960 is an arbitrary date. In many spheres of learning and thought it marks an important threshold, one often characterised by belligerence and a spirit of outright revolt. Right across the earth, people were trying to throw off the shackles of centuries of slavery. I deliberately have chosen this word, and the reasons become apparent in subsequent chapters.

Whether we choose the 300-year backdrop of industrialisation with its utilitarian and functional control over every aspect of human and planetary life, or the 10,000-year epoch of patriarchy, with its insatiable masculine urge to 'conquer and control' (or a whole series of interpretative models situated between these two datings) is not immediately relevant. Probably, more to the point is the ability to acknowledge that we were undergoing a profound evolutionary shift, which in time may be perceived as being as momentous as the unprecedented outburst of cellular life in the Cambrian period. In other words, we were the recipients – or victims (depending on your understanding) – of a *transformation of creative energy* instigated not so much by humans as by the power of evolution itself, operating on a global scale.

Whatever the precise explanation – the desire for precision is itself a mechanism of the patriarchal will-to-control – power began to shift in a manner and to a degree that had not been known for many millennia. Initially, this instigated a climate of suspicion. We began to mistrust those whose word we had taken on trust for such a long time. Specialists became the primary target of this climate of suspicion. Did politicians really know what they were talking about? Was it appropriate to entrust your health care to a specialist called a doctor? If economists knew what they were doing, why was the world in such an economic mess? Are theologians talking on behalf of God or are they trying to play God themselves?

Might it not be the specialists themselves that have engineered the culture of exile?

From this climate of suspicion emerges a new quality of specialisation, one which feels more at home with questions than with answers, committed more to seeking rather than finding, engaging with the big picture of open horizons rather than the closed system of official boundaries. We are dealing here with a radical reversal, although it is not at all clear, even today, what we are seeking to reverse. Nor indeed does everybody agree that it is a task of reversal.

It is definitely a task of *recapitulation*, uncovering and reclaiming afresh ancient wisdom and understanding – often into prehistoric horizons, which in the pre-1960s era were almost inconceivable. More importantly, the exploration we are addressing involves a gigantic leap forward, which, increasingly, is being perceived and understood as an evolutionary shift, on which we humans are being carried along, for weal or for woe, depending – it would seem – on how aware we are of what is happening to us.

Beyond the climate of suspicion, is the call to a new sense of *participation*. Every human being has a right and a duty to that wisdom and learning which formerly was deemed to be the reserve of the specialist. And this is eminently true for the theologian. Theology claims to deal with ultimate questions on how God engages with us and our world. Consequently, *all* of us have something to say to that reality, since God works through, and is manifest in, every dimension of the created order. The theological task then is not about safeguarding *sacred boundaries* that the 'unworthy' or 'unlearned' should not transgress, but exploring *sacred horizons*, the holy ground on which God journeys with all created reality.

Why not revamp the old?

As I befriend these emerging questions of our time, intimating the probable decline of formal religion and the revival of spirituality as a central feature of our personal and planetary lives, I often find myself wanting to throw overboard most, if not all, of my inherited religious tradition. This also makes me impatient with, and at times cynical towards, those scholarly efforts that try to revamp the old so that we don't have to discard it. It often feels as if we must salvage the culture of exile and somehow transform it. My question is: But why not seek to outgrow it, even if that ultimately means abandoning it? Even contemporary theologians seem desperately concerned that we don't lose our past, that *continuity* is essential, that the tradition must somehow be preserved, albeit updated and worded afresh. And I ask: But why are we afraid to die to our past traditions? Why do they have to last for ever? Why do we consider so many of them to be above the provisional nature of all human inventions?

My dilemma is acutely felt when I read a work like Sandra Schneiders' *The Revelatory Text*, a study of contemporary biblical hermeneutics written with great lucidity, conviction and impeccable scholarly expertise. In the very last paragraph of the book, Schneiders (1991, p. 197) writes:

> Exclusiveness, domination, oppression and discrimination are embedded in the language and metaphors of our most sacred traditions. Ideology is pervasive and will not be exposed, recognized and repudiated except by incessant vigilance and courageous action.

I wonder why these words are not in the opening, instead of the closing, chapter of the book? Had they been written at the beginning and kept as a central focus right through, then I would expect a very different outcome. Instead of the painstaking (and genuinely motivated) effort to interpret afresh the language and metaphors of the Christian tradition, the author might be pushed to the realisation that they were invented in the first place to serve another purpose (namely, exclusiveness, domination, etc.) and consequently should now be discarded so that the deeper meaning of the tradition can be reborn afresh.

It also concerns me that this fine piece of scholarly work can be used as a type of academic collusion to maintain the *status quo* while giving the impression that we are modernising our faith tradition. It does provide a challenge to the *scholarly* world and its commitment to the study and transmission of faith and faith-values, but what has it to offer to the millions who are trying to make sense of faith in the contemporary world and for whom sacred texts, updated or otherwise, have little meaning or appeal? The scholars tend to accuse the spiritual seekers of being 'rootless' and reckless in throwing everything overboard, but surely it is quite a prophetic gesture to throw overboard that which has been largely about 'exclusiveness, domination, oppression and discrimination, etc.'.

I am myself the product of a biblical and theological tradition based on this painstaking quality of scholarship, and some of those same scholars have been, and continue to be, associates, whose friendship, support and challenge I deeply cherish. Without the grounding of that tradition, I would not be able to pursue the new horizons which this and my earlier books have explored. I am deeply indebted to that tradition. However, I must honestly admit that the tradition no longer nourishes nor sustains me; it is not 'big enough' for me. Nor does it resonate with the thousands of spiritual seekers I encounter in my daily life, some still affiliated to formal churches or religions, but most being people who have long outgrown the need for formal religion.

It is not a case of abandoning something precious and sacred; rather it is about following a call (or vocation) to work creatively with God and with people; a call, however, that invites me (and, apparently, millions of others) to grow beyond 'orthodoxy' in a way that does not eliminate everything that has gone before but in a way that assimilates the old into something that is essentially new.

Nor is it merely about *relativism*, the classical reaction from mainstream Churches and religious institutions, one that carries strong overtones of evangelical ideology. Patriarchal domination begets and breeds a quality and quantity of certitude. Specific ideas are construed to be certain, absolute and unquestioned, for example the divinity of Jesus. Any questioning of these ideas is quickly labelled as succumbing to *relativism*. As Brueggemann (1993, p. 10) suggests, the real threat is not relativism but that quality of dogmatic certitude that stymies deeper connection with the unfolding mystery: 'I regard relativism as less of a threat than objectivism, which I believe to be a very large threat among us precisely because it is such a deception.'

As a last desperate ploy, the spiritual seeker may be confronted with the choice of being within the Church or outside it. This is yet another dualism often used to label and categorise people, a subtle and at times devious way of exerting control over people's lives. It is a classical patriarchal ploy that needs to be exposed and denounced. As creatures of the universe and inhabitants of planet Earth, there are, in the eyes of God, no reserved places.

For most of our evolutionary story, we humans engaged with our planet, free of all those anthropocentric boundaries and divisions that the masculine will-to-power has put in place. The spiritual seekers of our time want all those barricades demolished, and while they continue to exist we'll either choose to ignore them or find subversive ways to circumvent them. We don't have any other choice if we are to come home to ourselves in the truth of our cosmic and planetary vocation.

Pushing the boundaries

We begin the theoretical reflections of this book by examining two of the dominant boundaries that mark off the space and experience of exile. I refer to the sacred traditions that focus on *place* and *word*. I wish to examine the undergirding of these two notions, along with the cultural and historical context out of which they have emerged.

Religion of the *place* attributes central (divine) importance to particular geographical places, such as Armistar, Jerusalem, Rome, or specific buildings considered essential to a particular religion, e.g. a church, temple, gurdvara, mosque, vihara. This quality of religion belongs primarily to the era of the Agricultural Revolution, with the focus on land or place; hence the significance of land to this day for the Jewish faith (the land of Israel), or for Catholicism (the *political* State of the Vatican in Rome).

Religion of the *word* seeks to preserve sacred story and legend, proclaiming the great deeds of the gods and their dealings with people. Many of these legends were committed to writing in what we Christians call 'Scriptures'. Subsequently, the sacred text assumed ideological weight whereby the words themselves were considered to be those of God (as Muslims interpret the Koran today), or observance of religious laws became the dominant expression of faithfulness to the land (as in the idea of the Torah as a portable Israel – see Davies, 1974, p. 219). All the religions have had a long epoch whereby *verbiage* (respectfully called 'preaching') has been used to hound people into fear and submission.

At this cultural moment, there is overwhelming evidence to suggest that those boundaries cannot hold the spiritual energy embodied in the religions. There are several cracks on the surface, the foundations are shaking and the threat of disintegration is all too apparent. The culture of exile is running out of steam.

Meanwhile, the guardians of the boundaries respond as they always did, as they were told they always should. They try to plaster over the fissures, plug the holes where water keeps seeping through and, most importantly of all, destroy the enemy whose external attack (e.g. Salman Rushdie) or internal disruption (the silenced theologians) allegedly caused the breakdown of the system in the first place.

And here we need to confront the great delusion: *nobody is causing the breakdown*, and it is a tragic waste of energy and resources playing such a futile defensive game. Religion is disintegrating because *it has served its purpose*. Its day is spent; it has become redundant. Seeking to preserve it serves no purpose other than the calcification of realities that were never intended to last in the first place. In fact the attempt at preservation is the greatest contradiction possible, guaranteeing the eventual annihilation of that which it seeks to preserve.

Religion today is rapidly outgrowing all its boundaries, and particularly the foundational ones of place and word. The water seeping through the cracks is highly symbolic: the wisdom is seeking to pour out and over into the vast universe of life, so that it can interpenetrate with other life-forms and befriend that new sense of *connectedness* and *interdependence* which seems to characterise the spiritual revival – the home-coming – following on the demise of the old order.

I'd like to conclude the reflections of this chapter with what I consider to be a parable for our time. In 1953, the British explorer and scientist, Edmund Hillary, reached the top of Mount Everest. His guide for the expedition was a Buddhist monk, Tenzing Norgay. On reaching the summit, Hillary thrust the British flag (the Union Jack) deep into the snow-capped peak and proclaimed in loud exuberance that he had conquered the mountain. Meanwhile, his companion knelt knee-deep in the snow and prayed for forgiveness from the gods of the mountain for having disturbed their peace.

The two concepts which will recur throughout the pages of this book – *exile* and *home-coming* – are poignantly illustrated in this story. Trying to conquer territories without, never satisfies the deep, inner search for meaning: it only exacerbates our sense of exile and estrangement. It is precisely when we acknowledge the deep 'withinness' of every thing in life – assuredly mountains have their inner sacredness which the religions have long suspected (see Lane, 1998) – then we know what home-coming is all about.

— 2 —

Religion and the Sacred Place

We mostly are scribes maintaining the order of the day. We mostly are appreciated by and paid by people who like it the way it is, who do not sense our exile and resist discerning it, who do not yearn for a home-coming because we have fooled ourselves into thinking this present arrangement is our home.

Walter Brueggemann

Without official leaders, ecofeminist organisation is a network within which actions spring up, disappear and emerge elsewhere like the branching elements of a fungal mycelium. This is . . . the organicist politics of chaos.

Melissa Raphael

As a young clergyman, I was invited to officiate at a Baptism in which the child's mother was a Catholic and the father a lapsed Methodist. The father consented willingly to have the child baptised and expressed a wish that the rite take place somewhere other than in a church. I felt quite excited about this challenge and duly approached the Parish Priest, asking if the ceremony could be performed in the couple's own home. My excitement was brought to an abrupt end, and my pastoral sensitivity hastily dismissed, in order to protect the accretions of canonical rectitude.

The Parish Priest, having upbraided me at some length for considering such a 'ridiculous idea', proceeded to inform me of the theological significance of the church building in the faith life of God's people as constituted in each particular parish; that Baptism, more than any other sacrament, needs to be celebrated as a visible reminder of the Church's life and sacramentality; that good liturgy, of its very nature, is public and not private worship; and that the welcome which the sacrament signifies should not be reduced to the privacy of the home, except for very serious reasons.

Theologically, nobody could disagree with such statements; except, of course, on the grounds of inclusiveness and pastoral sensitivity. And therein, I suggest, lie some vital clues to the deeper questions I am seeking to explore. The theological arguments, while valid in themselves (depending on how we define what theology is about – see Appendix 2) are a type of veneer for a form of religious power vested in building and structure. Not surprisingly, therefore, I was duly reminded by the Parish Priest that I could be initiating a dangerous precedent, whereby other parishioners also would be asking for such services in their own homes rather than in the parish church. And that was a risk that could not be entertained, because it might begin to shake the foundations of a structure which, respectfully, I suggest already rests on several shaky foundations.

The *building* has had a powerful grip on our religious consciousness. Even in the Jewish faith, although *Shabat* is celebrated weekly in the home, it is the synagogue and not the home that is considered to be the central place of worship. Scholars frequently seek to explore the Jewishness of Jesus by alluding to his frequenting the synagogue (temple), despite being critical of other things in the inherited religious system of his day; on the other hand, they attribute little significance to his several acts of table fellowship in people's homes, a phenomenon which arguably is much closer to the ritual of the *Shabat* meal and, therefore, a more coherent statement of his allegiance to the Jewish faith.

It is also noteworthy that in Judaism, as in Islam, the worship in the public place (synagogue, mosque) is predominantly *by* men and *for* men; women are relegated to a more private place, and often are completely excluded. The masculine will-to-power and the patriarchal value-system underpinning it, are deeply embedded in the tradition of the sacred building.

The building takes on religious and theological significance because of its relation to a sacred *place*. All the religions tend to be associated with a special place, either of pilgrimage or central administration: sometimes both. Examples that immediately spring to mind are Rome in the case of Catholicism, the land of Israel in the case of the Jewish people, Armistar for the Sikhs, Mecca for Muslims. Historically, such places are an integral dimension of the sacred story of each religion but, over the centuries, have assumed an importance and significance that often negates the very fundamentals of the religion they seek to propagate or represent.

Christian scholars (e.g. Edwards, 1995; Hessel, 1996) try to develop a more ecologically-grounded theology on the basis of the divine significance of land in the Hebrew Scriptures, where the focus is very much on the sacredness of life in the earthly realm rather than ultimate fulfilment in a place beyond this world. Davies (1974) examines in detail the religious significance of the land in both the Old and New Testaments. While the land was perceived as a gift from Yahweh to the people, political and religious forces progressively objectified the land (as did the dominant patriarchal culture); and, particularly in New Testament times, the land tends to lose much of its ecological and spiritual significance, as the new focus on place – Jerusalem, temple, church – tends to become more heavenly and, therefore, split off from the earthly foundation of all life forms.

In Christian times, Jerusalem is perceived to be the centre of the world (Davies, 1974, p. 202), just as the land of Israel was for ancient Hebrew culture. And for contemporary biblical scholars such as Meyer (1979) and Wright (1996), the close relationship of land (Israel) and sacred building (temple) is central to their understanding of the life and mission of Jesus.

A history of place

The most recent research in human evolution suggests that we humans – as a unique and distinctive species – have inhabited the earth for almost four-and-a-half million years. We evolved into our bipedal mode well over two million years ago, and in our presently developed state of *Homo Sapiens* we have been around for some 200,000 years. For most of that time, even during the *Homo Sapiens* phase, we humans lived in the open spaces in the midst of nature. That convivial bond with nature, developed over some millions of years, is far more fundamental to our human and spiritual well-being than contemporary scholarship seems capable of appreciating, the brilliant exposition of Abram (1996) being a notable exception.

It is estimated that cave-dwelling is probably no more than 150,000 years old and the earliest model of house is usually dated to 15,000 years ago. Independent dwellings, owned by specific families, is a feature of Agricultural times and was probably unknown before 7000 BCE.

The notion of private property, which today we take so much for granted, and consider to be a basic human right, is a relatively recent development in our evolution as a human species. For most of our time, we did not, nor did we even desire to, lay claim to a particular piece of land and property, and seek exclusive rights over its use and ownership. The transition to private property, and the shift in consciousness accompanying it, is central to the considerations of the present chapter.

Strange as it may sound, we humans are much more at home in the open spaces rather than in the confinements of a specific place or privately owned building. In our essential nature we are creatures of the entire planet, and for most of our evolutionary story we considered the Earth to be our *primary* home. For thousands of years, back into our ancient past, we roamed anywhere we wished on planet Earth, often using the natural resources of life (trees, woodlands, rock-shelters, etc.) for shelter and protection. Home did not mean a particular building, local area or a specific country; the whole planet was home and the relationship with planetary life, despite occasionally precarious conditions, seems to have been benign and positive.

To many readers these ideas will feel bizarre and totally irrelevant. As a people saturated in a world-denigrating culture of exile we are largely unable to reconnect with anything of depth and significance. Our minds are so cluttered with scientific reductionism and utilitarian functionalism that we are bereft of imagination and a supportive sense of history. The educational system of the past few hundred years has quite successfully convinced us that everything that existed before the age of civilisation (usually dated from about 3000 BCE) is primitive, archaic and totally irrelevant to our lives thereafter. Little wonder then that we have developed a highly sophisticated systemic psychology whereby we project onto our ancient ancestors all those deviant and destructive behaviours of our age; the ancient scapegoat excuses us from engaging meaningfully with this enormous cultural shadow.

Writing in this vein, there is a dual temptation for both writer and reader: either to dismiss our ancient past as barbaric and uncivilised, or – as tends to be more the case these days – to exaggerate the positive qualities of prehistoric times. My argument is somewhat different: we humans, like all other creatures, are essentially *cultural* and *historical* beings. We are the product of a magnificent evolutionary story, millions of years old, carrying in our very bodies the stardust of aeons past. Apart entirely from our religious significance (to be dealt with later), our very existence – and the *story* within which that is encapsulated – is profoundly mysterious and creative. The rediscovery of that story – and our urgent need to reclaim it – is my primary concern in this book.

What I wish to establish in the present chapter is our primordial connection with creation itself, in its expansive grandeur and universality (globality). This is a central element in our cultural and spiritual desire to 'come home'. It is much more fundamental to both our nature and identity than any of the more specific parameters we set around our sense of self. Most pedagogical and educational systems begin by acknowledging and affirming individual uniqueness within a specific family of origin, belonging to a local tribe and a particular nation-state; we then go on to emphasise differences in the name of national identity, ethnic uniqueness and religious heritage. The whole tenor is adversarial and competitive. Explanations tend to be offered, not in terms of what we hold in common, but how we are different from each other, and not merely different but *better* than everyone else.

This pedagogical and educational approach is so widely adopted and so resistant to criticism, re-examination and re-evaluation that it is now proving to be not merely a major blockage to progress, but may in fact be sowing the seeds of humankind's ultimate destructibility – not just of the Earth but of our very own species. Our world today is being held to ransom by a parasitic anthropocentricism which in its blindness and ruthlessness can no longer befriend either the alienation of exile nor the deep universal desire to come home to ourselves in peace and harmony.

The anthropocentric culture continues to offer partial and, at times, highly questionable solutions to the world's major problems. This is a patchwork approach, with little or no benefit either in the short or long term. The way forward requires much more drastic solutions; in fact, a radical reversal of what we take so much for granted.

The pedagogical and educational vision referred to above creates a dominant set of perceptions, a *world-view*, which underlies our current ways of acting of relating to creation in terms of space and time. It is the *perceptions* that need to change. Instead of the unquestioned linear approach of opening up the mind and heart from the local to the global, we need to begin with the universal nature of life and reclaim our particular identity (and place) in the light of the greater whole. Educationally, we need to begin by highlighting our universal and planetary identity as human beings – our primary home is planet Earth, not the actual house we inhabit in a particular town or village in a geographical area of a specific country. Our national, ethnic and religious identities then become relative values in terms of the greater whole to which we owe our primary allegiance.

Divide and conquer

It was not a growing sense of differentiation and maturity that led us to our present relationship with the creation around us, but rather a progressively deteriorating sense of alienation generated by the obsessional desire to divide and conquer. Our greed and selfishness catapulted us into a state of exile in the wake of which we have forgotten how to relate appropriately with our Earth Mother. Our 'progress' is a delusory veneer shielding us from the harsh reality that we are, in effect, a species that has lost its way.

I am not pursuing some new ideological or political utopia: I am merely highlighting, and suggesting that we reclaim, that quality of connection and relationship with planet Earth which we humans have known for over 90 per cent of our evolutionary time. The fragmentation of our planetary existence is – in evolutionary terms – a very recent phenomenon. It began about 10,000 years ago (keep in mind here that Homo Sapiens has been around for 200,000 years), when in the wake of the Agricultural Revolution, we humans set out to conquer and control the land to our own advantage. This, I suggest, is when we first opted for the demonic culture of exile.

In order to make that a manageable process we began to fragment the planet into sections, which progressively came to be known as nation-states. And in due course, we put in place a series of mechanisms to determine who should and should not own one or other piece of land; foremost among such mechanisms was a device called warfare. The urge to conquer and control had become a rather brutal business; it continues to be so ever since then.

It was only in the latter half of the twentieth century – thanks to more sophisticated anthropological and archaeological research – that we began to suspect the neat, linear outline of human, evolutionary development. For long, we had assumed that humans evolved progressively from being primitive, ignorant and barbaric beings, whose lives were governed by instinct and savagery, to becoming more enlightened, developed and culturally more refined. We now realise that evolution – either of planetary or human life – does not unfold in that linear sequence that humans of the twentieth century feel comfortable with; it tends to unfold in waves and troughs, along a trajectory that often looks irregular and even chaotic, following a rhythm of birth–death–rebirth, according to a logic greater and more mysterious than we humans are capable of devising.

It is far too simplistic – indeed, it reveals a frightening level of ignorance – to suggest that humans in ancient times were generally primitive and unenlightened, whereas people of recent centuries are more advanced, humanly and intellectually. It is we humans who have arbitrarily chosen the date 3500–3000 BCE as the onset of 'civilisation'. We discerned the rise of urbanised culture in the Tigris-Euphrates valley to be a significant step beyond all that preceded this development and we called it 'civilisation'; subsequently, influenced particularly by the tendency in Greek culture to divide everything into pairs of dualistic opposites, we began to attribute the label 'uncivilised' to everything that preceded the age of civilisation. Therein lies one of the great misapprehensions of all time, and a root cause of the alienation that makes us feel like exiles from home.

We now know that prior to the Agricultural Revolution humans related to the land in a very different way. The orientation to divide and conquer had not yet evolved. Consequently, humans roamed wherever they wished. The entire planet was theirs and all indications are that the resources of planetary life and indeed the very planet itself were shared in an egalitarian and non-destructive way. Moreover, people seem to have bonded with the Earth as if it were another living creature and connected with it in a relational, inter-dependent fashion (see Abram, 1996).

Theorists of later times perceive this to have been a co-dependent relationship in which humans were unable to attain their unique identity which, it is alleged, they could only have done by separating from the planetary web of life: hence the notion of differentiation that occurs frequently in both anthropological and psychological literature. This is the illusion (rather the delusion) that has created so much alienation and meaningless suffering for people and planet alike.

The dis-engagement from our planetary roots is the original sin to which all the religions allude, directly or indirectly. (As we shall see later, the religions themselves contribute to this alienation.) In modern jargon, we could refer to it as the 'shadow side' of the Agricultural Revolution. The participation in planetary life, which had prevailed for possibly the entire 4.4 million years that humanity has been around, provides the ambience without which we cannot experience in full what it means to be human. The bond with the wider creation is imprinted in every fibre of our being. Our lives make no sense without an intense connection with the earth itself, and until we reclaim that connection – in a radical way – we'll continue to feel like people in exile, expelled from their true home.

Some may wish to argue that the connection was only significant after we became consciously aware of it – and some will go on to argue that that could only have happened in the age of civilisation. Obviously, *our* awareness of the link intensified the sense of connectedness, but the meaningfulness of the connection is not dependent on our awareness of it. The gift of awareness enables us to name the experience and enter into a deeper dialogue with its meaning and significance.

Evolutionary studies inform us of various developments in which we progressively inter-related with planetary life (many texts still use the language: *mastered* planetary life). We learned to live in harmony with the elements, to procure food, shelter and other basic needs, to relate meaningfully among ourselves and with other creatures, communicate symbolically and linguistically. The acquisition of all these skills is itself a deeply spiritual dimension of our evolutionary story, which today we tend not to understand in terms of the survival of the fittest, but rather as the endowment of an intelligent and benevolent planet on those who learn to live convivially with it. Of particular interest for the present work, is our ancient burial customs, for which we have archaeological evidence now dating back at least 70,000 years (most researchers date it to 100,000 years ago).

Our ancient ancestors seem to have taken great care in laying their dead to rest, providing them with food for the ongoing journey and various ornaments as treasured memories, or possibly for other 'religious' reasons. This in itself should not be construed as belief in an afterlife; our ancient ancestors probably did not think in the dualistic terms of *this* life and the *next* life, but rather in a *continuity* of life through the medium of spirit, a factor that still underpins the reverence and love modern Africans show for their ancestors. Undoubtedly, they too felt the pain of suffering, loss and tragedy, but probably understood these experiences in a more holistic way than we today are capable of.

As yet, we know little of other religious factors that prevailed in these ancient times. Did people believe in God and, if so, what understanding of God prevailed? Did people worship and pray? And what type of ethical code – if any – did they operate out of?

The answers to these questions become somewhat more focused when we review the religious consciousness of the paleolithic era (40000–10000 BCE). Thanks to scholarship and research of the past 30 years particularly, this is an epoch for which we now have a great deal of information, and which is central to the considerations of this book. More than that, it provides us with some of the most compelling evidence for the human urge to be creative and for the transformation we humans can bring about when we release the wellsprings of that creativity.

Ice Age art and the Great Goddess

Ice Age art was first discovered about 150 years ago but is now largely associated with the findings made in the middle of the present century in the Dordogne region of Southern France (especially Lascaux), Vogelherd (West Germany), Altamira (Northern Spain), Willendorf (Austria) and Mezin (Ukraine); it is now generally accepted that rock-shelter paintings discovered in Australia, Tasmania, Tanzania and South Africa – in all more than 10,000 sculpted and engraved objects – belong to the same genre (cf. Leakey, 1992, pp. 314ff and the excellent resume by Michael D. Lemonick (1995, pp. 40–2).

Several interpretations have been offered, ranging from sympathetic magic focused on the hunt (hence the animal figures) to idol worship of various types, to infantile and primitive projections born out of fear and ignorance. Today most interpreters (of whom Margaret Conkey of the University of California at Berkeley is a leading authority) acknowledge that the motifs are both complex and profound and require deep spiritual sensitivity to grasp their ultimate significance.

One of the better-known scholars, Leroi-Gourhan (1968), suggests that an appreciation of ancient mythology is essential for a comprehensive interpretation, revealing (in all probability) a cosmological synthesis imbued with a highly developed holistic, intuitive and spiritual consciousness. Many contemporary interpreters – James Mellart, H. W. F. Saggs, Alexander Marshack, Marija Gimbutas, Elinor Gadon – believe that paleolithic art opens up a whole new world of spirituality and religion with the worship of the Great Mother Goddess as its central inspiration (see Appendix 1). Although some commentators give prior attention to the *animal* drawings and images, all allude to the female figurines (often called *venuses*) which outnumber male figures by ten to one.

The fact that some of the images depict grotesquely large and obese females may be a device to highlight the creative potential of the Goddess through such themes as fertility, menstruation, copulation, pregnancy, birth and lactation. The archaeological discoveries of Catal Huyuk (in southern Turkey), excavated by James Mellaart in 1961–63, suggest a long tradition of worshipping God as woman, the Great Goddess whom the ancient artists seem to be depicting (or worshipping) in the exaggerated form of the cave drawings.

Although the evidence is still tentative, indications are that humans across the populated world of paleolithic times (from at least 40000 BCE) understood God to be a woman of prodigious fertility, and worshipped her for it. Moreover, the Great Goddess was not perceived to inhabit a supernatural realm called heaven or a world beyond, but was identified as embodying the Earth itself, impregnating the whole of creation with creative energy, and more specifically the entire Earth as the abode of the Great Mother. The Earth, therefore, was a sacred place on which one should tread lightly, respectfully, fearfully and joyfully. The Earth was the crucial link with divinity, with that ultimate 'reality' that somehow or other held everything in being.

How our ancient ancestors felt about this divine life-force, how they understood it, is largely open to conjecture. What I wish to emphasise, for the purposes of this book, is the *earthly* dimension. The earthly creation itself was the foundational clue to everything that 'divinity' meant. And it was not creation in its piecemeal fashion as we encounter the Earth today – divided into nation states, ethnic groups, different religions, etc. – but the Earth as *one, indivisible, organic (alive), spiritual* reality.

The sacred had not yet been reduced into the fragmented units of the patriarchal compulsion to divide and conquer: wholeness was the essential dimension of all life-experience, and that wholeness is what we humans have known and experienced for well over 99 per cent of our evolutionary history. The dualistic opposition of the sacred and the secular, of Earth and heaven, was unknown to us until a few thousand years ago. In our inner beings, we identify much more readily and deeply with connectedness and not with that quality of *separation* that characterises our state of spiritual and human exile (see the excellent analysis of Keller, 1986).

Contemporary commentators tend to view the paleolithic way of life as an amorphous, undifferentiated, unenlightened, pre-verbal, primitive (the list of adjectives is quite lengthy) way of being that humans transcended when civilisation began to evolve (about 5,000 years ago – less than 0.1 per cent of our existence as a human species). Civilisation, in this context, signifies, among other things, that humans not merely differentiate themselves from the rest of creation, but set themselves over and against it. Creation – and more specifically the Earth – is not a life-force which we are asked to befriend, but an enemy to be conquered and dominated.

As already indicated, this, I believe, is what the theology of *original sin* is really about: not some flawed state that existed from the beginning, but the distaste for the created order that we our-selves developed with the evolution of patriarchal consciousness. It was not God or Satan who invented original sin: it was human beings! We did it out of the confusion and pain of being people in exile and it was *we ourselves* who invented that estranged state!

The alienation is particularly striking on two levels.

First, following the lead of the French cleric and paleontologist Abbe Breuil, scholars for long assumed that the prevalence of animal forms in Ice Age art reflected the hunting society of the time and the precarious concerns around procuring meat for survival. Therefore, hunting magic was often invoked as the predominant underlying motif for the art work – the assumption being that it was *men* who did the drawings, whereas the prevailing view today is that it was *women* who did them.

Important new insights are provided by the pioneering work of Marshack (1991) whose thorough and sophisticated analysis of the cave drawings suggests that they mark seasonal celebrations and rites (especially of springtime), related more to a food-*gathering* rather than a food-*hunting* culture.[1]

The notion that our ancestors in paleolithic times foraged and hunted for food in a spirit of adversarial competition seems to be another patriarchal projection from the present onto our ancient past. The more *feminine* relationship with the Earth, possibly inspired and animated by the worship of the Great Mother Goddess, suggests ways of procuring food that are less violent, more sustainable and more sensitive to the Earth's own needs. Why resort to violence and domination over other life forms on a planet which is perceived to be the womb of prodigious fertility? Much of our spiritual history as a species is one of relating harmoniously and not in an alienated way with our planet and its resources. Perhaps this provides the archetypal evidence for the central significance of food in all the great world religions.

Second, many of the images from paleolithic art arc quite sexually explicit. There is much to suggest that sexuality was perceived not just as a source for procreation but as a medium of spiritual (mystical) exploration. The erotic seems to have been perceived as an aspect of the spiritual: indeed, a central aspect of it. Devoid of much of the guilt and shame of recent centuries, human sexuality was a joyful and spiritual experience in which people seem to have engaged in an open but respectful way. Eisler (1995, p. 57) makes a similar observation:

> To our prehistoric ancestors, for whom sex was integral to the cosmic order – and for whom the body of woman was *not*, as the medieval Church proclaimed, a source of carnal evil but an attribute of the Great Goddess herself – erotic rites would have had a very different meaning. For them, erotic rites would have been rituals of alignment with the life-giving female and male powers of the cosmos often represented in paleolithic art. So for them, partaking in the pleasures of sex would not have been sinful but, on the contrary, a way of coming closer to their Goddess.

Undoubtedly, our ancient ancestors, too, endured their share of meaningless pain and suffering. And they had to live with unanswerable questions on which we, today, seem to be much more enlightened. But that is not the issue I am seeking to address. My concern is with our *total* history as a human species, the cumulative experience of which each one of us carries in the very depth of our being.

I truly believe that the alienation that has become so insidious and widespread in our lives today is not just an inner, individualistic state – as spiritual writers like Nouwen (1986) and Rolheiser (1979) suggest – but primarily the result of our *evolutionary dislocation* from planet Earth itself. Because of the compulsive patriarchal drives of the past 10,000 years we have largely betrayed our interdependence within the natural world; we have become a nomadic, homeless species, engulfed in exilic waywardness; we have betrayed our basic identity as children of Mother Earth, and we will only rediscover it in the process of returning home to where we truly belong as cosmic–planetary citizens.

I am not suggesting a return to the ancient past. Rather my conviction is that we can only become whole once more by reclaiming the fullness of who and what we are as human beings. And that we can only do in the context of the planet and universe which we inhabit. As I shall explore in subsequent chapters, we humans are unavoidably *relational* creatures; our very identity – in its multi-faceted dimensions – is to be in relation with, not just other humans, but with all the creatures of earth, sea and sky, along with rocks, water, air and everything else that comprises life around us. In isolation, our lives have no meaning and the more we try to bring about a meaningful existence in our convoluted isolation, the surer we are to destroy ourselves – to the very point of extinction.

From our ancient ancestors – particularly in that inspiring epoch of Ice Age art – we can learn anew what it means to live interdependently. Obviously, we'll do it in ways that relate to our consciousness and identity as creatures of the twenty-first century, of the present time, and not as beings of prehistoric times. We can use the ancient wisdom as a type of mirror in which we can view and reclaim aspects of ourselves that have been subverted or lost in the intervening period. For instance, our sexualising of God into a monotheistic, patriarchal male which we claim and proclaim to be an unquestioned truth clearly does not resonate with much of our experience as a spiritual people. This is only one of several examples illustrating that it is religion itself which has thrown us into exile and remains largely responsible for keeping us there. We have been worshipping male God-figures for about 5,000 years, but prior to that time we worshipped a female figure for an estimated 30,000 years. Internally – in both a personal and collective sense – the female sense of God is much more congruent and inspiring than a male model ever could be – which, perhaps, enables us to understand why many contemporary feminists seek to reclaim the feminine face of God.

The shift towards mastery and control

These observations give context and substance to the notion of place and its central role in our religious beliefs. For most of our spiritual story as a human species the place was the entire creation itself, perceived to be the body of the Great Mother Goddess. As already indicated, we can surmise that worship tended to be in the open spaces and probably in circular formations, frequently gathered around the open fire.

That openness and inclusiveness (of the land and creation at large) was seriously undermined in the change of consciousness accompanying the Agricultural Revolution c. 8000 BCE. The reasons for this shift in consciousness – with its positive and negative outcomes – are far from clear. Even the factual information on what exactly happened is meagre, but the ensuing developments are now well substantiated and outlined in much of the relevant literature.

Around 8000 BCE, a profound shift happened in how humans perceived and understood the meaning of the land, and especially its ability to produce food for human well-being. More importantly, the land's ability to produce, itself became a bartering tool, whereby some people began to exchange goods for the food produced by others. This practice gave a feeling not merely of power over people, but certain 'rights' over the land itself. The more land one could acquire, the more one could sell and accumulate 'wealth' for one's own benefit. Land, contrary to the spiritual significance of the previous 30,000 years (at least), now became a commodity to be exploited, and menfolk emerged as the primary exploiters.

The first task was to explore the land's own potential to produce food. Various skills and techniques were developed to maximise production and, cumulatively, these came to be known as the Agricultural Revolution. Cattle-raising was another important dimension, and indeed may have been the initial factor in the move to divide up resources; firstly people began to claim that they owned the cattle and then they had to differentiate who owned which animals. In order to maintain such distinctions, it became necessary to divide up the land itself and to differentiate who owned what. And in a short while, it became necessary to defend and protect one's patch against those others who were now perceived as encroachers. Disagreements and skirmishes ensued, and within a few thousand years open warfare began.

The Agricultural Revolution took some time to unfold (some claim that there are parts of our world today that have not yet been affected by it). By the fifth century BCE, it had assumed global significance in that geographical area we now call Europe. I am not convinced that it was only happening in the European landmass; but to date, it is the only part of the then inhabited world for which we have substantial evidence.

This is what seems to have happened. Around 4500 BCE, nomadic bands, sometimes described as the Eurasian Steppe Pastoralists, set out to obtain more fertile lands for their cattle-herds. Best known of these roving groups were the Kurgans of Eastern Europe, the Aryans in India, the Luwains in Anatolia, the Achaeans (and subsequently, the Dorians) in Greece. Not long afterwards, we notice the Hebrews in Canaan (Palestine) adopting a similar strategy, echoes of which surface several times in the Hebrew Scriptures (the Old Testament).

The rather misleading term, 'Indo–European invaders', is often applied to this movement; others, like the anthropologist, Marija Gimbutas, tend to use the term 'Kurgan' invaders and go on to describe three major strands: Kurgan wave No. 1: c. 4300–4200 BCE; wave No. 2: 3400–3200 BCE; wave No. 3: 3000–2800 BCE. Led by warriors and powerful priests, these invaders sought to justify their desire to conquer and control in the name of a male, conquering God whom they sought to represent. With these invasions, the image of the conquering chief on horseback becomes a prevalent symbol, adopted by both religion and politics for many subsequent centuries.

Human culture and civilisation, as known up to this time, seems to have changed dramatically, and apparently quite rapidly. The nature of that change, briefly described above, is illustrated at greater length by scholars such as Childe (1958), Gimbutas (1982) and Eisler (1987, 1995). To quote from Gimbutas (p. 281):

> The old European and Kurgan cultures were the antithesis of one another. The old Europeans were sedentary horticulturalists prone to live in large well-planned townships. The absence of fortifications and weapons attests to the peaceful co-existence of this egalitarian civilisation that was probably matrilinear and matrilocal. The Kurgan system was composed of patrilineal, socially stratified, herding units which lived in small villages or seasonal settlements while grazing their animals over vast areas. One economy based on farming, the other on stock breeding and grazing, produced two contrasting ideologies. The Old European belief system focussed on the agricultural cycle of birth, death and regeneration, embodied in the feminine principle, a Mother Creatix. The Kurgan ideology as known from comparative Indo-European mythology, exalted virile, heroic warrior gods of the shining and thunderous sky. Weapons are non-existent in the old European imagery; whereas the dagger and battle-axe are dominant symbols of the Kurgans, who, like all historically known Indo-Europeans, glorified the lethal power of sharp blades.

On the part of humans, a new set of attitudes and perceptions began to evolve, largely focused on a subtle and sinister sense of divine power validating the subjugation, manipulation and destruction of other life forms and of the land itself. With such developments came the gradual erosion, possibly the deliberate subversion (as Eisler (1987) avers), of all that the culture of the Great Mother Goddess signified. Woman, and all that woman-power symbolises, was to become the greatest loser in this upheaval, with consequences that prevail to our own time.

The religious convictions of the invading forces are central to the entire strategy. The strategy itself – *divide and conquer* – belonged initially to the shadow-side of the Agricultural Revolution; it was more a cultural than a religious phenomenon. Progressively, the religious motivation – focused on the supreme male deity, a projection of the male dominators themselves – becomes the overwhelming justification for the destruction and conquest. It was a short step, and indeed a short time, before this vision became a formalised religious belief. It began to happen around 3000 BCE with the rise of Hinduism, and true to the spirit of 'divide and conquer' eventually evolved into a whole series of religious systems which, to this day, battle it out for the religious supremacy of the world.

Reductionism became a crucial weapon of control, just as it is in the scientific, political and religious world of our time. The diverse understanding of how the divine operated in the world (polytheism) posed a threat to those who wanted to be in charge. Consequently, *monotheism* (belief in one supreme God) was promoted as a more appropriate alternative. It was important for two reasons. First, it validated the human desire to structure all of life in hierarchical terms with one person ultimately in charge; in due course that power was invested in the *king*. Second, it facilitated an attitude of subservience among the people; ways of behaving could only be validated through the supreme human authority (the king on Earth), whose existence took all its meaning from the divine King in the sky.

To this day, kings within their respective nations or territories enjoy unquestioned jurisdiction (although frequently, these days, they are mere token figures within Western-style democracies). The ultimacy of the king's power tends to be symbolised in the royal palace, often the most elaborate and ornate building in the land. In many of the great religions, the king was considered divine; in the Anglican faith the king (or queen) automatically becomes head of the Church. Not surprisingly, therefore, the religions evolved very much along lines parallel with kingly standards, and in due course the palace of the earthly king was supplemented with the *temple* for the divine King.

With the evolution of special buildings devoted to the pursuit of religion – of which the temple is the universal prototype – the focus makes a subtle but important shift from the *land* to the *building*. Religion comes to be associated, especially in the public view, with expansive buildings, often erected on mountains or overlooking cities. And it was now the building and not the land that was deemed to be the primary residence of the god(s). Religion is still very much linked into place, but the focus has shifted significantly. In fact, it is another form of reductionism that enables the ruling patriarchs to be more firmly in charge.

A history of sacred building

Ironically, it is not temples but *caves* that humans first used for divine worship. It is impossible to establish when humans first began inhabiting caves; the earliest evidence suggests around 150,000 years ago. Not surprisingly, therefore, caves were also to be the first 'indoor' sanctuaries for ritual and worship, and with the discovery of cave art at Kununurra in Australia in 1996, we now believe that our ancient ancestors used art forms to express their religious sentiment possibly as far back as 75,000 years ago. The extensive use of 'sacred' art throughout the paleolithic era suggests quite strongly that caves were used as places of public communal worship; how far back that practice prevailed is difficult to establish, but it certainly pre-dates the formal religions by many thousands of years.

What we are seeking to trace here is the development of worship using a special or sacred building. The cave certainly is one of the older, if not the oldest, religious structures. Archaeological remains of ancient altars are dated back to about 7000 BCE, probably in the open rather than in a closed space (often on mountain tops), while the first temples are dated to about 3600 BCE, and many of these were of cave-like design hewn in rock (especially in Egypt and India). The temple seems to be the first and oldest formal religious building constructed by humans, and not surprisingly is still significant in many of the world's great religions.

It is noteworthy that in Hinduism, which first developed the notion of temple worship, the sacred building was visualised as a symbol of the cosmic life-force, with several dimensions (sections) all of which had to be interconnected (i.e., designed) in a way that expressed the universal harmony and oneness through which everything was held in being. The place of worship, in this ancient understanding, was not to identify one or other form of religious allegiance, but to depict the potential within religious belief to unify and celebrate the oneness of life. Worship, in the sacred space of the temple, was about celebrating life in its fullness above and beyond the dictates or guidelines of one or all the religions.

There is evidence that temple design followed closely the design and structure of kingly palaces, and since the king in many ancient cultures was deemed to be divinely chosen and endowed, he was the one that often built and subsidised the temples. Paradoxically, it was also under the king's tutelage that the temple's sacred function was often undermined, and at times virtually eroded as they became centres for legal, economic and commercial transactions. Temples also became the focus for warfare and bitter struggle as kings vied for the control of land and property. Almost from the beginning, the temple as primary symbol of God's 'royal' control, was seriously tainted by the insatiable whims of patriarchal, human control and thus progressively lost the original cosmic significance which underpinned its existence and development.

All the formal religions of the Far East used the temple as the central place for worship, and as time passed each religion developed its own unique forms of worship and began to emphasise not the common, but the adversarial, elements which set them in opposition to one another. A whole range of religious structures began to ensue, e.g. the stupas and viharas of Buddhism, the pagodas of China, the ziggurats of Mesopotamia, the synagogues of Judaism; and in more recent centuries the churches of Christianity, the mosques of Islam and the gurdwaras of Shikism. All are expressions of the temple tradition, the original sacred building from which all the others have sprung.

Historically and architecturally, temples, churches, mosques, etc. embody some of the most exquisite design and religious expression ever known to the human imagination. Right down to our own time, our sacred buildings awaken deep religious sentiment in the heart of believer and non-believer alike. They embody a tradition that needs to be cherished and preserved for posterity: living emblems of undying faith.

And yet we need to be aware of the shadow side of this illustrious symbol, the dominance and rigidity of religious dogma perceived to be as stable and as unchanging as the buildings themselves. We need to be aware of the patriarchal figureheads who inhabited and controlled the masses, from the divine royal palace, whether it be the original kings or their several 'clerical' successors, down through the ages. We need to be aware too of the painful contradictions embodied in the so-called beacon of light on the hill-top which, historically, embodies some of the most outrageous corruption and destruction in the history of humankind (in the past 5,000 years).

Sacred buildings of one type or another will continue as a dimension of our faith practice and experience, but with a greatly diminished significance. They are likely to become much more simple and adaptable to several uses at the disposal of local communities. We will divest our sacred buildings of the moralism and religious dominance that has characterised them for so long. And, perhaps, most significantly and disturbingly for many, we will *de-clericalise* them significantly.

The sacred dwells in space, not just in place

Learning anew to worship our God 'in spirit and in truth' involves the transcendence of the controlling grip of land and buildings. God and the divine energy cannot be reduced (confined) to any piece of land or to any sacred building. God dwells in prodigious creativity in the entire creation; there are not, and must not be, any limits on God's radical cosmic and planetary presence to the whole of evolutionary life.

All sacred landmarks – place or building – are transitory in their religious significance. As we shall suggest in later chapters, God exists first and foremost as the 'go-between' that makes all connections and relationships possible. Any attempt to restrain the divine interconnectedness undermines the essential freedom and creativity of God. It also undermines the integrity and freedom of humanity whose primary spiritual home was never intended to be a sacred nation or a holy building.

Humans are created to inhabit the whole of planet Earth; without a real connection with the entire planet we try in vain to come out of exile and to come home to where we really belong. We belong to where God first encountered us, where God continues to meet us today: in the unrestricted spaces of God's universe, where the divine creativity continues to birth forth new possibilities for life and meaning. Therein, and in nowhere less, do we truly come home to ourselves and to our God.

— 3 —

Words About the Word

Anyone that claims that the biblical text can be read 'at face value', without interpretation, does not understand the nature of texts in general or of this text in particular. The question is not whether to interpret the text, but only how to interpret it.

Sandra M. Schneiders

Literalism prevents mystery by narrowing the multiple ambiguity of meanings into one definition. By treating the words we use as ambiguities, seeing them again as metaphors, we restore to them their original mystery . . . Rather than an increase of certainty there is a spread of mystery, which is both the precondition and consequence of revelation.

James Hilliman

M Y ARGUMENT THUS FAR suggests that religion in its formal sense is characterised primarily by a sense of *place*, concretised in a particular sacred structure called church, temple, mosque, etc. In keeping with the adversarial and dualistic mind-set of the post-Agricultural era, all the religions go to great lengths to defend their respective places, buildings and tangible achievements. The religions, in line with the nation states, also go to war to defend their properties or strive to retrieve them when they have been attacked by alien forces. Central to this strategy of defending the place, and in order to justify such defence (or counter-attack), the religions developed *rhetorical statements*; in time they become known as Scriptures and tend to be encapsulated in one or more sacred books.

In the present chapter I want to explore the evolution of the *word* and its central role in the development of formal religion. It is difficult to determine how significant human language was in the spiritual consciousness of our ancestors prior to the Agricultural

Revolution. Whereas we have inherited a rich repertoire of image and symbol (in the Ice Age art of paleolithic times), we have no written or verbal record from the ancient past.

The reader may retort: 'How could we when writing had not yet been invented?' We usually trace the origin of writing to the cuneiform script of the Sumerians around 3000 BCE, and we tend to ignore the fact that the Sanskrit alphabet is thought to pre-date it, possibly by a thousand years; either way, the invention of writing cannot be dated before 5000 BCE.

Although writing had not been formally invented, the creative imagination expressed religious sentiment and intent in a vast range of expressions, especially in dance and art, image and symbol. It is, therefore, surprising that there are no traces of hieroglyphic expression of the type we find in Egypt in the second millennium BCE. The main reason being, I suggest, is that the rational and linear mind-set of the Agricultural era had not yet evolved. While we have an elaborate and widespread spiritual enculturation, it has been neither formally recorded nor codified, except in the form of *story*. And we have good reason to believe that it was *stories* rather than *a story*, which enjoyed a great range of narrative embellishment until the rational linear mind felt it necessary to curtail the unlimited possibility of the fascination with mystery.

Our religious traditions – in *all* the world religions – lead us to believe that the focus on the word belongs to a very ancient and archetypal religious consciousness. In fact, once more, we are dealing with something of very recent origin, and like the attachment to place (or building) it is based on unexamined and rather misleading assumptions.

The development of sacred speech, leading to sacred text (Scriptures), became another patriarchal device to augment the insatiable desire for control. What could be put into print – and especially when we began to claim that it was *God's own* word(s) – was endowed with an unchangeable permanence and was there for all to see. Whereas the narrative structure of story could be changed and modified as the creative imagination saw fit, the written word could not be altered. Human imagination and divine creativity were both strangulated. The urge to divide and conquer was in the process of becoming a divinely-validated strategy; it has remained so ever since.

The word in the various religions

We will sketch briefly the evolution of word (*logos*) in the various religions leading to the major Scriptures we know today. All the religions view language as a manifestation of the sacred; spoken words have a special power to convey religious sentiment, and religious text is regarded as an embodiment not just of divine power but of divine form itself. There is an extensive religious belief – in both the formal and native (tribal) religions – that the cosmos was brought into being by a divine *verbal* pronouncement.

At this juncture the reader needs to remember that spoken, verbal language evolved about 100,000 years ago, whereas God's creativity, in the known cosmos, has been operative for billions of years. Addressing this dilemma, Hodgson (1994, p. 140) states:

A word-of-God theology is an extension of anthropocentrism since only human beings can hear and respond to God verbally . . . Finding alternative, cosmological metaphors and developing them conceptually is a difficult task, which theology is only beginning to address.

Language comes to be understood as a favoured medium for God's relationship with the whole of creation, but since only humans can use language (at least for the greater part) access to the divine is perceived to be a special human privilege, only partially available, if at all, to other creatures and to the rest of creation. Hodgson (1989, 1994), following an approach closely similar to the present work, sets out to retrieve the cosmological context, inspirited by the divine energy that enlivens and sustains everything that exists.

It is this divine energy that nurtures and sustains creativity in evolution's unfolding process for billions of years before either humans or verbal language ever evolved. Endorsing the vision of Rosemary Radford Ruether, Hodgson suggests we adopt the twin metaphors of 'primal matrix' (from primal energy) and 'historical liberator' as the foundation stones for a new theological vision for our time.

In the great written traditions of Hinduism and Buddhism, silence always takes priority over the spoken or written word. (Here is primary evidence for the older spiritual tradition of humankind.) The path to enlightenment is through the focused mind (and heart) rather than through external ritual, verbally or symbolically enacted. Nonetheless, speech remains a significant force, and almost in spite of the primary commitment to the non-verbal, assumes a superior role. Thus we find that the ancient Vedic Creation God, Prajapati, speaks the primal symbols *bhur*, *bhuvah* and *svar* to create heaven and Earth. He is said to have given name and form (*nama-rupa*) to the world, two elements to which there are several allusions in the Vedic Scriptures. Moreover, Prajapati's wife is named *Vac* (which means 'speech'), the Goddess who, in some traditions, begets the entire creation and even *becomes* the universe itself – again re-echoing central elements of the paleolithic spirituality of the Great Mother Goddess.

One prominent esoteric or mystical development within both Hinduism and Buddhism is known as *tantrism*. The supreme deity of Hindu tantrism is known as Siva, considered to be pure consciousness and thus silent. In one of his manifestations, Siva consorts with Vac (speech), through whom Siva's creative power (*sakti*) is awakened, and activates the creation of the universe. Accordingly, creation begins with a subtle vibration (from within the universal silence) that develops into the multi-form expressions of creation, with the Sanskrit alphabet itself as foundational to the meaning and naming of all form. To this day, all Eastern *mantras* used in meditation practice are grounded in the various sound qualities of the Sanskrit alphabet and are considered to be endowed with vibrational qualities of divine energy.

Buddhism, it seems, was founded as a reform movement, seeking to reclaim those ancient spiritual values that Hinduism was considered to have usurped and undermined. More than anything else Buddhism sought to subsume all forms of discourse into the category and experience of discursive thought. The Buddha is said to have lived his entire life in 'the silence of the sage' and never spoke a word. We know of course that even Buddhism, considered to be a *non-theistic* religion, developed elaborate Scriptures known as the *Pali* Canon, with its classical tripartite division: the *Vinaya-pitaka* (mainly on monastic discipline); the *Sutta-pitaka* (from which are derived discourses with the Buddha also known as *sutras*) and the *Abhidhamma-pitaka* (a process-oriented view of experience).

Even in the rather sober Theravada tradition, the pronouncements of the Scriptures are considered to be *ipissima verba* of the Buddha himself. In the Mahayana tradition, the Scriptures are deemed to be an embodiment of the Buddha, and any location where the text is read or studied becomes a sacred place. As in Hinduism, the ritual incantation of the Scriptures is considered to be a rich source of merit accelerating the attainment of Nirvana. The evolving centrality of the word within Buddhism is nowhere more apparent than in the Zen tradition, in the well-attested practice of the *koan* (Chinese: *kung-an*) as a means of attaining enlightenment.

Although a rather diminished force today, Zoroastrianism, founded between 1400 and 1200 BCE (in present-day Iran), relates significantly to the considerations of this chapter. The earlier followers refused to write down the *oral* teachings of its founder considering this a deviation from the power of the sacred word. The *Avesta*, their collection of holy texts, was finally compiled with the aid of a specially invented alphabet in the fifth/sixth century BCE. Not only does Zoroastrianism affirm the divine creation by the power of the word, but outlines the seven-stage process we retain to this day in the Hebrew Scriptures. Several other features, including a strong ascetical, dualistic and patriarchal value-system, have also been incorporated into Judaism and subsequently into the tradition of Christendom.

The Hebrew Scriptures open with the story of God breathing over the formless void and pronouncing in poetic regularity the words: 'Let there be . . .' This is the creative *word*, translated as *dabhar* in Hebrew and *logos* in Greek. But the Hebrew term does not mean 'word' in its current usage. *Dabhar* signifies an outburst of creative energy endowing the recipient with truth, love and meaning. It denotes a release of liberating power that awakens into being what previously either did not exist at all or existed in some type of chaotic and disordered state. In modern parlance, the word *eros* describes this quality of energy and creativity (see Hodgson, 1994, pp. 94–8, 193–6; also Brock, 1992).

Dabhar does not impose meaning and sacredness on something pre-existing, but rather liberates from within the embryonic life awaiting its fuller realisation. To translate it with the word 'wisdom' (*sophia*), is much closer to the intended meaning, as long as we remember that the wisdom referred to in many of the world's Scriptures is itself not merely an intellectual quality but a highly charged emotion of potential and unlimited creativity (see Murphy, 1990).

The corresponding New Testament term, *logos*, while retaining a strong wisdom flavour, has been used for more subtle and questionable purposes. Aldredge-Clanton (1995, p. 24) writes:

To the earliest readers of the Gospel of John, the Greek word *Logos* carried rich and complex connotations. No word in English can translate it adequately. It is like the concept of the Tao, or cosmic order, in Chinese philosophy. *Logos* includes the power that created and rules all of nature, God's plan for all of human history, and the moral law.

Greek philosophy in general and in particular the neo-Platonic influence of Philo of Alexandria contributed to a progressive gendering of the *logos* away from the original feminine attribution of *sophia* (wisdom) towards a concept of masculine power. Instead of the invitation to celebrate the innate order which divine *sophia* makes possible, the focus shifted to a sense of *imposed* order, requiring a patriarchal, male-dominated system.

Logos is very much about clear-headed, linear and logical rationality. It depicts an overseer who is primarily a thinker, working with the intellect to ensure that all is in order and equally determined to punish those who create any imbalance in the logical ordering of life. Although many commentators link the usage of the term *logos* in John's Gospel to the wisdom (*sophia*) tradition in the Old Testament (Brown, 1966, pp. 519–24; Johnson, 1992, pp. 97–9; Edwards, 1995, pp. 36–7), this provides a dangerous theological veneer for a cultural concept that quite unambiguously supports the dominant patriarchal value system of the surrounding culture. The *logos* of John's Gospel may be intended to be a bearer of light, but shrouded in the masculine urge to control and conquer, it becomes a rather dark and sinister undercurrent.

The meaning of sacred story

As we review the evolution of the word – whether in the cultural or religious context – we note that spoken language pre-dates the written form by at least 95,000 years. The oral tradition, that characterises most of our history as a species, was not based on the factual and functional interchange that dominates human speech today. The prevalent mode of communication seems to have been that of story, a narrative infrastructure that held and conveyed meaning in regard to every aspect of human and planetary life.

Story-telling has little place or significance in our contemporary Western world. Our rationality on the one hand, and the projections of fantasy and imagination on to television and video on the other, has severed us quite seriously from our inherent need for narrative and myth. We have been brainwashed into a relational mode of co-dependency, whereby we expect *answers* from on high, thus depriving us of the use of the creative imagination to figure things out for ourselves. We have largely lost the individual capacity to dream and the collective capacity to discern, which is precisely the function of story in prehistoric times and in native (tribal) groups to this day.

Story has been relegated to the realm of childish play, as indicated in the popularity of bedtime story-telling, nursery school pedagogy or the type of 'gossip' that prevails in social recreation. In other words, stories are not meant to be taken seriously, so we end up with a repertoire of trivialised and banalised stories. The end result is a lot of empty language – the cult of the verbose – denuded of that quality of narrative that sets the imagination on fire, namely *myth*.

In popular parlance, 'myth' denotes a legendary fable belonging to the world of the imagination, but with no foundation in the world of reality. This, in turn, begs the question: What do we mean by *reality*? For most people it refers to what we can see, hear and touch in the observable world around us; more precisely, what we can measure and quantify with the aid of modern science and mathematics (economics). Reality, therefore, is about facts; rather, what we humans consider to be facts. But what is the factuality of the facts we encounter in our daily lives? The following examples will help to highlight the significance of this question.

As I write these words, I sit on a chair, the measurement and structure of which is clearly delineated in terms of dimension and solidity. And at the commonsense level, nobody can dispute that it is a functional timber object, the fundamental essence of which can be described predominantly with the aid of two senses: sight and touch.

Adopting the same commonsense approach, a particle physicist looks very much like every other human being, but offers a totally different description of the chair:

> My chair is a blur of uncertainty which I am allowed to think
> of as imaginably tiny particles whizzing around in a fuzzy
> manner. I know I mustn't think of these particles as 'things' in

exactly the sense I think of the chair as a 'thing' – something that can be pinned down in the accurate way we expect to pin things down. I wonder whether a chair consisting of 'non-things' can itself fairly be called a 'thing', and why I see it as such. (Ferguson, 1994, p. 5)

It sounds like I should call my chair an *event* rather than a *thing*, something that is 'alive' (in some sense) rather than dead inert matter. And where does that leave my *factual* certainty?

Before sitting down to write this chapter I did some work in my garden. At one juncture I held a handful of earth, noting some tiny ant-like creatures burrowing their way about. Apart from the tiny ants, that earth too felt dead and inert and could be described as a soft clingy substance which, when enriched with some fertiliser, water and air, will enable my plants to grow – a fairly simple factual description. And then I thought of those poetic words by world-renowned microbiologist, Edward O. Wilson (1992, p. 329):

> Organisms are all the more remarkable in combination. The flower in the crannied wall – it *is* a miracle . . . Pull out the flower from its crannied retreat, shake the soil from the roots into the cupped hand, magnify it for close examination. The black earth is alive with a riot of algae, fungi, nematodes, mites, springtails, enchytraeid worms, thousands of species of bacteria. The handful may be only a tiny handful of one ecosystem, but because of the genetic codes of its residents it holds more order than can be found on the surface of all the planets combined. It is a sample of the living force that runs the earth – and will continue to do so with or without us.

Now the handful of garden clay takes on a totally different meaning. What previously seemed simple and ordinary now becomes complex and extraordinary. The *facts* are not really relevant any more – and, anyhow, what are the facts? Wilson's description is *factual*, but more importantly, it resembles a parable, a story loaded with meaning to a degree that almost makes the facts redundant. Here we are verging on *myth*, and are now in a situation to describe in greater detail the contemporary understanding of this phenomenon.

Panikkar (1993, p. 15) offers a cryptic description: 'Myth is what you believe in without believing that you believe in it.' It is a state of inner resonance, a touchstone of truth by which facts are recognised as truths. The inner conviction, however, is not merely personal, but simultaneously interpersonal, planetary (cosmic) and open to the influence of the divine. 'This is one of the values of mythology', writes Moore (1992, p. 221) '– its way of cutting through personal differences in order to get to the great themes of human experience.'

In the state of mythic awareness, the human, the global and the divine all interact to produce a quality of coherence and intelligibility. In the mythic moment, meaning awakens; a creative restlessness ensues, requiring a new quality of engagement with reality. Out of this engagement, *story* is born.

While we can use standard prose to describe what myth does, we require a different quality of language to engage mythically with our world. Story provides the psychic, emotional and spiritual ambience to unravel our engagement with mystery, with ultimate meaning, with the really real. Story works on the imagination and penetrates right through to the depth of soul. And it is not merely in the listening or in the speaking that transformation happens, but in that quality of immersion which the story-teller evokes.

Stories don't have to make sense. Their message and meaning is in that unspeakable realm where spirit relates to spirit, and the 'greater whole' is apprehended. More precisely, meaning *overflows* rather than *ensues*.

The power of story hinges very much on symbolic narrative and the use of *metaphor*. The description provided by Riceour (1977) is adopted by many contemporary scholars: nothing other than the application of a familiar label to a new object which first resists and then surrenders to its application. A metaphor is a semantic device which discloses a new world of human possibility and existence, apprehending the hearer with a 'surplus of meaning'.

Taken literally, metaphors are stripped of their meaning and power; hence a statement like: 'Individualism is the cancer of our society'. A society cannot have cancer in the colloquial sense of a person having cancer, and cancer medically understood consists of certain medical and scientifically based conditions that cannot affect an abstract concept like individualism. Yet, the statement embodies a profound truth illustrated all the more graphically precisely because of the choice of metaphor. To get the right metaphor is very often what the creative imagination is pursuing.

Not alone does it provide a more creative quality of description; in fact, it also provides us with a more *truthful* one. A great deal of human discourse – verbal, and especially non-verbal – is not about facts but about the *meaning of life that undergirds the facts*. Facts are best understood as provisional statements of how we perceive things to be, until we arrive at a better understanding, one that will serve us more effectively at a further stage of our planetary/personal evolution.

In evolutionary terms, there are no ultimate facts about anything in life; there are no final answers nor perfect solutions. Indeed, contemporary science, itself dogmatically committed to factual, verifiable truth, verifies the fundamental uncertainty and unpredictability of all reality (as in the uncertainty principle). And it is by entering more deeply into the unfolding story of our universe – and all its constituent life forms – that we encounter the truth that sets us free: to become the type of people our creative God intends us to be.

A word about language

The acquisition of human language has been extensively studied by scholars from a range of different disciplines, and the learning mechanisms by which we acquire linguistic competence are quite well understood. What is rarely highlighted is that verbal language is quite a recent visitor to our planet, surfacing about 100,000 years ago, and not developing into the contemporary spoken idiom possibly as late as 40000 BCE, as Corballis (1992) claims.

This means that for an estimated 90 per cent of our time on Earth, we humans communicated in a *non-verbal* fashion. This observation alone has enormous consequences for our growth and education as a human people, but like many other dimensions of our deep story, it receives virtually no attention in our upbringing or education. Even the simple awareness that we can survive, and indeed thrive, in our relation with the planet and the cosmos, *without verbal communication*, is in itself something that requires contemplative attention. Little wonder that the non-verbal is so fundamental to all our personal and planetary lives, and often unlocks the doors to the deep inner search for meaning in psychotherapy, prayer and in our experiences of tragedy or ecstatic joy.

Tracing our human story throughout the 100,000 years in which we have used verbal language, there is a widespread erroneous belief (another misleading *fact*) that we progressed from a language of literalism (Piaget's concrete thought-patterns), based on ignorance of the world around us, to a more imaginative use of language when we acquired the ability to think *abstractly*. Several contemporary studies, especially in anthropology and archaeology, belie this long-held belief.

Mithen (1996), accumulates a substantive body of evidence indicating that what he calls 'cognitive fluidity' is more basic to our human nature than anything else. We are reflective, enlightened beings whose basic orientation is towards intelligent and creative action. Mithen goes on to suggest that it is this innate cognitive fluidity – which I suspect is more about spirituality than mere cognition – that led to some of the most sophisticated and elegant creations of prehistoric times, e.g. Ice Age art and creation-centred spirituality.

We often work with the unexamined assumption that intelligent human behaviour only first unfolded with the rise of civilisation, some 5,000 years ago. Not only is this a perceptual intellectual error, based on a totally false reading of history and culture, it is an enormously destructive indictment of humanity itself. It exonerates, and even divinises, that dimension of human evolutionary experience that belongs to the age of patriarchy, and in the process seeks to trivialise and even obliterate all that went before.

Central to that trivialisation is the tendency to use human language to argue your way against all who disagree with you, and over all those you wish to obliterate. Conveniently, we employ language as a central element of mainstream religion and unwittingly adopt the linguistic oppression of the wider culture, turning religion into yet another powerfully oppressive weapon of elimination. Little wonder that women often feel that they are being made invisible by formal religion.

Without wishing to disregard the genuine sincerity of those scholars who devote – in some cases – their entire lives to the study and exposition of sacred text and language, and to the promotion of sacred text as the very Word of God, our evolutionary unfolding today requires a much more radical investigation into how language has been used to engage and promote religious belief. My intention is not to undermine what we have been about for the past 5,000 years, but to underwrite it with that quality of faith that reconnects us with our ancient past. I wish to rediscover, and reclaim afresh, that quality of spirituality that transcends both place and word and empowers us to engage anew with the creative God who co-creates at the heart of creation.

In many fields of scholarship, it is widely assumed that language acquisition (some 100,000 years ago) is a precondition for the development of imagination, symbolic expression and the use of abstract thought. In other words, prior to that time, we humans were unable to think or perceive in a creative, imaginative or symbolic fashion. Allegedly, our minds were darkened; we lived in a state of ignorance. In a sense we were not really human.

Only in recent years has this view been challenged. In a work of substantial scholarly research, Deacon (1997) collates extensive evidence to indicate that the acquisition of language, contrary to being the precondition for symbolic behaviour, is itself the final outcome of a species that had been behaving symbolically for thousands (perhaps a few million) years previously. Language itself is the fruit of symbolic engagement with life, not the mechanism that releases the power of the symbolic imagination. Language is the final outcome of a richly endowed species engaging the creative imagination for thousands of years previously.

Abram (1996) makes a similar claim but develops his ideas along very different lines. He considers our closeness to the Earth and our attunement to the processes of nature to be the foundations both of our linguistic and literary abilities. Our eventual achievement of structuring sound into words and sentences comes after thousands of years of absorbing and internalising the music of bird-song, the gurgling of streams, the whishing of wind through the trees. The sound which evolved in human speech is itself an extension of the many sounds which nature produces. Precisely because we are an intelligent, creative and imaginative species, long before formal speech evolved we allowed nature to teach us the rudiments of our developing linguisting ability. Indeed, that same observation is also foundational evidence for our spiritual *raison d'être*, a topic I shall explore in later chapters.

The evolution of language, like many features of our human evolutionary story, is loaded with meaning and with profound interconnectedness. Religion of the word somehow bypasses that ancient engagement with mystery; in fact, it is difficult to avoid the conclusion that religion seeks to undermine this tradition, often labelling it 'animism', 'paganism' or 'spiritual darkness'. Once again, we are hurled into exile, disconnected from our deep story, where the co-creative God has been wonderfully at work, long before formal religion ever began to evolve.

The tradition of the Word

In our Christian tradition, the priority of the Word became the penchant of the Reformers in the sixteenth century. This was the icing on the cake for a development that had lasted at least 4,000 years. The Word had assumed not merely a descriptive and analytical power, but had now assumed a divine symbolism which gave the ruling male class the right to impose an oppressive value system to foment the patriarchal wish to be totally in charge.

The sixteenth century also marks the rise of classical science, with the machine emerging as the dominant metaphor to understand every aspect of human and planetary life. The mechanistic culture strictly adhered to the principle: the whole equals the sum of the parts; the machine consists of nothing more than its constituent parts. How the parts function in unison for the benefit of the whole machine, how they are to be repaired or replaced when they fail to function, became the major preoccupation of the scientific consciousness of the sixteenth century. And the metaphor of the machine was applied to everything, animate and inanimate alike.

The seventeenth century follows with a logical development often referred to as the *age of enlightenment*. The ability to use *reason* constructively, to think rationally and logically, became a prized capacity. A clear head and a succinct mental state were considered to be the primary assets to function effectively in a mechanised world: what O'Hear (1997, p. 203) call 'the normativity of the mental'. No dreaming or imagining: stick with what can be observed by the human senses, tested by human experiment, and verified by science and mathematics.

The clear thinking required a clarity of concept and language. And language was assumed to describe reality as it is. Analytical philosophy had a hey-day, and the names of Rene Descartes, Immanuel Kant, David Hume, Friedrich Nietzsche and Bertrand Russell are all too well known. These are the final generation of those who propagated the power of the word. From the nineteenth century onwards, even philosophers became suspicious of the power and influence of both written and spoken word, down to our own time when many, notably Ludwig Wittgenstein, Jacques Derrida and Michel Foucault call for the deconstruction of language and its insidious power in the hands of those still pursuing the vision of 'divide and conquer'.

Meanwhile, the religious significance of the Word (usually spelt with a capital W) grew in prominence. The nineteenth and twentieth centuries produced an enormous upsurge in biblical studies, the vast majority of scholars believing the Scriptures to be the primary (and for some the exclusive) source of God's design for humanity and the world. The Muslim faith spread across the world, claiming the Koran to be the one and only way to God (indeed, the very Word of God *him*self). The interest in the great Eastern religions led to a renewed interest in such religious classics as the Bhagavadgita and the great Sutras. Religion – all religion – was perceived as having a special affinity with words; that the Word has the *power* of the divine within it, characterises the nineteenth and twentieth centuries more than any other epoch in religious history.

But this does not mean a more spiritual and humane society. Indeed, quite the contrary; as the religions claim stronger allegiance for their respective sacred texts, the more they tend to vie for superiority in the world. And this search for dominance is not just in the religious sphere, but in the social, economic and political one also. All feed off the same misguided source: the culture of exile!

It is well known that many of the evangelical sects in North and South America command huge economic resources. The Dutch Reformed Church quite unashamedly reinforced the apartheid system in South Africa for several decades. And the Islamic alliance of the religious and political spheres does not produce a more wholesome human or earthly society, but quite a sinister, oppressive and dangerous ideology.

The focus on the Word, when examined closely, has little to do with genuine faith or spirituality, but everything to do with patriarchal dominance, the masculine will-to-power, and the culture of exile and alienation. Prior to 1960, in both the Protestant and Catholic Churches, only male clergy were allowed to study scripture or theology. Since 1960 that picture has changed dramatically, and it is now estimated that by the year 2010, 60 per cent of all theologians in the Catholic Church will be lay people, and at least three-quarters of those will be women. What this essentially means is that the traditional power-structure will be undermined significantly; a new egalitarian consciousness will be set free and theology will assume a radically new shape, the contours of which we will explore in subsequent chapters.

Meanwhile, the traditional Churches and religions continue to emphasise a religion of *preaching* and *proclaiming*, while an ever-decreasing remnant of faithful followers look to the Churches for 'the truth' in terms of faith adherence and moral obligation. It is the Church's rigid allegiance to the communication of the Word that contributes largely to religion's demise in today's world.

The present generation believes in action and not in mere words. In a sense, our world is so bombarded with empty rhetoric – from politicians, economists, social planners, media consumers and religious manipulators – that many reflective people are becoming highly suspicious of any strategy that relies too heavily on the *spoken* word. Most of what is said, we suspect, has ulterior motives, which ultimately are not in the best interests of person or planet.

The growing irrelevance of the word is also accentuated by the power and impact of multi-media. A speech-content on television carries so much more impact than that delivered from a podium or pulpit. The effect of image, and the variations made possible through a TV channel, makes the lone speaker anachronistic and ineffective. In an age of mass communication, where knowledge itself is the primary and most powerful commodity, verbiage and rhetoric cuts little ice for many of our contemporaries.

In fact, the revolution taking place is even more profound. It is not uncommon today for people in therapeutic work, e.g. counselling or therapy, to explore deep feelings and emotions using a *non-verbal* mode. A client may experience an inability to express in words an internal dream or struggle; invite that person to adopt a non-verbal medium, e.g. art, clay, movement, music, etc. and quite quickly something deep within is released. What could not be spoken to (or about) unfolds when something more than the verbal mode is adopted. In fact, for some clients, words seem to get in the way. In terms of their internal process they seem to be transcending the need for verbal communication; what serves them better is the non-verbal, or more appropriately the *super*-verbal.

Something quite important seems to be transpiring here, one that may have enormous implications for history and evolution itself. As already indicated, we humans have been using the verbal mode for approximately 100,000 years, about 5 per cent of our time on Earth since the emergence of *Homo Erectus* some two million years ago. We know that throughout that two million-year span, we have been a highly innovative and creative species, and many of the achievements of that time required close collaboration with one another and with our Earth. Undoubtedly, communication took place, and much of it was both intelligent and sophisticated. From an evolutionary point of view, the *non-verbal* potential is more natural, innate and deeply rooted in our collective psyche than the propensity for spoken language. Perhaps, today, evolution is pushing us to a new threshold in which we can transcend the rigidity and structure of the spoken form and reclaim in a more explicit way the liberation and creativity of the non-verbal mode!

For some readers, these ideas may seem speculative and even supercilious. For a spirituality of the twenty-first century, however, they may be of central importance. The external structures of building and spoken word do not inspire or awaken religious sentiment in people of our age; yet, people continue to search for spiritual meaning, and explore spiritual outlets.

The widespread interest in meditation, especially since about 1960, may be further evidence that spirituality has become more inward – which is very different from becoming more introverted. A weariness prevails around all the external facade, pomp and ceremony; it does not speak to the heart any more. And as people become more enlightened, the more they perceive (or at least suspect) that the foundations – of building and word especially – are indeed very shaky!

The time is ripe for a type of religious quantum leap – not into some vast unknown, but into the deep *story*, the well-spring of spiritual awakening which existed before, and will continue to flourish long after, every religion known to humankind will have faded into history. The time is ripe to forgo and outgrow the amnesia imposed by the culture of exile and to reclaim the great subverted story of who we really are as a human spiritual species. When we choose to come out of our alienation, then we liberate the Spirit within: that's the beginning of the long journey home!

— 4 —

Exiled from the Earth

We are not even aware of our loss, consequently, the pain of our
spiritual exile is more intense in being largely unintelligible.

John O'Donohue

The emptiness that many people complain dominates their lives comes
in part from a failure to let the world in, to perceive it, and engage it fully.

Thomas Moore

THE REFLECTIONS OF PREVIOUS chapters highlight the
source of that *exile* I wish to describe in more detail in the
present chapter. There are two fundamental strands to this
experience of exile: firstly, from the Earth itself, with which
humans have felt an inseparable bond and sense of connectedness
for millions of years, and, secondly, our imposed separation from
the cosmos with which we maintain a psychic connection because
of our groundedness in the created world that surrounds us.

Generally speaking, religion has nothing to offer us to make
sense of either of those primordial connections with 'home'.
Much more serious is the fact that religion seems to set out to
alienate us into exile from those ancient and primal connections.
All the religions, as already indicated, breed an anti-world polemic,
with varying degrees of distrust, antagonism and denunciation of
the created order.

A central element of our sense of exile is the fragmentation of
space and time about which Abram (1996) and Goodenough (1998)
writes so elegantly. For at least 90 per cent of our time on Earth,
we humans related with life as a space–time continuum; for much
of our history, we measured time by the rhythms we encountered in
the space around us. And we interpreted time cyclically long
before the linear and piecemeal understanding which is little more
than a few thousand years old.

The experience of exile wrought in the name of religion attacks time, however, in an even more destructive way. It colludes with the patriarchal perception that civilisation is no more than 5,000 years old, thus creating a time capsule which undermines not merely human sacredness but radically desacralises the spiritual potential of the universe itself.

Disconnection becomes the order of the day; *divide and conquer* becomes the governing politics and the ruling ideology (theology). The sacred story of previous millennia – the immediacy of spiritual connection with the elements of nature, with the rhythms of wind and sea, with the changing and cyclic seasons, with the tradition of the Great Earth Mother Goddess – is subjected to the barbaric forces of patriarchal domination. Humans are expelled from the garden of life; we become strangers in a foreign land.

Exiled from God

All the religions try to convince us that the alienation we often feel is because of our distance from God, and our refusal to follow God's way. Therefore, we overcome our sense of estrangement by returning to God, *as the religion indicates.*

This is the bait on which billions have been hooked throughout the dark age of civilisation. This is what Karl Marx quite accurately called the 'opium of the people'. It is the blind delusion that promises utopia in that home from home, variously called heaven or Nirvana. Only then, we are told, will we be at one with God. What is really meant is that we will be totally subservient to the great patriarchal father-God, the one that validates all patriarchal power in heaven and Earth alike.

The way of formal religion is not a way out of exile; we only reach the promised land when life is over! Religion condemns us to perpetual estrangement, and the more we examine the *redemption* doctrines of the various faiths, the more it becomes apparent that instead of liberating people towards *salvation*, they only plunge us deeper into despair and ennui.

Because the God of formal religion is modelled on the governing principles of the patriarchal system, this can never be the God of unconditional love purported by many of the religious Scriptures of the various traditions. A love that requires that you must first obey is not a free love, nor indeed is it a full love in any

meaningful sense. Rather it is the collusive type of love that often
begets destructive and abusive relationships, the type illustrated
in the required sacrifice of Abraham (Gen. 22:1–18), with apparently the boy's mother having no say whatever in the matter.

Within formal religion, one feels a sense of being exiled from
God, because the religion itself requires this form of alienation in
order to function effectively. An experience of being exiled is
endemic to religion. The ensuing sense of estrangement does not
arise because we lack a proper relationship with God. Rather it
arises from the other dysfunctional relationships that the religion
requires in order to be a follower of that God.

These dysfunctional relationships include the ambivalence
towards, and the disconnectedness from, one's earthiness, one's
sense of cosmic connectedness, and the freedom to act more
creatively. Fear, and not freedom, governs the value-system of
formal religion. The exile of religion thrives on the fear of never
being able to placate that loving but insatiable sky-God, who requires
us to bypass all our earthly homeliness to reach the utopia on high.

One begins to realise that the sense of exile is a self-perpetuated,
co-dependent state that alienates not merely from 'God', but also
from self, others, the Earth and the entire engagement of our
cosmic and planetary existence. It jeopardises everything of our
graced potential to become creatures of meaning, purpose and
imagination. It usurps energy and vitality, and in extreme cases,
sucks one into a deadly inferno of emptiness and despair.

What I wish to establish in the opening section of this chapter
is that the experience of exile is not really about God. For most of
our evolutionary history, we humans do not seem to have had a
major problem with God! In the absence of formal religion we
connected with the 'divine' through the processes of nature, and
we do not seem to have had great difficulty in holding together the
polarities of destruction and creation which always beget the
process of evolution.

And when life allowed, or encouraged, us to develop our creative
faculties, as in the artistic explorations of paleolithic times, we
personalised the divine, not as a male deity on some royal heavenly
throne, but as a prodigiously sexual and fertile woman whose body
was that of the Earth itself. The modern concept of humans being
co-creators with the divine was probably already well known and
well integrated by our ancestors in the paleolithic era.

Our sense of exile today is not about God, but rather about the alienation caused by our cosmic and planetary homelessness. It is our sense of being out of tune with the Earth, and the clay of our own bodies, that makes us feel like aliens in our own land. In the words of Abram (1996, p. 196), 'The pain, the sadness of this exile, is precisely the trace of what has been lost, the intimation of a forgotten intimacy.' Our meagre identity in such a vast universe also beleaguers us – largely because patriarchy creates a false and superficial opposition between us and the ground of our being and becoming.

Exile in the mainstream religions

All the religions thrive on the perception that they possess a special quality of divinely endowed wisdom which:

1. presupposes (rather than proves) that we humans have *always* felt a spiritual sense of estrangement; that God has so designed creation that alienation is built into the very fabric of the divine-human relationship;
2. enables us to resolve the estrangement that is part and parcel of human and planetary existence.

As a broad generalisation, the great Eastern religions seem more authentically connected with the spiritual culture of pre-patriarchal times and, therefore, employ a *cyclic* basis to religious belief; a person has to endure several cycles of suffering, struggle and longing before eventually achieving the state of enlightenment or liberation and thus escape into Nirvana. Contrary to the Calvinistic slant of Christendom, the Eastern religions attribute the release into Nirvana to humankind's own efforts, rather than having to throw oneself completely at the mercy of God. By way of comparison, Islam veers towards a mixture of the two, although the anthropocentric (and male) emphasis tends to take priority.

The monotheistic religions tend to opt for a once-off process, with a powerful intervention by God – at the personal and planetary levels – to rescue humanity from its alien state (formally known in theological jargon as the state of *original sin*). Volumes have been written on which of the two systems might be right, or what are the advantages of one over the other. I suggest both are best regarded as human projections – highly anthropomorphic ones – to abet the patriarchal drive for ultimate control over the whole of life, the divine included.

The Jewish faith, and in consequence Christianity, is where we see the notion of exile assume central importance. The historical context is that of the attack on Jerusalem by the Babylonian king, Nebuchadnezzar, in 586/587 BCE. The temple in Jerusalem was burned, the holy city was destroyed, the Davidic dynasty was terminated and the leading citizens, i.e. the political classes and the skilled workers, were deported to Babylon.[1]

In 538 BCE, Cyrus, the king of Persia, overcame the Babylonians, and permitted the Jews to return to their homeland; many chose to remain where they were. This attempt at return and restoration failed to actualise many of the grandiose expectations we read about in the prophetic literature of the Hebrew Scriptures.

Over the centuries, in fact right up to 1948 when Israel became a State in its own right, both Jews and Christians have used the concept of exile with a great deal of imperial rhetoric and spurious religious intent. Exile became a powerful metaphor, but as Neusner (in Scott, 1997, pp. 221–37) suggests, one that engendered resentment and regression rather than authentic spiritual progress. It also becomes a major contribution to the exclusive and sectarian notion of the 'chosen people' perceived to be superior and holier than the millions of others created by the same God.

Regarding the original historical basis for the notion of exile, we note some salient points:

1. It was only the leading citizens who were deported. The vast majority of the people remained, and indications are that they were well treated. The sense of loss expressed around the deportation of the leading citizens (all of whom were men, as far as we know) indicates the power of patriarchal rule, the utter dependency of the people on their leaders, and the insinuation that in the absence of these leading figures, God had also abandoned the people. In other words, God could not even be invoked, unless the patriarchal powers did the invoking.

2. As indicated above, the Jews in Babylon were offered the option to return, and the majority refused. They were content in the foreign land, and, seemingly, quite well treated there. The metaphor of exile thenceforth took on a whole new

meaning, one that flies in the face of all the historical facts, but is retained and augmented because it reinforces the power and prospect of the patriarchal governors.

3. What is most intriguing is the way in which God is depicted and described – presumably to suit the patriarchal rhetoric. For those in exile (i.e. the leaders), it feels like God has abandoned them, that God himself is gone into exile. When the exiles choose not to return, the notion of God's abandonment becomes quite convoluted, throwing into turmoil the patriarchal expectation that God should act as the ruling forces expect God to act. The shallow and idolatrous foundations of patriarchal religion have been exposed; and, not for the first time, the patriarchs chose not to see!

The notion of exile as described in the Hebrew Scriptures is both political and communal, yet as translated into religious observance and piety over the centuries became progressively individualised. The desert conditions of the Middle East became the metaphorical space for the idealised, heroic Christian life. Spiritual discipleship was depicted as a battle with the harsh elements of nature, a reminder that the spiritual life was an unrelenting struggle to regain 'paradise', the home from which humans had been expelled and which could only be reclaimed through a special divine favour combined by a life of asceticism and sacrifice.

Although the desert spirituality does not surface in the great Eastern religions, their monastic systems adopt an ascetical programme very similar to the West. In fact, Buddhist monastic life is a great deal more severe and frugal than the Western forms. And the notion that we humans are exiles in pilgrimage, aliens struggling to find our way back 'home', is a central theme of all the major religions.

In all cases the alienation we describe is not just about a global or cultural sense of being exiled or estranged. The sense of external fragmentation quickly invades the realms of inner being. Body and soul become disconnected; human wholeness becomes fragmented. The religion of 'divide and conquer' eats like a cancer into the very recesses of the human soul.

And so we note in all the religions the tendency to individualise both the notions of sin and salvation. We are each responsible before God for our exile and alienation, and the onus is on each one of us to save our individual souls and find our way into God's eternal life. Holiness then becomes a competitive battle, inspired by a litany of holy idealists (most of whom were male) each striving to be one up on everybody else in the crazy mutilation of the human self.

Were it not for the fact that many of these same saintly people were also outstanding in works of mercy, justice and compassion, most would have ended their days in idiotic madness. Yet, in many cases, what has been recorded for posterity is not their outstanding charity but their outlandish asceticism. The metaphor of the *hero* always takes priority in the rule of patriarchy; the central metaphor of the Christian Gospel (and, indeed, of all the great religions), the *helper*, is not merely side-tracked but often portrayed as the fruit of the ascetical ideal.

Heyward (1989, p. 11) names with pungent realism the under-lying energies of these two metaphors:

> Heroes show us who we are *not*. Helpers show us who we *are* . . . Heroes diminish our senses of relational, or shared, power. Helpers call us forth into our power in relation and strengthen our sense of ourselves . . . Heroes have brought us causes and crusades, flags and battles, soldiers and bombs. As our liberators and leaders, popes and presidents, mentors and gurus, heroes have brought us pipedreams and smokescreens and everything but salvation. And this, I am persuaded, is because we tend to search everywhere except among our selves-in-relation for peace.

In recent decades, all the religions are striving to reclaim a *communal* (i.e. relational) aspect to their life and mission. The robust individualism has currently gone out of fashion. Allegiance to religious authority tends to be spoken of in terms of 'fidelity', to God and to others. We speak of the 'fellowship of faith' and the 'family of the Church'. Yet, despite the warm and welcoming veneer, millions continue to feel a sense of alienation in life, and formal religion rarely provides a meaningful response.

Exile and disconnectedness

The Jewish notion of exile provides a type of crystallisation of a pervasive sense of alienation which dominated the world of the time. In fact, this sense of alienation had been building up for possibly 5,000 years and seems to have reached its zenith in the centuries immediately preceding the initiation of the Christian era. Some claim that it reached its apex in the mechanistic world-view of the sixteenth and seventeenth centuries.

The core element in that process of estrangement seems to have been alienation from the universal created order and specifically from planet Earth itself. Consequently all the religions, and particularly the monotheistic ones, associate the felt alienation with *land*. The people have become disconnected from their grounding, from their foothold in the Earth itself. Because of the patriarchal compulsion of conquering, dividing and portioning-out land, with its accompanying rivalries and hostilities, people had been uprooted. The human soul and the soul of the Earth, in harmony for millions of years, had been torn apart:

> The Jewish sense of exile was never merely a state of separation from a specific locale, from a particular ground; it was (and is) also a sense of separation from the very possibility of being placed, from the very *possibility* of being entirely at home. (Abram, 1996, p. 196)

The religions, in trying to address the alienation from the Earth, offer the only solution patriarchy knows: reconnect the people with *a portion* of land, which the patriarchs have named the 'nation–state', and which under their patriarchal view of God they believe is the way God wants them to deal with land. But for millions of years, the people have befriended the land in its totality, in all its global and universal dimensions. They have never known a restricted space called a 'nation–state' and they don't want to know it. The people want to relate to the *whole* of the land; the entire Earth is home, and nothing short of this planetary home-coming will satisfy the yearnings of the human heart.

The alienation is also about the loss of *mother* (cf. Pirani, 1991). Our ancestors looked to the Earth as the great nourishing mother, a robust figure that at times could be fiercely protective and paradoxically destructive (hence the strange notion in Rev. 12:4 of the mother giving birth and immediately consuming its offspring). Patriarchal religion could not even hear these yearnings, since one of its main functions was to undermine the power of the great

Goddess. Religious disconnection seeks to dismember, above all else, the power of the feminine.

The religious response is also one of congesting reductionism. In the ancient spiritual wisdom the people looked to the elements and cycles of nature for wisdom and guidance. They tuned in to the flow of nature itself; they were able to listen deeply and drink from wells which provided spiritual and practical nourishment. Now all that is being castigated as paganism and idol worship. The umbilical link with universal wisdom is being severed. The people's innate sense of coherence is dislodged. The great universal wisdom embodied in the land and sky is reduced to the rituals of place and word. The spiritual energy is being choked to death.

Viewed in this light, it is neither brash nor exaggerated to suggest that people have never really taken to religion: it was imposed upon them; they had no choice. Progressively, they were deluded into thinking that religion would provide something of the sense of connection and 'being at home' that they had known of old; the only aspect of religion that marginally achieved this is *mysticism*. For human beings, formal religion is profoundly alienating.

The segregation and disconnection from the Earth is at the root of all human alienation, painfully displayed in the world today with millions of people driven from homes and loved ones. According to the UNHCR Report: *The State of the World's Refugees* (1997), there are 22,729,233 refugees in the world today; the true figure is at least double that.

Slavery is another major source of cultural and personal dislocation. According to Bales (1999) an estimated 27 million people are kept in slavery, robbed not merely of their freedom but of any hope of ever knowing what it means to feel at home on the Earth.

Ironically, the refugees may be the people that will enable us to reclaim the Earth as home once more. In their cruel and merciless ostracisation, they know no home other than planet Earth and those few nations that are willing to welcome them in. Were it not for the patriarchal invention of the nation–state, we may well not have a refugee problem at all. And with religion fuelling barbaric practices such as ethnic cleansing and the Islamic *Jihad*, one also wonders how much religion contributes to this great scandal of our age.

Renewed concern for the plight of the Earth, the revival of creation–centred spirituality, the reawakening of Green consciousness, are not just contemporary fads nor are they merely movements seeking to address the precarious ecology of our planet today. They symbolise a great deal more, something profoundly spiritual, but not necessarily religious. They express a deep yearning to come home to who we really are, children of Mother Earth, people whose interdependent existence requires a quality of relatedness that has been fragmented and disconnected by the forces of patriarchal power, of which formal religion is a major factor.

Evangelicals (of all religions) rightly perceive the religious connotations of the Green consciousness and the new ecological sensitivity. And their fears that this could be a new religious movement that would draw people away from mainstream religion are well founded. For the evangelicals, however, the problem is in their fears and not in their perceptions. Like all those immersed in formal religion, they read reality from a narrow, and usually defensive, perspective. They are already disconnected from the great story; consequently, they are unable to make the connections that millions are forging in our time.

The end of religion?

If religion is to survive its current crisis, and reverse its decline, it will have to connect with the spiritual hunger of our age, one that is profoundly searching for new earthly and global connections. The religious agenda of our time has long outgrown the central concerns of formal religion. Might this mean the end of religion itself? I suggest that this is a likely possibility, and a highly desirable one!

In that case, was religion a mistake in the first place? Probably not! Evolution is not a neat linear progression in which things build systematically on each other: it tends to work in starts and bursts, with a great mixture of light and shadow. Evolution embodies a great deal of darkness and destruction – which paradoxically seem essential to the grand scheme and the overall pattern. And many times throughout the course of evolution, major achievements of previous epochs have had to die (in total extinction) before a new and usually unprecedented leap could take place (see Eldredge, 1999).

The rise of formal religion fits uncomfortably into evolution's trajectory. It diminishes and tends to reify the elegance and magnificence of divine creativity manifested over the aeons of time. It congests reality into narrow functional categories that honour neither the grandeur of the divine nor the creativity of the human. Its tendency to undermine and disown the power of the feminine is a particularly disturbing aberration.

While religion has aided the development of the human species, it has done so in an unbalanced, ambiguous and misguided fashion. It has colluded with the patriarchal drive to exalt humanity over the rest of creation, thus breeding the ferocious anthropocentrism that reaps such havoc in our world today. Religion has contributed very little to the development of the Earth itself, and as Lynn White proffered many years ago, religion (he was alluding to the Judeao–Christian tradition) may well be the main cause of the current ecological crisis.

The great misconception on which religion has arisen – and will eventually collapse – is that humans are a species set apart to conquer and control the Earth. Religion seems to have no appreciation of the fact that we intimately belong to the Earth; and without a meaningful sense of our earthiness, our lives become quite meaningless.

Religion in its essential essence is about alienation from the Earth and from the cosmos. Yet, as Hodgson (1994, p. 375, n. 30) reminds us, 'Estrangement is not a necessary condition of creation; on the contrary, it is a distortion and disruption of what is essentially good.' Tragically, religion continues to adopt the patriarchal perception that the human life form is superior to all other life forms, and relativises every other form by setting itself up as the absolute and enduring reality. A mere glance at the story of evolution illustrates that creation thrived for billions of years before we ever existed, and will continue to do so long after we have become a redundant species.

Any allusion to the demise of religion engenders fears of pagan darkness and the prospect of even greater alienation. This is where the distinction noted earlier between religion and spirituality becomes important. We humans do not need religion in order to live religiously. Innately, we are spiritual beings with a transparency for meaning, mystery and the divine.

Religion restricts and restrains our spiritual capacity and, effectively, aborts our spiritual will-to-meaning. And in setting up the dualistic oppositions of flesh and spirit, sacred and secular, the human and the divine, we have fragmented the very foundations of our emergence and unfolding as spiritual people. This is the basis of our exile and alienation.

Initially, the decline of religion will lead to a cultural vacuum. Evidence for this is already widespread. We note it in the moral vacuum of the West, whereby greed, exploitation and economic expediency over-ride all other considerations. We see it in the escalating spiral of violence which respects neither people nor property. We evidence it even among many religious believers in which religion and daily life rarely, if ever, inform each other in a creative and constructive way. Nowhere is the vacuum more deleterious than in the distinction between Church and State, allowing politicians to fudge their moral and cultural responsibility to protect and foster people's deepest values – of which the *spiritual* is one of the most basic.

Exile and human restlessness

While religion continues to decline and disintegrate (a process that will take hundreds, perhaps thousands of years), a growing spiritual consciousness engages our attention and research. The key elements of this new upsurge I outline in a previous work (Ó Murchu, 1997b). This is a diffuse movement with a vast spectrum of expression and experience across the human world of our time. I conclude the present chapter with some reflections on that subversive restlessness which, on the one hand, is enabling us to name the exile for what it really is, and in that very process is empowering us to see a way through and beyond it.

In examining the major cultural shifts that have happened over time, the sociologist Pitrim Sorokin (1950) suggests that the primary catalysts of social and cultural change tend to be 'the restless middle classes'. Colinvaux (1980, p. 50) endorses this view:

> I suggest it is axiomatic of human history that social upheavals, even revolutions, do not emerge from the ranks of the poor, for all the claims of Marxists that they do. They come from the disaffected individuals of the middle classes, the people who experience real ecological crowding and who must compete for the right to live better than the mass.

These observations help us to identify the personal and social dynamics that characterise the culture of exile and provide the impetus to move beyond it. All the major religions support a 'preferential option for the poor'. While nobly intended, this can be a misguided and dangerous veneer for one of the most crippling collusions ever known to the human species.

For the poor of our world, *survival* is all that matters. All their energy is invested in this primary concern. The more precarious the human and material culture, the more they will look to external supports to give some semblance of hope and meaning. Religious 'faith' comes much easier to people whose existence is under threat than to those who are doing reasonably well.

This dependence on formal religion serves well the culture of patriarchal religiosity. People who live in fear of God are much more likely to be conducive to earthly authorities also. Respect for authority, politically and ecclesiastically, involves respect for God as the justification for such allegiance. There are several questionable and disturbing elements to this collusive package.

Ironically, the rich and powerful often exhibit strong religious adherence and strangely can keep their religious belief and practice totally separate from their political and economic lives. South American Catholicism of the twentieth century is saturated with 'loyal and faithful' rulers who butchered thousands of 'dissidents', often in the name of saving the world from the curse of communism; in many cases, bishops and high-ranking clerics fully supported the process.

When it comes to confronting the distorted culture of exile, the poor are too preoccupied with survival to even notice the corruption around them. As long as the religion will maintain a focus on the suffering Saviour on the Cross with whom the poor and suffering can identify, they don't feel a need to ask much more of the religion.[2] On the other hand, the rich use the religion, presumably because it helps in some way to enhance their power and their right to exercise authority.

As perceptive scholars like Sorokin and Colinvaux indicate, it is the *restless middle classes* that begin to raise suspicions, questions and subversive stories. And it is not merely for their own improvement, as Colinvaux intimates. There is something much deeper at work here, perhaps something akin to a systemic undercurrent fuelled by the power of the Jungian collective unconscious. Consequently, while one sector of the disaffected may resort to violence, others will veer more towards social opting out, of the type often associated with the New Age movement.

It seems to me that there is no such thing as a 'respectable' way to respond to the restlessness that characterises our time of transition. It is a complex phenomenon, driven by forces over which we do not exert rational control. And if we try to control it rationally, the chances are that we'll strip it of its real spiritual and cultural potential. The great C. S. Lewis (1964, pp. 222–3) probably had an intuitive glimpse of this phenomenon when he wrote:

> It is not impossible that our own model (of reality) will die a violent death, ruthlessly smashed by an unprovoked assault of new facts . . . But I think it is more likely to change when and because far-reaching changes in the mental temper of our descendants demand that it should. The new model will not be set up without evidence, but the evidence will turn up when the inner need for it becomes sufficiently great. It will be true evidence. But nature gives most of her evidence in answer to the questions we ask her. Here, as in the courts, the character of the evidence depends on the shape of the examination, and a good cross-examiner can do wonders.

Around our world, increasing numbers of people engage in the 'cross-examination'; they are no longer prepared to live with the culture of exile. This sense of disenchantment is no longer a feature of rebellious students of the 1960s, nor does it merely belong to the huge numbers of Americans disillusioned by the outcome of the Vietnam war. What we describe is a growing universal phenomenon, pioneered in many cases today – with disturbing levels of violence – by the emerging peoples of Africa and South East Asia. Perhaps it is here more than anywhere else that religion is the great loser. It is totally at a loss on how to respond to the emerging culture – and, for the disaffected at least, they no longer look to the religion for a hopeful response!

Admittedly, this does leave us with a dangerous moral and spiritual vacuum. More accurately, it leaves us with several such 'wastelands' in the now globally diffuse situations in which this new emergence is unfolding. But we are not without hope and fresh vision. Where we look for it, is the first major challenge; we won't find it from within the major institutions of Church or State, but rather in those liminal, marginal spaces where small creative networks dream new, innovative and subversive possibilities for the future.

These liminal spaces provide hope for the future, and the nature of their often chaotic and subversive explorations is what we'll explore in Part Two of this book. Meanwhile we need to trust this unfolding process and seek to engage with it at several levels of participation. We need to tolerate its untidiness and its occasional deviant slants. Above all, we need to learn to befriend its chaotic and creative emergence, as we would the birth of a newborn infant. Hopefully, the reflections in the second part of this book will help awaken in us a receptivity and welcome for that new spiritual vision that characterises the journey home from exile.

— 5 —

From Chaos to Cosmos

Science has been a process of differentiating our knowledge into an incredible wealth of precise details, but these details become ever more disconnected from one another and cry out for integration into coherent wholes.

Elizabet Sahtouris

Life can educate one to a belief in God.

Ludwig Wittgenstein

THE TITLE FOR THIS CHAPTER I borrow from a pioneering work of the Greek physicist, Elizabet Sahtouris (Sahtouris, 1989) whose vision embraces many disciplines and provides some valuable landmarks for our journey through and beyond the turbulent times in which we live. In terms of our human role in the evolutionary cosmic process, Sahtouris suggests that we behave like belligerent adolescents and that the time is now ripe for us to move toward the stage of young adulthood, thus learning to respond in more responsible and creative ways. In a word, our relationship with the creation around us needs to mature into a more creative and co-operative endeavour.

To assist us in taking this step towards adulthood, Sahtouris advocates a reassessment of how living systems operate within the process of evolution itself. Therein, she suggests, we will encounter valuable guidelines to direct our own behaviour so that we relate with our planet and the wider creation in a more harmonious and productive way.

In mythology, the place of exile is often associated with the *desert*, a place of dislocation, confusion, alienation, often accompanied by the bewildering sense that the surrounding world is in the grip of frightening evil forces. *Chaos* characterises every moment and experience of this bewildering place. There is no order, harmony or meaning. Everything seems to be falling apart, and the way out is far from clear.

A great deal of chaos prevails in the world of our time, often kept at bay by defensive tactics of denial and scapegoating. If you don't look you won't see, and if you do see what's going on, find somebody to blame for it. In that way you can direct the attention to the scapegoat, away from the reality itself. Our patriarchal culture will go to great lengths to keep the forces of chaos at bay. One wonders for how long!

It is fashionable these days to talk about chaos – in physics, biology, business organisation and even in economics! It sounds like we might be encountering a new wave of archetypal energy in which old realities are being tossed and torn loose from time-honoured moorings. Some scholars go so far as to claim that the theory of chaos may well be to the last decade of the twentieth century what relativity and quantum theory was to the opening decades. In a sense, the theory feels right, because, I suggest, the actual experience of being in chaos is so endemic to our times.

In contemporary science, two views prevail on how we understand this new theory. One seeks out the deep order which it claims underlines all forms of chaotic behaviour, while the other suggests that the order will unfold as the chaos is allowed to follow its natural course. Metaphorically, these may be seen as complementary rather than conflicting approaches to our understanding of chaos theory.

Attractions of the heart?

In the course of the present chapter I wish to adopt some key concepts from chaos theory to help us unravel some of our experiences in the situation of exile in which we find ourselves today. In daily life, chaos refers to those turbulent situations where disorder and disharmony prevail to varying degrees. When modelled with the aid of modern computers, we begin to encounter intriguing images that highlight the tendency towards order and structure within all forms of chaos. These discoveries not merely change the face of modern science but impact significantly on how we interpret the experience of our everyday lives, especially in those moments of cultural exile and spiritual dislocation.

A phenomenon known as a 'strange attractor' is particularly relevant to our reflections. For a number of years we have been aware of disorderly systems, e.g. weather patterns, cloud formation, smoke waves, stock-market prices, whose turbulence we could neither measure nor predict. Turbulence simply did not obey the laws of science, and for the scientist that means we wait until we discover the wisdom to test and interpret its real meaning.

Along come computers and we feed in our information! And things begin to happen that we had scarcely anticipated. When a system is first dislodged from its stable state, it moves into a period of oscillation, swinging back and forth between different states. If it becomes dislodged from the oscillation, then we expect full chaos, where everything should fall apart. In fact, it rarely does.

It is at this juncture that the system *spontaneously* re-organises. The computer-generated phase space magnetically pulls the system into various ordered patterns, often resembling firework displays or galactic formations. The energy that draws the system into an ordered pattern we call a strange attractor.

What phase space diagrams show is that chaos too has an 'attractor', a pattern that is neither a fixed point nor a limited cycle, but an orbit that always stays within certain bounds without ever crossing over or repeating itself (see Figure 5.1). A line that never doubles over itself loops round and round the computer screen in an infinitely deep and complex demonstration of the fine structure that constrains what we have thought of as a disorder. No two loops of the attractor are exact replicas; although there is convergence, there is no overlap or repetition.

Chaos is a science of pattern, not of predictability. It reminds us that in nature an exact replication of behaviour may lead to disaster rather than to progress. And in times of major transition, as in the current cultural journey of our turbulent age, relying on the predictable and well-tested truths of yesteryear may have disastrous consequences.

What are the 'basins of attraction' that characterise an age of religion in decline, a space of religious exile? Chaos theory suggests that these will not be found within the traditional religious institutions. Consequently, we need to look to the peripheries, and often well beyond them.

There are several cultural movements of our time that have a spiritual inspiration, although they quite explicitly shun religion

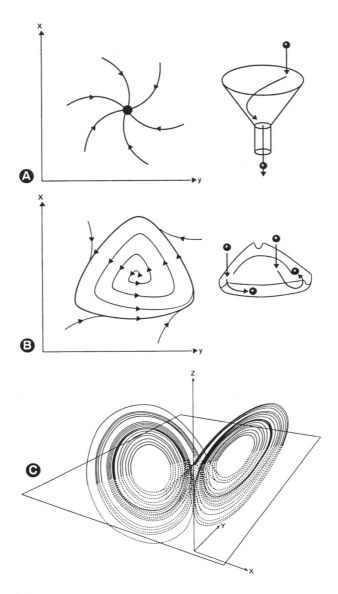

Figure 5.1: Strange Attractors Scientists use various types of attractors to model reality. The three illustrated here are the most widely used. (a) A fixed point attractor where movement is attracted to a fixed point; (b) A cyclic, or limit-cycle attractor, where the point of attraction is not stationary but follows a predictable, repeating cycle; (c) The strange attractor – here the system's movement seems chaotic and unpredictable, yet the system is being drawn towards an overall pattern as if 'in search' for a new solution to a novel situation. Source: Peter Coveney & Roger Highfield, *Frontiers of Complexity*, London: Faber & Faber; New York: Ballantine Books, 1995. Reproduced with permission.

in any formal context. *Ecological* and *feminist* movements carry a strange ring of spirit and of truth. They name our search and our pain with, at times, seering clarity. They awaken within us long-lost subverted values stretching the boundaries of the sacred far beyond the limits set by formal patriarchal religion. As I have suggested elsewhere (Ó Murchu, 1997) they may well be the most prophetic movements of our time.

There are several other movements which disturb and challenge our perceptual neatness and our religious sensitivities. The religions try to dampen or subvert their impact, but for those among us journeying through exile, and hopefully beyond it, they make a great deal of sense at times. These include various New Age movements, alternative technologies, alternative health movements, alternative life-style communities. If only they were not so ambiguous and ambivalent! In other words, if we felt 'in charge' of what they are about, we'd feel so much more comfortable with them. The point about 'strange attractors' is that you cannot be in charge; a wisdom higher than yourself is driving the system, and not everything in its evolution makes sense to our rational minds.

Whither predictability?

Chaos theory has other insights that may be useful to us as we try to find our way around in the place of exile. It has a lot to say about *non-linear dynamics*; in simple language, straight lines can be terribly deceptive. And the notion of following a trajectory from point A to point B is of little use in a liminal place.

According to the linear world-view, things follow logically upon one another. If the logic becomes disrupted, you try to go back to where the disruption happened and embark anew upon the course you were following. And essentially you always repeat an already set pattern, with definitive unquestioned ways on how things should be done. Disruption, conflict, surprise, novelty are all considered to be deviancies, blips which arise from some source which neither knows nor respects the rational, logical, predictable pattern which, allegedly, evolution follows at every level of life.

Chaos theory informs us that it is not as simple as that, and in fact never has been. Evolution is full of blips, some of them being troughs of decline and extinction that lasted for millions of years. And the evolution of new species, or new behaviours, rarely happens according to the combination of chance and necessity postulated by Darwinian theory. Unpredictability, creativity, surprise and a great deal of chaos characterise the unfolding process (more on this topic in Laszlo, 1996).

Of particular relevance for the present chapter is the notion of 'the edge of chaos', where predictability is no longer operating and, therefore, unforeseen outcomes arise. This is also known as a bifurcation point, illustrated in Figure 5.2 as a straight line which suddenly and unexpectedly breaks off in two new branches, each of which may branch off again several times.

Take for instance a leaf floating on a stream and encountering a boulder; it has to go to left or right of the boulder. Up to that moment, the trajectory of the leaf can be observed and predicted, but we cannot predict which course it will follow upon encountering the boulder. Unpredictability (or chaos) takes over at that juncture. Subsequently, the leaf may once more resume a predictable course, but it may find itself 'knocked off balance' for quite a long time after that.

I want to extend the concept of the bifurcation point to explore our reactions and responses to the current alienation we humans often feel in our dealings with the contemporary world. Our sense of exile is, in large measure, the result of our obsessional concern for order and predictability. At the bifurcation points of life – and there are several in all our lives – education, religion and all the dominant modes of knowledge alert us to a state of irregularity that is likely to be dangerous and deviant. Rarely are we told that it might be the opportunity for a new breakthrough.

When things are falling apart, the advice usually given is retrace our steps, reclaim the former wisdom and return to the sure, predictable pathway. Apart from often being downright impractical, this may be intellectually, emotionally and spiritually destructive. At the crisis points of life, regression is rarely healthy. The crisis is an opportunity to make new strides forward, often into unknown territory. Usually, the risks are substantial, and in a culture fixated on certainty and predictability, the repercussions can be shattering to self-image and personal morale. Rebuttal, castigation and social exclusion are all too common.

Two examples from daily life highlight the challenge and complexity of what we describe. John is still a relatively young man at 34 years of age. He has just been informed that his workplace is

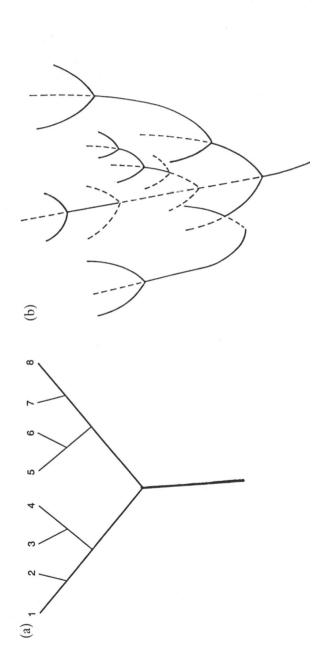

Figure 5.2: Bifurcation Points These diagrams illustrate the fork-in-the-road effect in which a system moves from a linear to a non-linear way of behaving. In (a) there is one major branching in which two new trajectories replace the original one and they in turn create other trajectories and are likely to continue doing so. In (b) the system is much more unpredictable and potentially more creative. The branching continues with both new and old expressions; several outcomes are possible.

closing one month from now. The promise and predictability of a long and promising career is suddenly smashed to pieces. His older friends bemoan the fact that 'a job for life' is a rare commodity these days. His trade union colleagues, on whom he relied so strongly, make loud noises about the injustice of the situation, and promise to make representation at the highest quarters. But John knows, and so do the trade union representatives, that they will not be able to reverse the decision. Somehow they feel they must go through the motions – a bargaining process that itself is also archaic and irrelevant. Everybody is trying to halt the chaos, but halting it will not work to anybody's advantage. Somehow, we have to find ways to befriend it.

In the Western world today, John's plight is all too common; yet we don't seem to have developed creative or dynamic skills to cope more constructively. Much more bewildering, and rarely explored in the open forum, is the bifurcation point whereby a married couple splits up and files for a divorce, often leaving a trail of betrayal, hurt and pain behind them. This situation is a great deal more complex because what may be a breakthrough for one partner (e.g., a new relationship) may be totally devastating for the other. Yet, in most cases, close examination will reveal that dynamics were at work in the relationship which, sooner or later, would lead to a serious breakdown.

The learnings for our time from this sensitive and complex example are even more urgent than that of the worker who is made redundant. It is in close relationships more than anywhere else that we form bonds of intimacy and trust that defy termination. Relationships thrive on long-term idealism, but require a great deal more if they are to continue to be enriching and sustainable. Like other aspects of human life, relationships have inbuilt limitations and fragilities. Many relationships stagnate, and remain stable over long periods of time on the strength of that stagnation. Increasingly, people tend not to remain in such relationships, no matter how binding the cultural or religious ties may be.

The lifelong commitment we assume to underpin serious relationships, such as marriage, requires of us today a radical reappraisal. The institution of marriage belongs to the sixteenth and seventeenth centuries when people often died in their 40s or early 50s. Most of their marital years were devoted to rearing their children. Stability was a key quality to understanding life at every level. Lifelong commitments reflected more the culture of the day rather than any noble religious ideals that we assume to have existed from time immemorial.

Today, people often live into their 70s and 80s. *Change* characterises our era. It is not uncommon to hear people say: 'S(he) is no longer the person I married.' Women particularly acknowledge that by mid-life they have often outgrown their male partners, developmentally and emotionally. I am not suggesting that the termination of a particular relationship is the solution to this predicament. I am simply trying to highlight the changed cultural conditions and the altered perceptions that ensue.

The tyranny of continuity

Our linear rational consciousness takes as normative the idea that things flow logically, one upon the other, in a sequence that we assume moves in one of two directions, forward or backward. This consciousness also assumes that there are wise people at the top whose task it is to ensure that things always move along the predictable route. People who operate on the basis of these perceptions have great difficulty in seeing the relevance of the bifurcation diagram above (Figure 5.2). The idea of splitting into two possible new directions – and the suggestion that these two trajectories might be *totally* new – feels like an assault on human intelligence.

Our Western culture suffers from a tyranny of *continuity* which, in fact, is a mask for a tyranny of stability. Patriarchal control requires us to have such a perception in place and to accord it un-questioned allegiance. But it flies in the face of everything that evolution evidences, and I am not merely alluding to the Darwinian notions of chance and necessity. Rather I am seeking to highlight what Eldredge and Gould (1985) call 'punctuated equilibria', an unfolding pattern, broken by surprising and unpredictable even-tualities, evidenced most poignantly in the great extinctions and the sudden outbursts of new life forms that often ensued.

Evolution illustrates the paradox of discontinuity on the grand scale; quantum theory does so on the microscopic level. The quantum leap describes an infinitesimally small change in the atom's trajectory, but one that affects all measurements thereafter, bringing into play the variables of uncertainty and unpredictability. Chaos theory helps us to grasp this same variance at many stages between the micro and macro levels of reality.

The Christian narrative of the death and resurrection of Jesus serves as a powerful illustration of the paradox we are considering. Theologically, we claim that Christ had to suffer and die before experiencing resurrection. Why it had to be this way, Jesus never explained to us. Nor do theologians do so in a convincing way, because in most cases they are encountering an *archetypal* story which sadly is often treated as if it was primarily an historical event.

Viewed in archetypal context, Jesus undergoes in his own life an experience that belongs to the whole of creation and reflects dynamics that are central to the course of evolution itself. Nowhere is this view of evolution spelt out so succinctly and imaginatively than in the classic work of Swimme and Berry (1992); consistently, they refer to this process as one characterised by the complementary dynamics of creation and destruction.

In the Christian model, there is no logical connection between death and resurrection. In the crucifixion of Jesus, everything of the known world falls apart. The dream of Jesus is in shatters, and, not surprisingly, his followers are scattered in despair and disillusionment. The fragmentation is vividly expressed in the words of the two disciples on the road to Emmaus: 'We had thought that he was the one who was going to set Israel free' (Luke 24:21). That had been their dream. That was the linear, logical, cause-and-effect line on which they had placed all their hopes. Now, they knew only hopelessness!

Yet the Jesus story ends in hope! In fact, all great archetypal stories end in hope, because ultimately hope characterises the very energy of evolution itself. The research of contemporary biblical scholars points increasingly to the poverty of reliable historical data around the actual event of the resurrection of Jesus. Paradoxically, the more we penetrate beyond the veneer of historical fact, the more we touch into the archetypal power of the experience which ultimately rescued the disillusioned apostles from their despair and disbelief.

In its archetypal meaning, resurrection is not about something that happened to Jesus, but about a radical change of perception in his followers. And it begins not with the dominant males (the twelve apostles) but with the marginalised females. All the Gospels agree on the central role played by the women in the initial encounter with the resurrection of Jesus. It was a small group of women that, amid great fear and confusion, began to recognize that something dramatically new and different had happened. For them the story of Jesus had not ended; rather it had undergone a massive paradigm shift. They could feel among them the presence of Jesus in a way that far exceeded what they had known of his physical embodied presence.

Ironically, in its initial moments this was not a pleasant or reassuring experience. The synoptic Gospels are at one in emphasising the fear and confusion of the women; these are exactly the feelings we all experience at the 'edge of chaos', when a known world has fallen apart and we can't make sense of the new one we are encountering. The new is radically different; it is not in continuity with the old. But if we have the intuition and wisdom to probe the ancient tradition, we will discover valuable insights toward understanding what is happening to us.

In the Gospel of Luke (24:6–8), we read the intriguing connection which the women make with the ancient story. The angelic voice (i.e. the wisdom voice) reminds the women of Jesus' own prediction of his suffering, death and subsequent resurrection using the formula cited on three crucial occasions in Mark's Gospel (Mark 8:31; 9:31; 10:33–34) – all of which were addressed to the *apostles*, traditionally assumed to be the male followers of Jesus. Are we to believe, therefore, that the women also heard, or possibly overheard, the words? Or is it possible that they 'heard' the message intuitively, through the power of feminine wisdom, and in the experience of chaos were able to invoke it in interpreting what was happening around them? Whatever the explanation, the writer of Luke's Gospel informs us that 'they remembered his words'. From thereon they are connected with deeper meaning, and the imperceptible order within the chaos gradually becomes transparent.

Are we dealing here with a metaphorical mode of memory as in *re-membering*, putting back together the pieces of a fragmented story and seeing – maybe for the first time – the meaning that ensues as the story is reconstructed? Luke's Gospel suggests that there is a distinctive energy shift at that moment: the women move away from the 'tomb', the context of chaos. They go to seek out the apostles and tell them what they have experienced. But the apostles do not believe them and allege that the women are talking nonsense (Luke 24:11).

Because the apostles have not been through the 'dark night', since they have not engaged with the chaos, they are unable to comprehend what the women have discovered. Rationality and creativity are in collision. In fact the dissonance probably continued for many years subsequently, since the patriarchal influence insists on keeping the apostles centre-stage, invoking the *symbolic* 40 days (which in reality may have been ten or twenty years) to bring about a change of heart, thus making redundant the original and more authentic witness of the women, without whom the transformation may never have happened in the first place.

In the Christian narrative of Calvary and resurrection we have a classic example of the shift named in the title of this chapter: from chaos to cosmos. The chaos of the Calvary event is measurable and verifiable even in some of its specific historical details. Crucifixion was extensively used in the Middle East by the occupying Roman forces. And the information we have about the death of Jesus makes a great deal of historical sense.

We're on a totally different plane in dealing with resurrection. The truth is that we have no precise historical details for anything that happened on that occasion. We rely totally on the story that was passed on which, traditionally, we have tended to interpret in literalist fashion – in keeping with our patriarchal need to control the information. Increasingly, these days scholars question the wisdom of this approach.

At an archetypal level the death–resurrection paradigm represents the shift from chaos to cosmos. Chaos is quantifiable, a here-and-now realm of experience. Cosmos characterises the shattering of all the here-and-now boundaries, and depicts a world of unlimited possibility. A whole new world is opened up; in the light of which the old order is no longer sustainable; in fact, it no longer makes any sense. Yes, assuredly, the old order was a necessary precondition for the new to emerge, but with the emergence of the new, the old is not renewed or revamped; rather, the old is declared to be redundant and, therefore, no longer relevant or useful.

It is this break between the old and the new, this lack of continuity, that meets with enormous resistance from the patriarchal guardians of our values and institutions. The resistance, I suggest, is all about *lack of control*. If we agree that something radically new can evolve, where does that leave the old guard who know how to manage current reality but may not be able to manage reality in a different guise. And if they can't manage it, who then will end up managing it? And could that mean that patriarchal power itself is under threat – even permanently?

Chaos theory is a welcome development as long as it is left at the level of conceptualisation. Although relativity and quantum theory have been with us for almost 80 years now, scholars still go to great pains to emphasise that they are not comprehensible at a rational level like classical theories were. Why not? Basically because scholars choose a language and jargon that tries to keep the general public in the dark. (In adopting abstract philosophical ideas and language, theologians do exactly the same thing.) Meanwhile, relativity theory has significantly advanced our understanding of the larger cosmos, while quantum theory provides the foundations for a great deal of contemporary technology, especially in the computer, electrical and medical spheres. Yet, we seem determined to safeguard the supremacy of the intellectual ruling class.

We confront a similar dilemma in engaging with chaos theory and its invitation to us to embrace unpredictability, untidiness and discontinuity as essential ingredients of evolution at every level of life. The scholars would do well to abandon the ivory towers of scholarship for a while and abide in the valley of exile. Quickly, they would discover that all the sophisticated theories have feet of clay. The real world is a rather chaotic place in which to be, but it is precisely from within the depths of that chaos that well-springs of creativity spring forth.

Standing on the bridge

This chapter is an attempt at building bridges between the exile that has forced us to forget who we essentially are as a human species, and the journey back home where we can begin to reclaim our true selves once more. In a sense, formal religion is the icing on the cake of our cultural alienation. It has given divine validation to our basic sense of estrangement. It has blessed that asceticism that sets us over against creation and purports the created order (our planet and the cosmos) to be a barrier between us and the God who will guarantee our ultimate fulfilment.

Religion, like modern science, thrives on reductionism. Although it claims to open us up to the mystery of God and to the mystery of life, it attempts to do so through a series of religious and legal requirements which stymie our spiritual creativity. Religion leaves us with an anthropocentric image of God, and seriously fractures the essential oneness of reality. We are left with a fragmented sense of who we are and what our role in the world is all about.

The awakening spiritual consciousness, through which we are struggling to rename our reality and tell afresh our true story, is based on a deep desire to build bridges. The alienations put in place to satisfy the patriarchal urge to divide and conquer no longer make sense to growing numbers of people. Pride in our individual national identities lags behind our desire to come together as one human family. We are no longer interested in the borders that divide and separate. We find ourselves encompassed by a layer of consciousness whereby we want to reclaim the freedom and creativity of former time when we roamed freely anywhere we wished on planet Earth.

Culture, language, religion, custom are often explained and expressed as important factors in achieving identity. What identity are we referring to? We take as given the fact that each of us is identified according to national, religious and ethnic lineage, whether it be French, Protestant, Asian, etc. Such categorisation is assumed to contribute to a more highly developed state, humanly and culturally, than that of the person who claims to be a spiritual seeker for whom the whole Earth is home. But this later claim is the one that characterises our human self-identity for well over 90 per cent of our time on Earth; the other – with its nationalistic, linguistic and religious specifity – is little more than 5,000 years old.

The driving forces of reductionism – separation, isolation, difference, atomism – do not contribute to creative self-discovery.[1] Those very things we cherish so deeply: nationalism, language, religion – the things we use to establish how we are different from everybody else, and especially from our *primitive* ancestors – may well be the things that alienate us painfully from God, from creation, from our own species and even from our inner selves. Coming home to who we really are will involve huge sacrifices, along with a radical reassessment of what it means to be cosmic planetary creatures.

While there are no easy solutions to this identity crisis, there is one fundamental dynamic that underpins our every effort:

connectedness! Its meaning is powerfully illustrated in astronaut
Michael Collins' description of being Earthstruck:

> The more we see of other planets, the better this one looks.
> When I travelled to the moon, it wasn't my proximity to that
> battered rock pile I remember so vividly, but rather what I saw
> when I looked back at my fragile home – a glistening, inviting
> beacon, delicate blue and white, a tiny outpost suspended in the
> black infinity. Earth is to be treasured and nurtured, something
> precious that *must* endure. (Quoted in Van Ness, 1996, p. 408)

At a deeply primal and primordial level we are creatures who
yearn for connection and relationality. Spiritual writers tend to
attribute this desire to a longing for God and for eternal life in
God's heavenly company. As I indicate many times in this book,
my conviction is that the connection with God is not the problem;
connection with creation *is* the problem. The fragmentation and
dis-membering that wounds the soul arises from the forceful
splitting-off from the womb that nourishes and sustains us. We
are like orphaned children disconnected from our origins.

We began this chapter alluding to the evolutionary call of our
time to outgrow our adolescent belligerence and learn to befriend
our world with that creative interdependence that belongs to
mature adulthood. This is where many of the religions remain
stuck, employing a dominant language of the parent–child
relationship. The loyal devotee, in any of the faith systems, tends
to be described as a faithful *child* of God. The Christian faith takes
the parental imagery even further, inviting us to be faithful
children, not merely of God, but of the Church as well. The
clergy are the parents; the faithful assume child-like roles.

To some readers this may seem a triviality; in fact, it has very
serious consequences. Those who command power from within
the religious systems have enormous difficulties in relating to their
followers in an adult-to-adult mode. It sounds very threatening
and, consequently, co-dependency becomes the order of the day.
Women in particular have been degraded by this ordering of
reality and, understandably, feel that they often have to move out
of the religious system to retain their adult integrity.

The homeward journey, which is the subject for the remainder
of this book, calls on adult selves, with all the creativity and vision

we can muster as cosmic–planetary citizens. It will not be an exhaustive treatment. I will attempt to raise the critical consciousness and indicate some of the pathways that lead us homeward. I am not trying to point out where or what the pathways are; that's best done by those who walk them. I see my role as something of a sensor and a catalyst: listening to the stories the people tell as they journey along, the innate wisdom that irrupts from liminal places. From the cumulative wisdom of the homeward journey – rather than from the learning and scholarship of specialists – we are likely to discern the 'truths' that will point us to the promised land of new tomorrow.

In fact, when we arrive there, we'll discover that it's not entirely new: some things look strangely familiar. In the oft-quoted words of T. S. Eliot, we will have arrived where we really belong, and we begin to recognise the place as if for the first time. When that happens, we know we will have left behind the culture of exile and alienation!

Part Two

Returning From Exile

— 6 —

After Exile – The Pilgrim's Journey Home

> Be-ing at home on the road means summoning the Courage to Be, the Courage to See and the Courage to Sin.
>
> *Mary Daly*

> It is essentially meaningless to talk about a complex adaptive system being in equilibrium: the system can never get there. It is always unfolding, always in transition. In fact if the system ever does reach equilibrium, it isn't just stable. It is dead.
>
> *Mitchell Waldrop*

As a human species, we have inhabited planet Earth for an estimated 4.4 million years. Throughout that entire time, we have co-evolved with our evolving universe. And God has been creatively at work in the growth and maturation of the human spirit. *Incarnation* has been happening for at least 4.4 million years.

The religions have been enormously successful in subverting our true story, in denying our real identity, in catapulting us into alienation. Why? Because religion itself, being a patriarchal invention, is primarily concerned about *control*, and not about *liberation*, although the word is liberally sprayed across the pages of all the great Scriptures.

It is religion more than anything else that has forced us to forget who we are. All the main religions suffer from a suffocating sense of culture and history and contribute significantly to our cultural and spiritual amnesia. They collude unquestioningly with the patriarchal conviction that civilisation began about 5,000 years ago and that everything prior to that time must be dismissed as irrelevant, uncivilised, barbaric, primitive and pagan! That God has been at work throughout the entire course of evolution and within the unfolding of the human spirit is a consideration that religion scarcely entertains. Religion itself stands knee-deep in blasphemy, seeking to subvert even the creativity of the Godhead itself.

To many readers, these will seem extraordinary, even outrageous, claims. I invite the reader to take the facts at their face value. Are we really serious when we confess that God has been at work in creation from the beginning? If so, why don't we take God at God's word? There in front of our eyes is all the evidence for God's creativity – except of course in all the eyesores that we, humans, have created in our obsessional desire to divide and conquer.

It is in the wonder and marvel of creation itself that we firstly encounter the living face of God. That is the great revelation made accessible to all humans, and to all other creatures too. We do not need a religion to mediate its meaning for us. Simply, we need to stop and see! And the ability to encounter the living God in the face of nature is a gift, given in radical freedom and generosity. We don't need a special religious system or sacramental experience to mediate it for us:

> Contemplation is there when a person is walking, and then suddenly stops and turns, the senses wide open, the spirit exposed. The contemplative desires only to become so totally one with the experience that at that moment the experience itself becomes a message . . . Through contemplative vision a person experiences for oneself something of the perfection inherent in the most insignificant of things and events. Thus there develops out of contemplative vision, that which is entrusted to all people who have become inward – the kingdom of God: that kingdom of danger and audacity, of eternal beginning and becoming, of the spirit that is open and inward. (Boros, 1968, pp. 82, 83)

As a species, we are innately tuned to be receptive to the divine invitation (to become co-creators – with God and with life). We are all called to be contemplatives; only when we gaze deeply upon the wonder of creation will we truly appreciate the wonder of our own being. The problem is that that 'natural' propensity has been undermined and subverted by the cruel manipulation of religious and political indoctrination, and by the insidious impact of educational systems that stifle the questioning and critical power of the human imagination.

Our state of exile is not from God – in fact, it is impossible to be alienated (totally) from a God of unconditional love – but from God's creation of which we ourselves are an integral dimension. As the book of Genesis highlights, we are a species that has been expelled from the garden, and that garden is not some idyllic place in a world to come, but the landscape of creation itself. We have been uprooted and displaced – not by God, but by our own misguided crave to become the masters of everything that exists.

Because we are at heart an intelligent species, as well as being highly creative and deeply spiritual, we know only too well that things are badly out of kilter! And growing numbers among us suspect that the 'wise' people at the top – whether religiously, politically, or otherwise – are not acting wisely any more. They have their own agenda, which is not about wisdom, but about *power*! And our hunch also is that enhancing their power does not empower the rest of us; in fact, quite the opposite: it only plunges us further into the meaningless abyss of alienation and helplessness.

We have a growing understanding of what is wrong; it is much more difficult to discern how we make the pilgrim's journey out of this condition of exile as we seek to reclaim a cultural space called 'home'. We are, therefore, very much a species in transition, and for growing numbers among us that means refugees in the full sense of the word. Some travel the journey with lighter hearts, sensing that the whole planet is home, and that somehow the point of departure is also the place of arrival. But since the vast majority have been indoctrinated by the 'education' of patriarchal management, we find it hard to muster the self-confidence to think differently, dream differently, and eventually act differently.

Reframing the points of reference

We find ourselves struggling to befriend many questions and a great deal of uncertainty. In fact, nothing can be taken for granted any more. The basic identity question: 'Who am I?' is up for major re-evaluation (cf. Chapter 9). And that question cannot be encountered without a fresh look at what it means to be *in relationship* – creatures whose fundamental *raison d'être* is about relationality. At every level of our existence we are an interdependent species, and our relationships are not just about other human beings, but about other species as well, and in a special way about the planet we inhabit (Chapter 8).

One of the great delusions of our exilic state is the view that politics belongs to the secular realm, and that questions of meaning and purpose in life belong to the spiritual sphere. The dynamics of exile thrive on dualisms; they are essential to the strategy of 'divide and conquer', the primary ploy of patriarchal management. And of all the dualisms, perhaps none is more destructive than the opposition of politics and religion. It suits each side to keep the dualism in place, but the consequences for both person and planet are extremely serious. The journey out of exile requires of us a radical re-visioning on how to be political in a truly spiritual way (see Chapter 11).

Some readers will come to this book seeking clues on new ways to be Church. It seems to me that this is not a major concern for the majority of our contemporaries seeking a way home from exile. Most have given up on the old idea of Church, and no longer feel guilty about it. Many are wandering in a spiritual wasteland, but re-invented versions of the Church don't have any great appeal as a means of finding one's way around, or out of, the wasteland. People certainly feel a need to talk about 'God' and about the 'spiritual', but 'Church' is only of concern to those who already are attached and would like to remain attached, although often their hearts are indicating otherwise.

The idea of Church, and its equivalents in the other great religions, is very much based on a human and spiritual need *to be in communion with significant others*. Church in that sense does have a universal appeal, but any attempt to link that felt need with the concept of *institutional Church* immediately evokes a sense of alienation for several seekers of our time. The Church seems to be reaping the fruit of its own oppression; it seems to me that it will take something akin to a miracle to salvage the Church from this negative fall-out.

Pastorally, we are encountering a new situation, one we frequently encounter on the way home from exile. People of our time do not talk about leaving the Church or abandoning the faith; rather they talk about *outgrowing the need for* Church or formal religion. Recently, a colleague used this rather vivid analogy: 'For me to remain in the Church feels like continuing to wear a coat I was given as a child; it feels tight and congested and desperately uncomfortable. I have long outgrown it and I need to discard it.'

It seems to me that there is a real pastoral urgency to engage those who feel they are outgrowing the need for the Church right where they are. These could well be prophetic people of our time and important companions on the journey home from exile. They tend to be reflective people, who have often given many years of love and loyalty to the Church or to formal religion. In general, they are not embittered or disillusioned people. They do not have an axe to grind over some moral, theological or ecclesiastical directive. Instead they are people who acknowledge the process of growth and seek to respond responsibly and creatively.

However, they detect a caveat, in fact a gaping chasm! Certainly, they would like to talk with the local pastor, rabbi or iman, but instinctively they know they will not be understood. Worse still, they might become the victims of projected guilt; they have seen this happen to others, they see no point in allowing it to happen to themselves!

This leaves many spiritual seekers of our time very much out in the cold. And many noble spiritual aspirations become dissipated in an atmosphere that often resembles a spiritual wasteland. It is commonly assumed that conversion to one or other of the mainstream religions is the strategy to reform the wasteland! This may well be the greatest delusion in the religious consciousness of our time.

It is unlikely that the mainstream religions can make a meaningful response to the spiritual hunger of the pilgrims journeying home from exile. That which projected people into exile in the first place, and kept them trapped there for so long, is unlikely to provide wisdom or animation for the homeward journey.

The *points of reference* that characterise the culture and context of formal religion are proving to be increasingly inadequate and inappropriate to make sense out of the spiritual hunger of our time. For too long we have assumed that spirituality is a by-product of religion, that unless one first followed a formal religion, one could not possibly consider oneself to be spiritual. Human experience has long belied that conviction. We all have known, and increasingly encounter, people who are not religious in any formal sense of the word, but do hunger for that deeper meaning which, in another work (Ó Murchu, 1997b), I purport to be the essence of the spiritual life.

Theologians devote a great deal of rhetoric to the absence of God in this post-modern world. The fact that God is not easily included in the rather cerebral philosophy of post-modernism is a dangerously misleading guide to discern the presence or absence of the divine in the human population generally. To begin with, post-modernism is very much a Western development, carrying no small share of the intellectual imperialism which has characterised the West for much of the twentieth century. This often degrades the experience of the *two-thirds world* – and that means approximately 4,000 million people – into the realm of cultural, intellectual and spiritual invisibility; in fact, it often denounces it into total oblivion.

God is as present to creation now as God ever has been; perhaps even more so if we adopt the approach of process theology, which suggests that God co-creates with the evolving creation and, therefore, becomes more deeply known, and more transparently revealed, to us humans as evolution continues its unfolding course. The fact that increasing numbers of people no longer follow a formal religion – as they used to – is, in itself, no indication of how God works in the world and in the lives of people. Nor, indeed, is it even a useful guide to determine whether or not people are grappling with the experience of the divine in their daily existence: that requires a radically new mode of discernment for the times in which we live.

Our evolutionary story suggests that we humans were never intended to be primarily people of action. For most of our time on Earth, we *prayed* and *played*, just for the sheer joy of it, and not to make money out of it. Our lives were never intended to be absorbed in one-dimensional functionalism. Humans, deprived of the nourishing input of mind and spirit, quickly become inhuman monsters. The compulsion to control is a sure road to human disaster.

Our spirituality, more than anything else, serves to keep us on our toes and focused on our priorities. The workaholic stupor, once known as the 'work ethic', has become a type of international epidemic, breeding a functional robot – Marcuse's 'one-dimensional man' – deprived of imagination of mind and enthusiasm of spirit. The market economy, now the powerhouse of the multi-national corporations, has no room for the dreamer or the prophet, unless of course they can be domesticated for the service of those forces that seek to control more and more for the sake of the international handful (estimated to be no more than 500 men) who control more wealth than 50 per cent of the human family.

Patriarchy is very much about *doing* – achieving, attaining, competing, outdoing, overcoming and, if need be, eliminating. It is very much an orientation of *action*. In one sense it does not matter much what you are doing, as long as you are doing something. And better still, if you can produce results – whether products, money or statistics – your action is deemed to be worthwhile (even if you experience it as being quite meaningless). Little wonder, then, that work itself contributes to so much exile and alienation: in the West, millions of workers are agitated, restless and unfulfilled, while billions in the two-thirds world atrophy from boredom and the meaninglessness that comes from being unable to work at all.

Towards a new mysticism

I have already referred to the contemplative giftedness with which every person is endowed. The contemplative gaze is itself one expression of a particular way of seeing, of looking at reality. It is the ability to see beyond the surface, beyond the labels, beyond the veneer of respectability and control. It is that disturbing vision that penetrates beyond all the superficialities and all the limitations that give the semblance of control and the claim to speak in the name of truth.

Ultimately, truth is in life itself, in all its complexity and grandeur, as well as in its simplicity and utter invisibility. The wisdom I allude to verges on that great spiritual well-spring known to all religions and for long experienced before formal religion ever evolved: the wisdom of the *mystic*.

A great deal has been written about this topic, and many efforts have been made to incorporate it into the structures of mainstream religion. The failure to do so possibly explains why many of the great mystics of Catholicism, e.g. Meister Eckhart, Hildegarde of Bingen, Mechtild of Magdeburg, Julian of Norwich, were never considered seriously for sainthood. The mystics read reality writ large. Their God is truly universal and yet closer than even the heart itself can envisage. And the dualisms of sacred and secular, body and spirit, all break down in the mystical encounter with life. Consequently, one cannot control mystical experience as one can control religious experience. Mysticism tends to escape the manipulative power of religious patriarchy!

The wisdom of the contemplative and the perceptiveness of the mystic are important resources for the journey back from exile. They both empower us to keep our gaze on the big picture; by keeping the focus on the hope that beckons forth, we are challenged to transcend the temptation to fall back on the support structures of the culture of exile. The mystical vision also helps us to embrace the darkness that at times can be overwhelming and the light that occasionally can frighten us because of its sheer luminosity. We need a wisdom that sustains both the greatness and ordinariness of our pilgrim experience.

In seeking to develop an ecological theology of liberation, Boff (1995, pp. 162–3, 70), offers us the following outline of the mystic's vocation:

> Mysticism is life itself apprehended in its radicalism and extreme density. Existence is endowed with gravity and depth when thus conceived and known appropriately. Mysticism always leads to the transcendence of all limits. It persuades us to examine other aspects of things than those we know and to suspect that reality is more than a mere structure concealing the realm of the absurd and the abyss, which can strike fear and anguish into our hearts. Mysticism teaches us instead that reality is where tenderness, receptivity and the mystery of loving kindness can triumph and are encountered as joyful living, meaningful accomplishment, and a fruitful dream . . .
>
> The mystic is not detached from history but committed to it as transformation, starting from a nucleus of transcendent meaning and a minimal utopian dimension which, in as much as it is religious, enables the mystic to be *more perceptive than anyone else*. (Emphasis mine)

To nurture the mystical vision, to sustain us on the journey home from exile, I suggest the following are some key elements that will need a great deal of reflection, dialogue and discernment:

- a time to be suspicious;
- a time to pose and befriend questions;
- a time to listen;
- a time to gaze into the depths;
- a time to dream and think big;

- a time for dialogue;
- a time to pray — with others and alone.

A hermeneutic of suspicion

Perhaps the greatest burden many people carry today is an impoverished imagination and a critical capacity, well subverted by the educational brain-washing we pursue in the West. Neither children nor adults in our culture are encouraged to ask perceptive or penetrating questions; in fact, we're not encouraged to ask questions at all. Our educational systems are well tuned — overtly and covertly — to safeguard and foster the values of Western capitalism.

Primary among such values are acquisition of power; competition; survival of the fittest (and diminution of the weakest); conceptual clarity; respect for hierarchical authority. The rebel, the questioner, the creative one tends to be weaned out, and where this is not possible, promoted — in the hope that they might shut up and stop rocking the boat!

A primary contemplative gift for our time is the need to be *highly suspicious*. We need to be suspicious of almost everything in our daily existence. The food we eat is probably far more contaminated than we even suspect; 90 per cent of media news is inaccurate, misleading, sensationalised and, frequently, nothing short of a pack of lies; doctors dole out pills which give temporary relief but frequently create long-term problems; economists try to blind us with convoluted rhetoric which is all about power and not the good of people or planet; politicians are grossly out of touch with the real state of human and earthly affairs; promoters of religion spawn off the naivety and vulnerability of insecure people, offering a utopia of salvation in a distant heaven, but no realistic hope or meaning for life on Earth.

I suggest that we need to assume that reality as currently construed is to the advantage of those who seek to lord it over others for their own self-aggrandisement. We need to assume that all the promises to feed the hungry and shelter the homeless are empty formulae that will never address the *causes* of these and several other major problems of our time. We need to assume that those we have entrusted with the governance of our world and the affairs of humankind are largely incapable of serving us in a constructive and creative way. We need to acknowledge that the current relationship of us humans to our planet, the Earth, is severely undernourished and, as a consequence, highly destructive both to ourselves and to the planet. And finally, and perhaps most important of all, we need to acknowledge that we have been robbed (by all those in whom we placed our trust) of our natural, God-given birthright to be creative and proactive people, betrayed into being robot-like functionaries within the false political structuring imposed upon our world.

And we need to develop the courage to speak aloud those suspicions we hold which are too easily and inappropriately resolved in media chat-shows or in the empty rhetoric of our public institutions. We need to nurture our suspicions so that they become the instigation for a different quality of dialogue and engagement aimed at surfacing the questions that have long been asked but scarcely never heard nor responded to in a responsible way.

Live the questions themselves

The words of the poet Rilke are often quoted: 'Live the questions now. Perhaps you will then gradually, without noticing it, live along some distant day into the answer.' To ask the right questions and ask them in the right way – that is, explore them in their deeper context – is one of the survival skills in today's world. And not merely survival: it is also a precondition to render unto life – personally and cosmically – that service of engagement which connects us meaningfully with the source of our existence.

Brueggemann (1993) claims that domination requires *certitude* as a central aspect of the will-to-power. The dominator provides a set of answers which are open neither to interpretation nor question. There is no truth other than the truth delivered from on high, all of which we associate with imperialist government and tyrannical dictatorships, but in fact it is extensively practised by the governing bodies operating within our so-called democratic and ecclesiastical institutions.

That the questioner can raise such strong fears, and evoke quite devious strategies to deflect the questions, vividly indicates the shaky ground on which so much 'reality' is established. We cannot afford to let the light of scrutiny penetrate too deeply; the sham is not far beneath the surface. In many ways, power is the most fragile of all forces; it is essentially kept in place by the compulsive crave of the power-seekers themselves.

The tendency to *absolutise* is the religious version of this compulsion. And questioning of the absolute values is often countered by the charge of *relativism*. Domination requires one truth above and beyond all others, and when validated by religion, Christians consider theirs to be the primary revelation, and Muslims consider theirs to be the only true way, while Judaism for the Jews is the ultimate source of truth. Indeed, all religion nurtures a form of absolutism born not of God but of the compulsion of the domination itself.

Consequently, relativism, the fruit of open and sincere questioning, is our surest safeguard against idolatry and that dogmatism that undermines both the creativity of God and the spiritual versatility of human beings. It is our capacity to question that safeguards us from the answers that stifle – and ultimately stultify – the pursuit of truth and the attainment of that adult growth that belongs to spiritual maturity.

The listening heart

People who question a lot tend to be receptive to what their questions open up. The genuine searcher is not necessarily pursuing a simplistic answer. Questions beget their own quality of meaning, itself largely dependent on whether the questioner can listen to the inner resonances that beget the questions in the first place.

Our capacity to listen is both undernourished and seriously infiltrated in the contemporary world. From infancy we are bombarded with noise, much of it cacophonous and disconnected from the natural sounds of the natural world. As O'Donohue (1997, p. 109) points out, we are also bombarded by the searching glare of neon lights, desensitising us to the contour and variety of shadow, under whose shade so much creativity evolves. Our internal world is also bombarded by the overload of information; the inner psyche is serrated by the ruthless edginess of so much input, infuriated by the crazy crave of our competitive educational system.

Our capacity to listen, receive, perceive and be porous to the mystery that surrounds us is an experience the majority of humankind have never encountered. We live beneath a cloud of enormous alienation which, fortunately, is the very force that drives some people to question the whole thing and choose alternatives for the sake of their sanity and sanctity. For some, the discovery can be frightening and often feels like a high price to pay for what should be a natural birthright.

Reclaiming our role as listeners is a multi-pronged challenge. All at once, many voices seek our attention, and they are all interconnected. We cannot listen to our own inner being without simultaneously attending to the pulsations of the universe itself. We cannot tune in to the power of the divine, until we first listen to the small, quiet voice, or perhaps the thundering tornado, within our own hearts.

Without a well-developed capacity to listen, we will fail to touch the deep layers that underpin our lifelong search for meaning. Listening is about depth, and that depth is the sacred space, the holy ground, where we weave the tapestry that holds together the various and often scattered strands of our existence. That tapestry is what the religions call *revelation*.

Gazing into the depths

The scientific method, with its focus on observation, measurement and verification, has stripped human perception of its grandeur and elegance. Our linear, rational and logical way of viewing the world has left us with a bland and deflated imagination. Beauty has been usurped by duty, depth has been overwhelmed by super-ficiality.

In recent years, it has become painfully obvious, particularly from the perspective of exile, that those to whom we have tradi-tionally looked for wisdom and guidance – governments, religions, etc. – are no longer capable of delivering a sense of hope or meaning. Nor are they capable of discerning the deeper aspirations of the human heart as people struggle to find their way home again. All the analyses, all the convoluted rhetoric, feels empty and lacking in substance: it merely scratches the surface of what today's world yearns for.

Silence is a rare commodity in our time. The ability to be – and be still – before the encapsulating mystery of life is largely unknown. Consequently, both our analysis (political, social, reli-gious) and the solutions we propose appear to be superficial, even false, lacking depth and wholeness. Increasingly, people recognise this shallowness, veer toward different perceptions, and desire alternative outcomes.

Enlarged horizons

Of all the faulty perceptions of our time, none is more destructive than the widespread assumption that meaning rests primarily in 'the ultimate building blocks'. We maintain the emphasis on the constituent parts of the machine, safeguarding the human need to analyse them to death. In seeking to understand the parts, we assume it will lead us to a comprehensive view of the whole: it rarely does.

Pedagogically and educationally we follow the same misguided approach. We begin with the familiar, the local, the small, what *we* can manage, and, rigidly faithful to our linear, rational logic, we expect to be able to embrace a larger picture of reality. But in a world where 'the whole is greater than the sum of the parts' the reductionistic approach is inadequate and, rather than facilitating access to truth, often catapults us into the depths of confusion and despair.

To do justice to the holistic world-view, from a very early age we need to introduce our children to a *multi-disciplinary* way of understanding life. We also need to inculcate in them a sense of their identity as cosmic–planetary citizens above and beyond the national context which, currently, we promote as the primary ambience of personal and global identity.

The ability to comprehend the big picture is enriching and liberating. We begin to see connections that facilitate meaning. We perceive qualities of interdependence that expose us to the beauty and power of mystery. We discern possibilities for growth – personal and global – that offer hope because they forge relationships of deeper belonging.

The emphasis on national identity, and specific denominational allegiance, is fundamentally flawed. Our prehistoric closeness to the Earth superseded all national boundaries we know today. It is quite possible that our worship of the Great Earth Mother Goddess, throughout the paleolithic era, united us spiritually and culturally to a degree that formal religion never could. Beyond the fragmentation caused by nationalism and the alienation arising from formal religion is a species far more centred and far more whole in its primordial self-understanding. Deep within our psyche – individually and collectively – we carry the imprint of that ancient formation. There are many indications, today, that humans are yearning to reclaim that ancient spirituality with its global and inclusive potentials.

A time for dialogue

This new spiritual and cultural awakening manifests in several ways, despite the political – and nationalistic – pressure to sustain a climate of competition. Many people are weary of competition, particularly the powerless billions who have nothing to gain from it. A new yearning for the co-operative mode surfaces in several quarters. It does not make headlines nor sensational news; it exerts a largely subdued but nonetheless powerful influence.

Enhanced by recent developments of mass communication, the desire to connect and dialogue is stronger now than it has been for several thousand years. As more people travel, encounter other cultures and expand the circles of friendship, the global family is enveloped in a new desire for connectedness. While there are several obvious barriers to its practical realisation, the shift in consciousness cannot, and will not, be arrested. In time, it is the consciousness, more than anything else, that will catalyse the transformation.

Currently, dialogue between cultures and nations is fuelled by economic and political forces. This is yet another significant example where the *informal* process is outpacing the formal strategy. National governments cannot set limits to the power of global communication. In fact, many governments today have great difficulty in persuading their citizenry to adopt and retain *one* national identity for an entire lifetime.

And yet the commitment to dialogue requires more sustained attention from the human family in general. Apart from the divisiveness of competitive market forces and the enmity fomented by warfare, a great deal of rancour and division prevails within regional and local communities – tribal rivalries in the African subcontinent being an obvious example. The forces of sexism and racism are still all too common in our world today.

Tribal feuds and family strife beget a great deal of bitterness and division, the frightening potential of which we saw in the Rwanda massacre of 1994. The slow and sensitive process of reconciliation, which has been courageously pursued in South Africa, is a model that needs to be activated in many spheres of contemporary life.

A time to pray – with others and alone

It is a Sunday morning in the city of Accra (Ghana). To my right, loud blaring music emanates from a charismatic prayer-group, while to my left I hear a male voice declaring the certainty of God's judgement coming like a flash in the night. Charismatic-type gatherings seem to be happening in every street; the air is filled with music and prayer.

And no doubt visitors like myself are often deeply impressed. Momentarily I feel a tinge of guilt and a nostalgia for a bygone time when I, a good Western Christian, also prayed assiduously on a Sunday morning. In fact, I experience many emotions: curiosity, admiration, cynicism; and to resolve my restless feelings, I decide to go and investigate.

Firstly, I head in the direction of the male preacher with his old-fashioned rhetoric of hell, fire and fury. The banner informs me that it is the Women's Free Church of Christ. So, why a male preacher? I am told that ever since the female founder died in 1986, the pastor has been a man: a fairly common phenomenon in African charismatic-led churches, I later discover (cf. King, 1995).

At the other end of the street, I am lured by the loud drumming where an ecstatic congregation (consisting predominantly of women and children) revel in dance and chant. Quite spontaneously, I find myself joining in, and I begin to register a distinctive sense of annoyance at the frequent interruption of a bellowing male voice declaring Jesus blessed as Lord, King, powerful one, majestic and worthy of honour.

I find myself wondering, as perhaps the young Jesus did when he first visited the temple, what God is being worshipped here, and what, if anything, is the connection with the Jesus of the Christian Gospel! And what does *prayer* mean here? A spiritual relationship with the living God, or a form of mass hysteria, an escape, or an opium, to keep people sane and hopeful amid their poverty and their struggle to survive?

A great deal has been written about prayer. For many it is the heart and soul of the spiritual life. In the past it was closely linked with asceticism (especially fasting) and with that quality of discipline and order we associate with the monastic and vowed life. What prayer means to 'ordinary' people at the heart of the world received scant attention before the 1970s. Prayer and immersion in the world just did not go together – at least that is what most of the 'experts' led us to believe – and in the subjugated state of exile, we took them at their word!

The false perfectionism that became associated with prayer led to various forms of exile and estrangement. Those in the vowed life multiplied prayers in great abundance – a type of spiritual production machine – while the ordinary people never knew where they stood with God, no matter how much they prayed. In a sense, those at the heart of the world, with their simple and at times bizarre devotional practices, had a more tangible sense of God's closeness to them than many of those devoted to the monastic experience of intense prayer.

The major flaw, still reflected in much of what is written about prayer, is an underlying patriarchal tendency, what the patriarchs tend to do with everything: organise it in every detail, so that we know where *we* stand with it. Although spiritual writers allude to the sense of divine abandonment – which translated more positively would mean radical trust in God's unconditional love for all life – in the patriarchal construal, that is not the primary guideline to a meaningful prayer-life.

In essence, prayer is about a radical transparency to the mystery within which all is held and sustained. Prayer is the name for that special relationship to the ground of our being within which we live and move. *Saying* prayers is a consequence of being a person of prayer, not the other way round. And since relationship is at the heart of prayer – as indeed it is at the heart of all life – true prayer will always lead us into connection with others, all aspects of creation, and not merely other human beings.

Our desire to pray, and our need to pray, is not merely a divine gift bestowed by special grace. Every moment of every day the universe to which we belong, and the planet we inhabit, pray in us and through us. God's creativity, which impregnates the whole of creation, is forever trying to break open the doors of the human heart, often bolted tight by the mechanistic conditioning of patriarchal control.

Innately, as with everything else in life, we are created transparent to God's wisdom, to God's invitation, and above all to God's love. Prayer is very much about letting go – of all the props, theories and theologies that have brainwashed us into patriarchal alienation. But in its essential nature, prayer is the great letting be: the Spirit of God who prays in us, so that the divine-becoming can continue its evolutionary unfolding through all the creatures that inhabit creation.

New ways of relating

In subsequent chapters, we try to unravel the dynamics that unfold as we travel the journey home from exile. We will find ourselves relating in several new ways as we try to leave behind the imposed models of the patriarchal age. Not all in patriarchy was bad; this leaves us with a delicate task of discerning what to hold on to and what to discard. This task will never be complete. Like the course of evolution itself, it weaves in and out along the paradoxical cycles of creation and destruction, the Christian enigma of death and resurrection.

In subsequent chapters, we examine the consequences of moving from a *hierarchical* ordering of reality to a *relational* one. To those in charge of our world, this is not a welcome development, because relationality essentially entails an egalitarian sharing of resources, choices and ideas, and it is not always clear who is making the choices and why. But those on the homeward journey often wonder what all the fuss is about, because it is blatantly obvious to them that the relational mode is the obvious one to opt for anyhow.

While not wishing to encourage yet another dualism, the ensuing polarisation here seems unavoidable. Today, it is most pronounced between the so-called New Age movement and the mainstream culture, the former making a radical option for the relational approach, with several aspects of life apparently 'out of control', and the latter denouncing the movement as reckless and irresponsible (see the comprehensive coverage by Hanegraaff, 1996).

The tension between these two approaches surfaces several times in the ensuing chapters. For instance, the concept of *embodiment* takes on several new meanings. Already I have made several allusions to the ecological one, looking at planet Earth (and the universe itself) as a living organism. Chapter 9 portrays the body within the fluidity of growing and changing relationships among humans themselves and in the context of the wider creation. Chapter 10 seeks to reclaim the subverted sacredness of the human body in its erotic propensity to connect and impassion. And finally, we look anew at the political body (the 'polis') and investigate some fresh ways of engaging with the major social and economic questions of our time.

Within and beneath all these paradigmatic shifts, we work with two assumptions, neither of which are outlined in detail in the present work, but extensively covered by other researchers:

1. As a species, we are undergoing a major evolutionary shift, explored by contemporary scholars such as Capra (1982), Jantsch (1980), Sahtouris (1989) and Laszlo (1993).
2. Accompanying this shift is a whole new understanding of *consciousness*. The ways in which we perceive, feel and think about our world are changing dramatically. Intuition, imagination and contemplation are beginning to outpace rationality and linear logic. Action always follows thought, and thought tends to move more rapidly than action. As thought-patterns gather greater momentum, we will need to be ready for whole new ways of engaging with the world of our existence. (On the changing nature of consciousness, I recommend Jantsch and Waddington 1976; Goertzel 1993, and Ceruti 1994.)

The relational and interdependent world-view, the primary concern of those homeward bound from exile, is a real enigma for those in charge of patriarchal reality. It is something that has come about in spite of us humans, and that is both incomprehensible and totally unacceptable to those who believe they are in charge of the world's destiny. Fortunately, the world attends to her own destiny, leaving us humans with basically two choices: we follow on the pathway of evolution, or we are left behind. The culture of exile tries to convince us that we should stay behind; the culture of home-coming informs us that the only life-giving choice is the option to move with it.

As we explore the new landscape opening out before us, let's begin with that ever new, yet ever old, underlying energy that is at the basis of all our relationships, personal and otherwise. I refer to creation's own innate propensity to foster and promote relationships. *Interconnection* is the landmark that will enable us to negotiate many a difficult hurdle on the journey home from exile.

— 7 —

The Homeward Journey:
From Separation to Connection

(Spirituality is) the aspect of human existence that explores the subtle forces of energy in and around us and reveals to us profound inter-connectedness.

Charlene Spretnak

Evolution is not a blind groping towards non-existent goals, a haphazard play with chance and accident. It is a systematic, indeed a systemic, development towards goals generated in the process itself.

Erwin Laszlo

IN THE EXPERIENCE OF EXILE, everything feels out of kilter. Disconnection abounds. People often feel lost and lonely, estranged from loved ones, and from the experience of being at home.

The journey back home has a metaphorical and spiritual sense of things falling into place once more. People re-connect afresh, not just with each other but also with the wider creation. And people tend to become more suspicious and critical of the imposed normalcy. We no longer accept that this is the way things have to be. We learn to feel at ease with questioning. It's OK to ask awkward questions and even to disagree with those who think they know it all.

The journey back home provides a kind of liminal space in which dangerous ideas can be entertained, and outrageous things can be talked about. Suspicions can be voiced and orthodoxies can be queried. Our doubts and anxieties become the very stuff that enables us to connect in new ways. Our shared vulnerability is the doorway to a new sense of connectedness.

And the liminal space is often an open one. Strangers in exile, especially refugees, often have to survive in the open spaces, even in harsh weather conditions. Paradoxically, this experience does not highlight the cruelty of creation. In fact creation, and the elements of the open space, sometimes feel more benevolent and supportive than do fellow human beings. Planet Earth, and the cosmic creation, can be perceived as being quite friendly, even in the depths of our estrangement and struggle. So, let's visit our cosmic space in a little more detail!

Connecting with the cosmos

Before religion came to be identified with specific places (whether understood globally or locally) and with certain oral and written traditions of the word, the prevailing primal conviction seems to have been one of a sense of connection with a universal life-force which inhabited the whole of creation. Our ancient ancestors are unlikely to have thought in the dualistic terms of sacred v. secular, matter v. spirit, divine v. human, and while not considering the life-force to be divine (as we understand that word today), it certainly was construed as *supernatural*.

For our ancient ancestors, however, the supernatural did not require a sacred place outside the world from which to rule and govern; on the contrary, it was unambiguously and radically present *within* the whole of cosmic life. Therefore the supernatural was seen to be operative in the many movements and rhythms of nature, whether it be the cycle of the seasons, the warmth of sunshine, the light of the moon, the force of wind and storm, the productivity of Earth. Long before *homo religiousus* described these experiences as forms of *pagan* worship, people related to the supernatural life-force – sometimes in fear (probably not nearly as frequently as popularly thought), often in awe, and always in the awareness and conviction that ultimately life was held in the embrace of a *benign* supernatural power.

Despite the occasional harshness of climatic conditions and other struggles for survival, our ancient ancestors seem to have been imbued with an unshakeable conviction that the supernatural is benevolent to humankind. It is from this conviction that humans began to comprehend that a reciprocal relationship with the divine also had to include a mutually respectful treatment of creation in all its life and diversity. The cosmos was considered to be first and foremost a sacred place, and planet Earth provided the immediate context in which humans had to negotiate responsible and creative engagement with the supernatural.

What today we call 'creation-centred spirituality' is in a sense the oldest form of religion known to humankind. Long before we came to personify the deity (whether in polytheistic or monotheistic form), we learned to connect with divine life in and through the surrounding creation. We have no concrete evidence to indicate how we negotiated that relationship, in terms of prayer and worship. There are good reasons to believe that we did so primarily through *movement* and *dance*.

Dance is a very ancient form of worship, probably pre-dating articulate speech by about 100,000 years. If the behaviours of existing tribal peoples are reliable, then circular dance movements would have been particularly widespread. The worship sought to express the sense of connection with humans among themselves, along with the connection with the divine. And in most cases the dance would have taken place in open space, thus forging the sense of connection with creation at large.

Although music is very much a development of paleolithic times, and bears an undoubtable spiritual significance, *drumming* is probably a much earlier development and would have been a widespread form of worship among our prehistoric ancestors.[1] *Droning*, and subsequently *chanting*, would also have been extensively used.

It is the creation itself, therefore, that provides the earliest context for the development and evolution of human belief. The cosmos, and our primary connection with it through the home planet, the Earth, awakens us to faith and evokes from deep within a reciprocal response. The 'withinness' from which this response arises is not just human; it is also cosmic and planetary. Were it not for the fact that the divine pulsates in the first place at the heart of creation, it would not awaken in our human hearts. We are blessed with an innate, spiritual capacity because we are the products of a universe itself endowed and impregnated with the power and love of the divine.

It is our disconnectedness from creation, the spirituality of 'abandoning', 'fleeing' and even 'hating' the world, more than anything else, that jeopardises our evolution as a human species, and as indicated in previous chapters begets what religionists call exile or alienation. Not only does it undermine our spiritual understanding of life, it alienates us from everything that makes us genuinely human.

In *all* its dimensions, ours is a humanity inexorably linked to, and connected with, the whole of creation. The carbon in our bodies we have received from the stars; our health and well-being are heavily dependent upon sunlight; the very oxygen we breathe, day in and day out, is dependent upon the animals and trees of the world. Our entire identity is wrapped up in the universal will-to-life.

As relational creatures we do not live *in* the world but rather *with* the world. In the anthropological studies of the past 100 years there has been a tendency to depict our ancient ancestors as being so enmeshed in the material creation around them that they were unable to develop that quality of self-identity deemed to be appropriate for civilised human beings. Allegedly, we had not developed the intellectual and self-reflective capacity to differentiate ourselves in that uniqueness which makes us different and separate from everything else in creation.

Parallels are frequently made with child development: if the child is not empowered to separate from the parents, and transcend its childhood sense of dependency, then it can never hope to engage with the world in a meaningful adult way. In a similar vein, we make the assumption that humans in pre-civilised times (i.e. prior to 3000 BCE) were essentially childish, infantile, unenlightened, incapable of reflection, ego-less, at the mercy of cosmic forces within which their individual identities were absorbed and usurped.

With recent advances in anthropological and archaeological research (cf. Mithen, 1990, 1996), we are beginning to see that such perceptions are both false and misleading. While, allegedly, such views are often extrapolations made on the basis of the behaviours exemplified by currently extant tribal peoples, they also contain very powerful projections whereby we, the self-righteous of patriarchal supremacy, choose to dump our dark and sinister shadow on the ancients rather than take ownership of it for ourselves.

There is ample evidence to indicate that it is *we* who are the barbaric, unenlightened savages, and not our prehistoric ancestors for whom the emerging evidence (tentative though it still is) verifies a people who had a highly developed *intuitive* and *spiritual* capacity. The fact that they did not develop a robust individualism similar to ours is our problem and not theirs. For them it was not a felt need; indeed, all indications are that they would have experienced such a status as a gross aberration.[2]

Whatever their limitations (which we tend to highlight) our ancient ancestors were endowed with a unique awareness of their interdependent relationship with planetary and cosmic life. There may have been hardship, suffering, deprivation, but probably not the sense of alienation or exile that we experience today. The shared perception that everything was interconnected, coupled with the innate conviction that a benign life-force was holding everything together, enabled people to feel at home in, and at one with, the enveloping universe. Precisely for this reason, an appreciation and understanding of the divine at work in the world does not seem to have been a problem. The problems began when *we* tried to reduce the spiritual to the religion of place and word.

Connecting with the empowering divinity

We need, however, to review another misguided development: the personalising of the divine life-force. Because we have tended to view our prehistoric ancestors as an inferior breed, and particularly as being incapable of making individual personal choices, we also live with another naive and misguided perception: namely, that they could not conceive of, nor relate to, a *personal* God.

Our ancient ancestors apparently did not consider God to be personal, as we understand that concept today. Indications are that philosophical or theological considerations of this nature were of no consequence for prehistoric peoples. In their hearts they knew that the life-force related to them, intimately and personally, but because their primary perception was one of the grandeur and globality of the life-force, it would be considered reductionistic, and therefore idolatrous, to attribute personal attributes to it.

Although the life-force was also the 'cause' of storm, destruction, suffering and death, our ancestors of old seem to have had a more integrated understanding of these realities than we have today. The complementarity of destruction and creation, the cycle of birth–death–rebirth, meant a great deal more in ancient times than it does in our time. People then were certainly not as intellectually versatile and academically developed as we are today, but they do seem to have been blessed with a quality of psychic awareness and spiritual intuition that we have lost in subsequent millennia. They could live with paradox, precisely because they were spiritually attuned. In our spiritual deprivation, we fail to comprehend the deeper meaning of so many things in life, particularly the recurring cycle of birth–death–rebirth which occurs all around us.

In terms of the personal sense of the divine, the major difference seems to be an apprehension of personhood that only makes sense interdependently with *planethood*. Consequently, an understanding of the divine as imminent within the whole of creation (but not confined to it, as in pantheism), at a time when humans seem to have perceived themselves as an integral dimension of that same creation, made a separatist notion of person both superfluous and unnecessary.

We have no way of establishing when we began to personify the divine life-force. The conviction that humans understood the divine to be something akin to a *woman of prodigious fertility*, possibly as far back as 40000 BCE, is an extrapolation rather than an established fact. However, indications are that Ice Age art was developed on a universal scale (in terms of the populated world of that time), and probably dominated thought and worship for at least 30,000 years. We are only beginning to explore the rich reservoirs of spiritual intent and expression that belong to our prehistoric past.

Remnants of this ancient Goddess culture remain in many of the great religions: the Hindu Shiva, the Chinese Kan Yin, the Egyptian Isis, the Greek Demeter, the Christian Virgin Mary, often revered as the Black Madonna in many non-European cultures. In the personification of the great Goddess, the focus was not on the person as person, nor on the person as autonomous from, and superior to, the rest of creation, but on her ability and capacity for creativity and generativity. The concern is not on who she *is*, but on what she *does*. What she does is prototypical for what everybody and, indeed everything, does and should do, in the collaborative process of co-creation.

Contrary to later personifications of the deity, especially in the mainstream religions, there seems to be no hierarchical allegiance, no supernatural realm beyond this world, and no priesthood to facilitate contact with the Goddess.[3] The relationship with the Goddess was equally accessible to all (despite the fact that the

Shaman and Shamaness do seem to have had a special quality of access), reflecting the egalitarian understanding of all relationships which was probably more widespread than we can ever hope to verify scientifically. Therefore a superior, more extraordinary type of personal God was not perceived to be necessary. The interdependent, relational nature of life already ensured a personal and interpersonal ambience to the unfolding sense of God's co-creativity within creation.

It is with the evolution of the monotheistic religions that the notion of a personal God becomes paramount. Monotheism is usually depicted as an antidote to the pantheon of gods (many of whom were female) that was promoted and worshipped in the 'pagan' cultures. Whether these were gods in their own right or merely several manifestations of a unified sense of God (which had prevailed for thousands of years previously) is an issue awaiting some thorough research.

Here we are moving in territory of many unexamined assumptions, made by human beings who at this stage were trapped in an anthropology which set humans over against creation and needed a supreme 'adversarial' deity to validate the attack on 'the forces of evil'. We therefore created a God *in our own image*, to justify our compulsive craving to divide and conquer the world. As already indicated, this patriarchal will-to-power is the foundation stone of the religion of *place*, of the subsequent developments around the religion of *word*, and the driving force behind the close connection that religion holds with the notion of *exile*.

With the development of the monotheistic, personal God, the radical *relational* nature of religion (and spirituality) has been perforated. The egalitarian relational mode has been subverted (but not conquered) by the patriarchal mode. The 'discipleship of equals' (Schusler Fiorenza) has become a hierarchy of dependents and progressively an institution that requires co-dependency in order to survive. Although, arguably, it has some sense of historical timeliness, nonetheless a radical reversal has taken place.

Connecting afresh with the relational Trinity

Of course, the relational dimension has not been totally obliterated. In fact, it has not been obliterated at all, merely subverted, and will in time regain its primordial priority. Hidden amid the plethora of dogmatism and ritualism, and all the other accretions of time and culture, it holds its rightful place. I allude to what Christians call the doctrine or mystery of the Trinity.

Christians consider this doctrine, the God who is three-in-one, to be uniquely theirs, while Muslims regard it as idolatrous and often use it to denounce Christians for doing essentially the same thing as the pagans did: worshipping many Gods. In fact, the doctrine of the Trinity is an ancient archetypal belief that long pre-dates formal religion, and tends to surface in many of the major religions (see the pioneering work of Panikkar, 1973).

Abraham (1994) maintains that a primordial triune structure, with *chaos, gaia* and *eros* as its ultimate foundation, characterises the spiritual vision of paleolithic times. And the emerging culture of the Great Earth Mother Goddess came to be understood as that of a Triple Goddess (cf. Wilshire, 1994). The late Neolithic times are populated with religious Triads, including the Christian one. Abraham (1994, p. 93) provides the following outline:

TRIVIAL	Crone	Mother	Maid
EGYPTIAN	Osiris	Isis	Horus
SUMERIAN	Inanna	Erishkegal	Dumuzi
BABYLONIAN	Anu	Ea	Enlil
BABYLONIAN	Apsu	Tiamat	Mummu
UGARITIC	El	Ashtoret	Baal
CRETAN	Zeus	Semele	Dionysos
HINDU	Brahma	Vishnu	Shiva
EARLY GREEK	Chaos	Gaia	Eros
CLASSICAL GREEK	Pluto	Demeter	Persephone
ALEXANDRIAN	Serapis	Isis	Anubis
PHILONIC	Yahweh	Sophia	Logos
NEOPLATONIC	Soul	Body	Spirit
CHRISTIAN	Father	Son	Spirit.

In all the above versions, three principles seem to be under consideration: first, a *unifying* principle, often considered to be the creative energy; second, a statement about the essential *diversity*, often incorporating the dark and destructive side of life; and third, a *feminine* principle that liberates and facilitates creative interaction between the unity and the diversity. We are dealing with something profoundly primordial; we are attempting to *name* life processes that underpin all life forms and life in its more universal meaning and eternal destiny. Personalising these archetypal forces will tend to blur rather than illuminate the deeper meaning. Developing the doctrine of the Trinity into a theological quagmire, as Christianity has done, seems to miss the deeper message of this profound mystery.

Whatever else the doctrine of the Trinity is trying to articulate, one inescapable feature seems to be the *relational* dimension; it is highlighted by several contemporary theologians (see Cunningham, 1998). In all the meanderings and speculations of the human mind, the conviction that seems to surface time and time again is that, whatever else God is about, God is primarily about *the capacity to relate*. Therefore, all our primordial attempts at articulating the divine essence culminate in a statement about relatedness. The primal divine energy has to do with relating and, consequently, the relational framework is the one in which we stand the best chance of engaging with God in a meaningful way.

But why the number 3? It probably arose from within the power of the collective unconscious, and contemporary science provides us with some important clues. As already highlighted, our prehistoric ancestors were deeply attuned to the universal will-to-meaning, and probably had an innate sense of the predominance of the number 3 in the overall fabric of creation. At the subatomic level, we know that combinations of three predominate in the quark world, the most basic form of elementary particle known to contemporary science. Scientists who have long been searching for the basic building-blocks of matter, which they have always considered to be objective and isolated, are now confronted with a quark-soup of wave-like movement in which the quarks will only manifest in combinations of two or three. It seems there are no such things as isolated quarks. Nature itself seems to be telling us that its essential meaning is to be discovered in how things *relate* and not in autonomous, independent entities vying for survival.

On the microcosmic scale, explored in modern science, the priority of connectedness is inescapable. But it is even more impressive on the grand, macro scale. Greenstein (1988) and Barrow and Tippler (1986) highlight that the three-dimensional nature of space–time is necessary to maintain appropriate distances between the planets, and between planets and their suns.

Without the three-dimensional structure, the force of gravity would be such that our sun would not be able to exist in a stable state; it would either fall apart or it would collapse to form a black hole. On a smaller scale, the electrical forces that cause electrons to orbit round the nucleus in an atom require a three-dimensional space – time configuration; without it, the electrons would either escape from the atom altogether, or would spiral into the nucleus, thus destroying the basic elements on which everything is constructed.

On a human level, daily experiences like the digestion of food, the circulation of blood and the functioning of the nervous system all require a three-dimensional operational base. Throughout the entire range of creation, the number 3 seems more basic to the fabric of life than any other combination. Is this merely accidental, or is it evidence of a divine imprint? We may never know the ultimate answer, but meanwhile we cannot avoid the profound trinitarian configuration that, in the words of Panikkar (1993, pp. 17, 59, 121) makes both monism and dualism obsolete and irrelevant.

Trinity, therefore, is not so much a religious dogma as an archetypal movement that permeates the whole of creation facilitating mutual interaction as the primary medium to enhance life, thus inviting us to transcend the 'paranoia of monism and the schizophrenia of dualism' (Panikkar 1993, p. 59). Today, there is no shortage of scientific and psychological explanations for animal and human attraction, and for the ensuing behaviours that culminate in intimate relationships. Yet there is a more basic driving force, forging the attraction of intimacy and love; it is as earthly as it is heavenly, as basic as it is all–encompassing, and its inherent primordial meaning is embodied above all else in that relational co-creative energy we name as 'Trinity'.

Relationship: the heart of all connection

Disconnectedness is the sin that underpins all others. It long predates the original sin of disobedience. Inherent to the process of evolution itself is a gradual (not linear) unfolding leading to greater complexity, coherence and harmony. Our human shortsightedness, our gross disconnectedness from the grand scale of evolution and history, seriously inhibits us from connecting with the meaning embodied in the greater whole. We view life partially, atomistically, and since the seventeenth century largely in mechanistic, utilitarian segments. We are a people in exile, precisely because we have lost the art of being able to see the connections. In terms of recent human evolution (the past 10,000 years), the major sin of disconnectedness is the disruption of the planetary inter-relatedness that characterised our unfolding for many previous millennia. I am not suggesting a previous golden age that we humans somehow abandoned. There are no golden ages in a universe that is in a state of perpetual evolution, but when we view the unfolding process on the grand scale we can point to shifts which either enhance or diminish the overall quality of life. If we are the enlightened species we claim to be, then surely a time must come when we choose to learn from our past, reclaim what has been life-giving for us and for our planet, and choose to outgrow that which has been deleterious and destructive.

Our present relationship with one another and with the planet we inhabit is still predominantly that of the estranged status of 'conquer and control'. As indicated in previous chapters, the masculine will-to-power is not an innate feature of 'human nature', but rather a learned response of post-Agricultural times, an orientation that may have a certain historical relevance to past times, but one which, today, sets humans on a sure road to perdition.

The masculine will-to-power is characterised by an insatiable desire to have power over, to dominate, to subdivide and fragment in order to impose this control from on high, and treat everything (and everybody) as an isolated, autonomous unit (to ensure a maximum amount of control). We have become so accustomed to, and brainwashed by, this model, that the bulk of humanity takes it completely for granted. Sanctioned by time, custom and religion, many people and governments consider it illegal and sinful to even question the assumptions on which this model is construed.

Even the Christian model of redemption is itself tainted by the philosophy of patriarchy and correspondingly flawed on several counts. The redeeming God is an external demanding father-figure, who chooses to use his 'beloved son' as a scapegoat for the sins of humanity. The whole doctrine of atonement is based on a type of cosmic co-dependency. In order to highlight the divine power of the omnipotent Father, the entire human offspring is deemed to be under the eternal blemish of 'original sin'.

Therefore, we must be dependent upon the perfect father to show us the way to a restored relationship with him and with each other. The punishment of one perfect child has to occur before the father can forgive the rest of his children and love them. In more benign atonement forms, the father does not punish the son. Instead the father allows the son to suffer the consequences of the evil created by his wayward creation. Hence, the father stands by in passive anguish as his most beloved son is killed, because the father refused to interfere with human freedom . . . The shadow of omnipotence haunts atonement. The ghost of the punitive father lurks in the corners. He never disappears even as he is transformed into an image of forgiving grace. (Brock, 1992, pp. 55, 56)

All the religions, in one shape or another, endorse a model of divine rescue based on the abusive relationships of victimisation and scapegoating. The notion of an external divine father-figure who intervenes in order to redeem, and the corollary that the redeeming process will require the sacrifice of an innocent victim, is quite a recent notion in the history of religious consciousness;[4] more precisely – to follow the definitions of terminology used right through this book – the notion of divine redemption belongs to formal religion, but not to the long history of spirituality which precedes religion by at least 70,000 years.

Spirituality arises as humans respond to what the Hebrew Scriptures call the God of the Covenant. Humans respond to the God who initiates a relationship – a relationship of unconditional love and not one based on any prior set of requirements. Humans, being themselves creatures with an innate capacity to relate, respond to the divine invitation, according to their evolutionary developmental potential. The ability to respond meaningfully to the divine relational invitation itself depends on how well we have integrated other dimensions of relationship: with self, other people, other creatures, our planet, etc. Enculturated in a climate and ethos of relatedness, we humans learn to relate with the God who relates with us through *all* the relational opportunities life provides for us. Reclaiming the central importance of such relationality is essentially what the journey home from exile is all about.

What does 'redemption' mean in this context? It is the invitation and responsibility to remain transparent to the transformation that authentic relationships make possible, as each relational context unravels (reveals) the divine intent of God's fundamental relationship with the whole of life. It is not about setting right something that has gone wrong along the way, or correcting a fundamental flaw built into the process from the beginning. There is no fundamental flaw, and there never has been. From the divine perspective, nothing has gone wrong. Therefore we don't need a 'theology' to set it all right, but rather an 'anthropology' to highlight how thwarted our human imaginations can become precisely when we disconnect from our spiritual inheritance.

What we need to redeem is the fundamental fact of our existence: that *relationship* is both the heart and soul of our very existence and the alienation that has brought about atonement doctrines in the first place arises because we have become disconnected from the pathway of authentic human and global inter-relatedness. And that is a *human* problem, not a *divine* one. We caused the problem; it is up to us to resolve it. It is we who have construed the notion of an all-powerful God in the face of whose power and perfection we are forever in exile; that myth is of our making, not of God's. Trying to construe a divine rescue package is a sure prescription for blasphemy in regard to God and for further alienation in regard to humans and creation.

As long as we pursue political, economic, religious and ideological policies of disconnectedness, setting ourselves over or against each other, other life forms, planet Earth and the cosmos, we continue to perpetuate the reign of sin. We continue to miss the mark, which is precisely what the Greek word for sin, *hamartia*, means. What we need to be redeemed from is not the wrong we do, but rather the myopic blindness, the ignorance that fuels our mis-guided perceptions, attitudes and actions. And we don't need divine intervention to bring about that change of heart. We have been endowed with all the resources we need to reach salvation – not in some distant heaven, but right here in the midst of our one and true home, the cosmic creation where the Cosmic Christ is already resurrected.

The God who relates *authentically* is not some type of divine parent wishing to rescue wayward children. The divine–human relationship is not a co-dependent one; the relationship of the covenant is *adult-to-adult*, a model that is largely unknown to the formal religions.

The work of redemption does not require an intervening or rescuing God, but rather a community of adult human beings who know what it is to participate collaboratively with our co-creative God. Adherents of a Calvanist vein will claim that this is only possible by the power of God's grace. I agree, but wish to acknowledge that in the very act of creation, initially, and in the case of everything that has unfolded since then, grace is bestowed with an abundance that we humans can scarcely visualise. We don't even have to ask for God's grace; we need to learn how to receive it with open hearts. A closed heart cannot receive, neither can it relate meaningfully. And the only thing that can break open a closed heart is loving, tender and healing relationships.

The work of redemption – from whatever religious persuasion we adopt – is about coming home to ourselves – from our self-imposed exile and alienation – as creatures of God endowed with an innate capacity to relate lovingly and meaningfully. It is not a technique to be mastered, but a process in which we participate – forever expanding into deeper and more inclusive horizons. That we make mistakes along the way is not a problem, as long as we learn to forgive ourselves and others, something humans generally are not good at – mainly because our masculine patriarchal modelling has hardened us for competition, conflict and antagonism.

The salvation of the future, particularly the future of *Homo Sapiens*, is very much in our own hands. And it all depends on how quickly and creatively we can reawaken to who we really are, and relearn the graced skill of coming home to ourselves as interdependent, relational human beings. In that very process, not only will we rediscover our true selves, but also the God whose presence radiates in the co-creative interaction of just and loving relationships.

Reconnecting with the Christian story

Since many readers of this book belong to a Christian culture, I wish to conclude the reflections of this chapter with some suggestions on how we might reclaim our Christian tradition. Feminist writers such as Mary Daly, Naomi Goldenberg and Daphne Hampson claim that Christianity is so saturated in patriarchy that it is beyond redemption and, consequently, should be totally abandoned, as they have chosen to do. In fact, many

Christians have chosen this route, and have tried to consign to silence and oblivion experiences, good and bad, that belonged to the religious phase of their lives.

Most feminist scholars claim that an original, more inclusive undercurrent of our Christian tradition can be retrieved, requiring a great deal of deconstruction, so that a more authentic Christian vision can be reconstructed. Consequently, the American theologian Elizabeth A. Johnson reclaims the Wisdom (*sophia*) tradition of the Hebrew Scriptures to reconstruct afresh the meaning and role of Jesus, the Christ. Elizabeth Schussler Fiorenza, having deconstructed the patriarchal device of making women invisible, suggests a radical reconstruction of the New Testament to show how women played a leading role in the discipleship of equals.

Scholars operating from within the Christian context tend to hold a conviction that Christianity is a faith tradition deeply imbued with primordial spiritual aspirations which, precisely because they are so fundamental, can and should be retrieved for the benefit of humanity. In large measure, I share this aspiration, although I believe that some key elements of the Christian 'faith', for example the end-of-the-world myth; the literalisation of the Virgin Birth and the 'event' of Christ's resurrection, are cultural accretions of a former age that we now need to abandon. This leaves some people wondering what then are we left with!

The main thing we are left with – the heart and core of the Jesus vision – is the *Basileia*, variously translated as the *Kingdom of God*, the New Reign of God, or my own favourite the Kindom of God. This phrase occurs over 140 times in the four Gospels and encapsulates everything that Jesus lived for, died for and represented in his very existence. Precisely because of our tendency to *personalise* great religious personages within the formal religions, and turn them into divine, individualistic heroes, it seems that we have misinterpreted the Jesus movement right from its origins. Already in New Testament times we get a strong sense of a close group of male followers (called apostles) who fundamentally misunderstand and misappropriate what Jesus is about. Consistently, they want to turn him into a heroic superman, modelled on the earthly, political king, in their desperate desire that he would be the one who could set Israel free (Luke 24:21).

Consistently, Jesus rejects this move, always pointing to the *mission* that he is about. And that mission subjugates even Jesus himself to the cause for which he is living and will die, namely the Kindom of God. It seems to me that Jesus never wanted himself viewed in personal isolation. His individual identity and existence has no meaning apart from the cause within which that life is lived out, namely the Kindom of God. Accordingly, Pannenberg (1977, pp. 52–3) can write:

> In the New Testament, however, Jesus' message of the imminent Kingdom of God precedes every Christology and every new qualification of human existence and thus becomes the foundation of both. Christological and anthropological interpretations cannot be imposed upon the preaching of the Kingdom, but must themselves be judged in the light of the Kingdom. This resounding motif of Jesus' message – the imminent Kingdom of God – must be recovered as a key to the whole of Christian theology.

Scholars (e.g. Feullenbach, 1995) argue that the vision of the Kindom makes no sense apart from Jesus, and should never be construed as some kind of social or reform movement in its own right. I agree, but that does not permit the popular interpretation that the Kindom is subservient to the person; in my opinion, the evidence points precisely to the opposite conclusion.

In striving to unravel what Jesus envisaged by the Kindom of God, it is our patriarchal tendency to exalt and exonerate the individual person as a type of divine hero – thus validating all forms of patriarchal rule – that sets us on a false track. It becomes further distorted when the Jesus vision becomes firmly ensconced within the Church; there is nothing in the Gospels to suggest that Jesus wished his dream for the Kindom of God to be confined within any formal religious movement or organisation. The Kindom of God is for everybody, and at the service of the whole of creation. Confining it to the Church or suggesting that the Church is the primary embodiment of the Kindom is a form of reductionism, engineered by Christendom, but not in tune with the Gospel vision of Christianity.

Once again, we need to confront our sense of disconnectedness and redeem ourselves from the theological (ideological) reductionism to which we have too often succumbed. We need to rediscover the Jesus whose entire life and mission is embedded in the Kindom of God at the heart of the world. The nineteenth-century liberal theologian, Ernst Troeltsch, states the challenge quite cryptically: 'Jesus did not bring the Kingdom of God; the Kingdom of God brought Jesus.' And the christological implications of that statement are nowhere more cogently stated than in these words from Peter Hodgson (1989, pp. 209–10):

> God was 'incarnate' not in the physical nature of Jesus as such, but in the gestalt that coalesced both in and around his person – with which his person did in some sense become identical, and by which, after his death, he took on a new communal identity . . . For Christians, the person of Jesus of Nazareth played, and continues to play a normative role in mediating the shape of God in history, which is the shape of love in freedom. Jesus' personal identity merged into this shape in so far as he simply *was* what he proclaimed and practiced. But Jesus' personal identity did not exhaust this shape, which is intrinsically a communal, not an individual shape . . . The *communal* shape of Spirit is the true and final gestalt of God in history.

Theologians still try to unravel what *person* and *personality* connoted for those who drew up the christological dogmas of Nicea and Chalcedon. I suggest that *connection* with present understandings rather than *clarification* of past ones would better serve the theological enterprise today. We have now moved away considerably from the notion of personal identity based on individual, autonomous characteristics to an understanding of personhood as fundamentally *relational* and *interdependent* (not just interpersonal, but also ecological and planetary).

In the modern view, each of us is at all times the sum of our relationships. Our personal identity is not something given once and for ever, but something continuously unfolding and evolving according to our ability to relate meaningfully and interdependently within the entire spectrum of personal and planetary life. And this seems to have been the sense of personhood out of which Jesus operated: a quality and quantity of personhood that required the global ambience of 'right relationships' for its full unfolding. That global ambience of right relationships is what the Gospels call the Kindom of God.

This more wholistic and inclusive sense of the personal is the first re-connection to be made, to be redeemed afresh. The second follows quite logically: the context for such re-connection is interpersonal, earthly, planetary, universal. It cannot and must not be reduced to any system or organisation – religious, political or otherwise. Christians may still wish to consider the Church as 'the means whereby the Kingdom is anticipated most concretely in the world' (Boff, 1985, p. 2), but we need to acknowledge that it will also unfold *in its fullness* wherever humans struggle for right relationships marked by justice, love, compassion and liberation.

How, therefore, do we redeem the connection between religion and the Kindom of God? Let's begin by asking: How did Jesus connect them? Did he connect them at all? In other words, did Jesus want to create a new religion in his name, in the name of the cause for which he lived and died? Probably not! It is Christians who invented Christianity (more accurately, *Christendom*) and not Jesus. Jesus called people into the fullness of life. The evidence for the view that Jesus was about a reform of Judaism is at best speculative, and there is nothing in the Gospels to suggest that Jesus wanted to replace it with a *better* type of religion.

As we connect more deeply with our faith tradition as a Christian people, we do in fact encounter even a greater shock, one enunciated by Sheehan (1986) with great clarity: not alone did Jesus try to transcend the closed religious systems of his day, but Jesus in enunciating the Kindom of God is trying to get rid of *all* religion. By implication, what Jesus is about is the retrieval of an *integral spirituality* that encompasses the whole of life in its personal, interpersonal, planetary and universal dimensions.

The call to the *fullness of life* (John 10:10) now takes on a radically new meaning, forges a whole new set of connections and resets the paschal experience (death and resurrection) in a radically new context. The implications of this new vision are the subject material for the remaining chapters of this book.

— 8 —

Creation is a Place Called Home

The control of nature is a phrase conceived in arrogance born of the Neanderthal age of biology and philosophy, when it was supposed that nature existed for the convenience of man.

Rachel Carson

Stars, planets, persons, with their bodies minds, spirits – all are warps in space–time; all rise up out of a mysterious energy pit. The nature we know has grown soft. Down below, there is something hazy that we can reach with our formulas but hardly imagine. There is a subsurface inaccessibility, plasticity, and mysteriousness that allows us more easily to be spiritual about this now than in the hard world of earlier physics.

Holmes Rolston III

COSMOLOGY – THE SCIENCE THAT studies how the universe came into being and continues to unfold – is as old as humanity itself. Humans have always been intrigued by the grandeur of life, whether understood cosmologically or in terms of the home planet, our Earth. It may well be that the astronauts who marvelled at the wonder of planet Earth from outer space were responding to an ancient, primordial inner awakening. They were giving external expression to something we have known internally for many thousands of years.

Outer space also provides an important context. There is something about the big vision – seeing totality in its essential oneness – that evokes a sense of wonder, mystery and divinity. Strangely, it is in the outer realms, amid the vastness of space, that humans did not feel lost or in exile. Quite the contrary: they often had profound experiences of being totally at home!

What the eye of the heart can see from a distance conveys a truth that neither scientific certitude nor religious dogmatism can ever comprehend. Creation radiates its own elegance and an embracing sense of intimacy; only by attending to its evolutionary flow can we hope to decipher its deeper meaning.

Those who drive us into exile – often the guardians of our political and religious institutions – tend to emphasise the precariousness of life and the impact of the alien forces that surround us. Life is construed as a *battle* – a favourite metaphor of patriarchal cultures – in which we spend most of our time struggling to overcome the forces of evil, and rarely enjoying any success.

As already indicated, the prevailing world-view of our time is heavily weighted towards estrangement and alienation. Both science and religion are caught in the same perceptual quagmire. Central to this dilemma is the conviction that our Earth (and the cosmos) is dead, inert matter, adversarily juxtaposed to alive and enlightened humans who somehow can make it malleable and more congenial to life.

Towards the end of the twentieth century, we began to adopt a less arrogant, although, some would claim, more anthropocentric orientation, by developing the Cosmological Anthropic Principle (see Barrow and Tippler, 1986). In its main outline it suggests that universal life is designed for the evolution of intelligent beings – and both science and religion tend to assume that we, in our present evolved state, are those beings. Implicit in this argument is the notion that we are the ultimate species to inhabit creation and, consequently, the future of creation is largely, if not exclusively, in our hands.

Harris (1991, p. 58) acknowledges the positive insights of the Anthropic Principle but invites us to rethink the ensuing anthropology:

> The earth is a planet of the right size, orbiting a star of the right kind, enveloped by an atmosphere with the right composition, and with a hydrosphere unique among the planets. It harbours elements and compounds with extraordinary properties, all propitious and most of them indispensable for the propagation and maintenance of life. None of this would be possible except in a universe as old and extensive as the one we observe, or in any but a space–time of four dimensions, or in any other than a physical world governed by the discovered fundamental constants of nature. These conditions are all interdependent . . .

Nothing is brought about by our ability to discover it. It is not because we are here that the world comes to be so disposed, but rather the opposite. So-called anthropic explanations are misused if they are understood to suggest such a reversal of causal connections.

The cosmic foundation

The previous chapter explored the foundational nature of reality as essentially *relational*. In other words, it is in connecting relationally – at *every level* of life – that we begin to come home once more to who we really are as a human–divine species. We assume that such relationships begin with humans and in the various interactions through which humans inter-relate. The suggestion of this book – perhaps its most original and controversial claim – is that such relationships are built into the fabric of cosmic creation itself and that it is from this source that we humans inherit the capacity to relate.

As already highlighted, all the major religions present an antagonistic and distrustful attitude towards the material creation in both its planetary and cosmic manifestations. The anti-world polemic features in all the religions. Although the religions often use the word 'world' in a metaphorical rather than in a literal sense, few can deny that experiencing God in the processes of nature has always been held suspect among the religions, and in fact is one of the major reasons why many mystics in the Catholic Church have never been considered for sainthood.

Religion also tends to ignore, bypass, and even subvert, a tradition of many millennia wherein people of no particular religious persuasion were obviously in touch with powerful spiritual energies, and often in relationship with the divine life-force. To view such development in a benign and transparent way has been virtually impossible because of the impact of such corrosive labels as 'pagan', 'heretic', 'agnostic', etc. Gradually, we are beginning to reclaim the central importance of spirituality, and its rich and complex evolution which pre-dates formal religion by several millennia – a topic I explore at length in a previous work (Ó Murchu, 1997b).

This distinction between religion and spirituality is crucial to the deliberations of the present chapter. Religion is essentially suspicious of creation, because ultimately religion is the offspring of post-Agricultural patriarchy, which considers the male species as superior to every other life form, creation included; in other words, everything is there to be conquered and controlled. Religionists stand outside creation; spirituality belongs to the inner realm.

This brings us to the central thesis of the present chapter, and indeed a hinge on which the whole book hangs: I am not trying to develop a spirituality that will help us to understand the universe as an object or organism out there. Rather, I wish to unravel and explore the *spiritual essence of the universe itself.* My conviction is that the universe is innately energised with a will-to-meaning; that everything in creation ultimately veers towards life-giving relationships (and this includes the paradoxical interaction of birth, death and rebirth). As a Christian, I believe God is the primary source of this co-creative energy and forever works co-creatively *within* creation and not as some external agent, activating and judging everything from afar.

Drawing mainly on recent research in cosmology, evolutionary theory and physics, I wish to highlight processes within the universe that point to this innate spiritual will-to-meaning. I have explored the topic at greater length in a previous work (Ó Murchu, 1997a). The reader needs to keep in mind that I consider the spiritual capacity of humans to be derived from the spiritual energy of creation, rather than it being some special form of endowment unique to humans and superior to that of the rest of creation. In other words, we are endowed with a spiritual giftedness because the creation from which we are created is innately spiritual, and without that creative unfolding, our lives are without meaning or purpose.

Spirituality does not try to establish that there is some type of divine spirits or beings enlivening everything that exists. Rather it pursues the sense of *relatedness that conveys meaning, elegance and beauty*. And it can also entertain and befriend the inevitable paradoxes, and even the contradictions that accompany any evolving process. As scientists probe more deeply the facts of universal life, they are – unknowingly for the greater part – weaving a powerful *story* that grips the hearts and imaginations of increasing numbers of people. Why? Because, I suggest, the more we discover about our universe, the more we learn about who we ourselves really are, and the more we come home to ourselves as cosmic and planetary creatures.

Contemporary cosmology highlights complex and autopoietic dynamics in the long evolutionary unfolding of universal life. An inner dynamism was at work (and I do not wish to suggest that everybody has to consider this to be a *divine* force) forever pushing the will-to-life to more complex and creative horizons. Scholars today are beginning to see that even the great extinctions are inherently congruent with the evolving process. The pioneering scholarship of Niles Eldredge (1985, 1999) in partnership with the renowned microbiologist, Stephen J. Gould (Eldridge and Gould, 1977), suggesting that we think of the great extinctions as 'moments of punctuated equilibrium', echoes a more Eastern notion of the balance of Yin and Yang, or the dynamic rhythm of rest and activity which we daily observe in all living species. Swimme and Berry (1992) write extensively about the mysterious blending of creation and destruction as complementary forces in the evolutionary story of our universe.

Erwin Laszlo (1996, 1998) is among the more daring and holistic evolutionary theorists of our time. He readily acknowledges that the dynamics of chance and necessity are essential to the creative, self-organising process that drives the course of evolution. But it is far from being a random process. Instead, (in Laszlo, 1998, p. 217), he writes:

> Evolution is not a blind groping towards non-existent goals, a haphazard play with chance and accident. It is a systematic, indeed systemic development toward goals generated in the process itself.

While not adopting the more explicit religious conviction that evolution has a clear sense of purpose, Laszlo (1998, p. 83) admits to a 'preferred direction' indicative of purpose rather than randomness, order rather than disorder, and creativity rather than entropy.

Energy that sustains and empowers

Spirituality also enables and empowers us to marvel at wonders which religion often dismisses as esoteric and irrelevant. Take for instance this fascinating description of the neutrino, the subatomic particle that may hold the clue to dark matter and to other, as yet undiscovered, wonders of our universe:

In the time it takes to read this sentence, millions and millions of neutrinos, pouring in from outer space, will zip through the body of every human being on earth. It's like a never-ending barrage of subatomic bullets, but with one important difference: unlike bullets, neutrinos are so ethereal that they pass through ordinary matter as though it were not there at all. Unless a neutrino scores a direct hit on an atomic nucleus, it leaves no hint of its passage. And such hits are so unlikely that the average neutrino can easily penetrate a slab of lead a trillion kilometers thick without grazing a single atom. (Lemonick 1996, p. 62)

Scientists frequently marvel at the improbable balances between chemical elements as life unfolded in the first few seconds after the 'Big Bang'. The probability that the energy levels of helium, beryllium, carbon and oxygen should be so finely tuned is considered to be extremely low. Yet, as Laszlo (1993, pp. 203–4) points out, this is true of the story of evolution not merely in its early 'Big Bang' stage but throughout the entire unfolding of universal life. Had the various forces and particles of nature exhibited values slightly higher or slightly lower than those that normally prevail, it is believed that life might have come to naught billions of years ago.

Of particular relevance to these reflections is the discovery of quantum theory in the 1920s. By introducing concepts like the wave/particle duality and the uncertainty principle into the mathematical calculations, scientists were forced to reconsider the rational, quantifiable and objective way they had viewed reality for the previous 300 years. God had become something of a non-issue for scientists, not because they were atheistic or agnostic, but because their scientific method was built on the exclusion of spiritual considerations. The quantum vision, with its fluid and liberating concepts, freed up the congealed system, and despite all efforts of the scientific community to keep quantum theory free of 'esoteric' speculations, it continues to engage the spiritual imagination of our time with renewed vitality and excitement.

The world-view of 'dead, inert matter' is no longer credible. Quantum theory provides added impetus to the basic hunch that there is more to life than meets the eye. Those strange and unexpected movements of the microscopic realm are not merely features of the 'subatomic' world, which make sense merely to the scientific mind. More accurately, they are scientific evidence of that spiritual energy, underpinning all reality and known to both sages and mystics down through the ages.

Even the emptiness of the space around us we now know is not empty at all. It is a fullness of pure energy, believed to be the primary stuff which constitutes life, the potential energy forever seeking form in everything we see and touch, including our own very selves (see the comprehensive overview in Laszlo, 1998, pp. 180ff). In the experience of exile, even from early childhood, we were brainwashed about the vastness and 'coldness' of space. The 'big, wide world' was rarely spoken about in endearing terms, of the type we find in the description of the vacuum offered by Von Baeyer (1992, pp. 105, 109):

> The dynamic vacuum is like a quiet lake on a summer night, its surface rippled in gentle fluctuations, while all around, electron–positron pairs twinkle on and off like fireflies. It is a wiser and friendlier place than the forbidding emptiness of Democritus or the glacial ether of Aristotle. Its restless activity is utterly fascinating to physicists and invites speculation about its nature and even its potential usefulness. As a theoretical conception the dynamic vacuum holds great appeal . . . It is empty of matter, but filled with surprises.

The creative vacuum is not some 'thing'; it is an event, an experience, a fullness overflowing, proclaiming the prolific nature of universal life. And there are other realms of connectedness activated by the underlying 'spiritualized' energy requiring the attention of those who imbibe this new awareness. Foremost among these is the notion of *fields*, one of the most intriguing and engaging concepts in contemporary science.

Field theory was first explored by Michael Faraday and James Clerk Maxwell in the nineteenth century, and by biologists Paul Weiss, C. H. Waddington and Rene Thom in the twentieth. In contemporary physics, there are four main fields, usually referred to as *gravity, electromagnetism, strong force* and *weak force*. Fields are non-material regions of influence, spheres of creative energy forever poised to express themselves in *form* – which can be physical, social, psychic, spiritual or structured in modes of consciousness which as yet we humans can scarcely imagine. And it appears that field-energy never becomes exhausted in its prodigious birthing, reminding us once more that this, too, is allegedly a dominant feature of the Great Earth Mother Goddess.

Take for instance the Earth's gravitational field. It is all around us. It gives things weight and makes things fall. It is holding us down to Earth at this moment, but also affecting the trajectory of the moon and the movements of other large bodies in space–time.

Fields may be considered as 'horizons of belonging' within which we live and move and have our being. We would like to know a great deal more about fields. Who or what created them, and where do they get their 'energy' from? Scientists believe they are an integral dimension of space–time and have existed from a very early stage of the evolving universe.

Is it God who created and still maintains them? Religionists would wish us to respond positively. But that feels like too simplistic an answer and carries with it the danger of creating a mechanistic God, acting behind the scenes like an executive manager. This is the God of exile often invented to assuage our alienation, but 'who' in fact only exacerbates our sense of estrangement.

Invoking once more the distinction between religion and spirituality, we may consider fields to be radiations of God's own creative energy, spiritual life-forces, with an inherent autopoietic (self-generating) potential which is fundamentally irreversible and essentially benign in its thrust to enhance life. This is not a deterministic movement, but we may wish to invoke religious language (which is no longer fashionable), and describe it as a movement of providence. Nor am I suggesting a *personalised* God-image of the type invoked by the major religions. The divine–cosmic–planetary–human grandeur being invoked here requires a trans-personal set of images which most theologians have not begun to imagine.

The connective tissue of universal life

The traditional belief that everything is made of atoms, also needs to be reconsidered. For some 30 years now, scientists under the pioneering vision of John Schwarz of Caltech and Michael Green of Queen Mary College in London have suggested an alternative metaphor, not one of isolated (and competitive) building-blocks, but something akin to a set of vibrational energies like those generated by plucking the strings of a musical instrument. For many millennia humans have believed that music could be the clue to the meaning of universal life. *Superstring theory* (popularly known as SUSY) is the latest rendition of that long-held belief. (More on this subject in Smolin, 1997, pp. 70–89.)

Conceptually, superstring theory lends itself more readily to the notion of an underlying relationality that has been referred to several times in the course of this book. The atomistic and mechanistic view of the world, which seeks to reduce everything to its constituent parts, no longer serves the best interests of either humankind or planet Earth. The 'survival of the fittest' has left many lonely heroes battling it out in the land of exile. Those among us who wish to abandon that land, or have already done so, know only too well that the co-operative, and not the competitive, mode is the only strategy that makes sense for the future. Increasingly, we realise that it may well be the strategy that sustained and nourished us for most of the 4.4 million years we have inhabited the Earth.

One time, we thought that nothing could travel faster than the speed of light; in fact, that is still the 'official' scientific position, since we believe that the principle of relativity cannot be violated. But several experiments of the past few decades, on the notion of 'non-locality' – the apparent ability of a particle to be simultaneously in more than one location – indicate otherwise.

Einstein himself described the idea (known as 'action-at-a-distance') as 'ghostly and absurd' and, in conjunction with his colleagues, Podolsky and Rosen, devised a thought experiment now known as the EPR Paradox to disprove the idea. Three decades later the Irish physicist John Bell designed an experimental method by which the level of correlation between photons could be measured. This opened the door for more detailed technological research of which Alain Aspect's experiment of 1982 is best known.

In a word, what Aspect proved is that identical particles emitted in opposite directions would respond simultaneously and instantaneously, although one may be on Earth and the other on the far side of the moon. The connective tissue holds life in an interdependent correlation that defies all the forces of fragmentation and all the anthropocentric desires to break things down into manageable segments.

So often in recent decades we have been reminded that the whole is greater than the sum of the parts. In fact, the phrase is becoming hackneyed from overuse. Yet there is an enormous resistance in the human community generally to integrate this principle into our way of relating with our world and with each other. We warm to the idea of relating more intimately and co-operatively, but deep within us a fierce competitiveness, an alienating sense of separation and a compulsive drive to conquer all before us, continue to drive most of humanity, still stuck in the land of exile.

Perhaps what most of us need is a pilgrimage to outer space, to have our eyes and hearts opened afresh to see the sacredness behind and above the appearances, and to have reawakened that inner light buried beneath layers of mechanistic brain-washing. The example of the astronauts continues to be paradigmatic for this new vision. Consider what it must have been like for Edgar Mitchell when he gazed down on the home planet (the Earth) and allowed poetry to exude from his heart:

> On the return trip home, gazing through 240,000 miles of space towards the stars and the planet from which I had come, I suddenly experienced the universe as intelligent, loving and harmonious. My view of the planet was a glimpse of divinity.

This is not the sentimental verbiage of some New Age mystic, but the words of a reputable scientist, schooled in the rigour and objectivity of the scientific method, well aware of the fact that he must not allow his feelings to blur his perceptions and must only work with data that can be checked and verified scientifically. Mitchell has not chosen to lay aside his scientific training, nor would it be appropriate for him to deviate from the strict procedures he is supposed to follow. He is overtaken by an experience: in fact, overwhelmed by it; and what we hear are words that come straight from the heart. Are they true? Are they accurate? Perhaps he is deluded!

It is worthy of note that Mitchell uses the word 'divinity' but not 'God'. What is at work here, I suggest, is spirituality and not religion. And ultimately, only the wisdom of spirituality can authenticate the perceptions and convictions of this experience. To access the experience, and discern its authenticity, spirituality will seek to explore the relationships – the connections forged between Mitchell and the planet he is encountering. At that moment the object-to-object connection breaks down and a subject-to-subject relationship takes over. Now, everything is seen in a new light. Such experiences are familiar to those on the journey home from exile, but it often feels a bit scary to say them out loud. It still feels risky to offend those safeguarding the land of exile!

Outgrowing the dominator/dominated paradigm

The strongest collusion between science and religion is that each considers the created world as an *object* placed at the disposal of human beings. It is a 'thing' to be used for the advantage of humanity, and how we use it is largely left to our own devices. The only 'relationship' thus permitted is a top-down, hierarchical one, with humans controlling all the power, know-how and dominance. It is a winner–loser relationship with the paradoxical irony that at the end of the day the superior force, i.e. humans themselves, is likely to endure the greatest loss. Those who inherit the prospect of conquering end up feeling the greatest depth of alienation and exile.

The only model of relationship that a patriarchal culture can tolerate is the dominator–dominated type. It is the father to all other relationships, itself validated by the supreme God on high. All the religions still cling tenaciously to this model; so does mainstream science (along with politics, economics, medicine, education, etc.), except that the central God has become a secularised figurehead. In their pristine teachings none of the religions agree with this paradigm, yet none are prepared to acknowledge the subversion that has taken place through religious enculturation. The fundamental values of the 'household' (*oikonomia*) have been betrayed; the religions themselves have not merely allowed this to happen, they have actually colluded with the very process.

Frequently, these days, it is the non-religious sciences that are confronting the religions with the call to reclaim the *right relationships* which they profess to uphold and foster. Scientist, Danah Zohar (1994, pp. 31, 40) writes:

In quantum physics, both the nature of being as a dynamic wave-particle dualism and the notion of transformation as a process through which things like electrons and photons are spread out all over space and time carry enormous implications for the kinds of relationships found between quantum systems.

It is here, in the realm of relationship, that quantum reality is truly most 'mind-boggling' and revolutionary . . .

Quantum holism may be telling us, for example, that power relations are not the only, or perhaps even the most effective, way that people and events can be linked in society. The politician or the manager who tries to influence or control events may be less effective than one who can be sensitive to the spontaneous emergence of social or political trends. The individual who realises that parts of his or her own identity emerge through relationship with others may be less guarded and defensive.

Being 'sensitive to the spontaneous emergence' sounds like a familiar signpost on the way home from exile. It is what constitutes a dynamic spirituality for our time, provided we don't reserve its application to humans and their influence on creation. Spontaneous emergence belongs first and foremost to cosmic evolution itself and to the intricate flow of interdependence and connectedness which characterises every moment of our self-organising universe. The intelligence which drives evolution does not require any sky-God endowed with supreme wisdom. The wisdom is inherent in the evolving process itself and becomes most accessible to us when we try to understand the inter-related dynamics birthing vast possibilities for life and growth.

On the grand scale we detect the relational foundation in the very structure of space–time itself, one of the great intuitive insights of Einstein's relativity theory. Space–time is curved, not shaped in the straight lines of Euclidean geometry. This simple structure of universal life profoundly affects everything contained within the curvature, and *everything* is contained within it! A flat universe allows, indeed encourages, us to envisage things being *stable* and *unmovable*. A curved universe conveys a very different set of ideas and perceptions: things move and encounter each other; they engage and inter-relate! In a curved universe, they cannot do otherwise. As Swimme and Berry (1992, pp. 77–8, 104–5) rightly emphasise *communion* is built into the very fabric of curved space–time, and in such a universe alienation is a theoretical impossibility!

Sadly, the symbolic significance of curved space–time has least impact on scientists themselves. Rational logic continues unabated, fuelling the 'war games' of 'divide and conquer'! Over the past

100 years we have successfully broken down atoms into several constituent parts. The pursuit has a relentless and compulsive feel to it; the scientists are convinced that one day they will isolate and identify the basic building-blocks of matter. With that discovery they will be able to re-assemble the master plan on which the whole universe is constructed. They are convinced that they will then have unlocked the mind of God. Patriarchy will have achieved its ultimate goal of total control over all the forces of life.

Few scientists would go along totally with these sentiments. Yet this is the subconscious driving force that underpins mainstream science today. It is a stubbornly resistant conviction built on centuries of a self-fulfilling prophesy validated by the unquestioned power of the supreme God of patriarchy. Therefore, evidence to the contrary is cleverly subverted, and those that persist in pursuing the deeper truths are weeded out, justly or unjustly.

The dogmatic conviction that the ultimate stuff of the universe consists of basic building-blocks was dealt a severe blow in the closing decades of the twentieth century. But the scientists made sure that it did not hit the headlines. The most recent family of subatomic particles, the quarks, deviated from all previous discoveries in the subatomic world. They refused to be isolated, manifesting only in pairs or triads (relationships); and, having tried every option at their disposal, the scientists failed to smash the quark into smaller building-blocks. And the response was predictable: build larger and more powerful particle accelerators which one day will smash the elusive quark, thus ensuring that the pursuit of the ultimate building-blocks continues unabated!

That the quarks may be witnesses to a very different picture of reality – highlighting the fundamental *relational* nature of all things – is not merely implausible for the majority of contemporary scientists, but is dismissed as abhorrent and despicable (Smolin, 1997, being one notable exception). That the quarks can have any significance other than that which scientists claim they should have is a matter that should not be subjected to consideration or debate. That somebody other than a scientist should offer interpretations is deemed to be an aberration. To perpetuate the culture of exile we need to maintain clear boundaries between those who understand and those who never could!

It is at this level that the scientist and theologian collude in the most blatant fashion. The certainty of truth is, and always should be, reserved to those formally delegated to explore and communicate ultimate truth. All those outside the enlightened circle should know their place (on the hierarchical ladder) and respectfully maintain it. In other words, only those relationships construed within the parameters of *exclusion* and *inclusion* are deemed to be authentic. The idea that relationships underpin the whole of reality, animate and inanimate alike, might be a nice philosophical or religious idea, but it is unlikely to be seriously entertained either in the field of science or in formal religion.

Spirituality is the wisdom for our age that can circumvent, and ultimately undermine, the sturdy barricades of rational knowledge. To circumvent and undermine suggests subversive action. It involves bypassing or ignoring the 'laws and regulations'; it means dreaming alternative ways of engaging with reality; it suggests pushing boundaries towards novel possibilities. Most importantly it means adopting the methods of dialogue and mutual enrichment across all the time-honoured boundaries of the intelligent v. the ignorant, the specialist v. the amateur, the wise v. the foolish, the divinely inspired v. the wisdom of creation. The spirituality that belongs to the journey home from exile seeks to break down all boundaries and forge new relationships in the mutual exploration of the truth that unites and liberates.

In a universe constructed and evolving on relational principles, the spirituality of home-coming challenges us to a subject-to-subject relationship with the whole of universal life, most of which we humans are only beginning to discover. It also invites us to come home to ourselves in our rootedness on planet Earth and reclaim something of that ancient sacredness known to our ancestors throughout paleolithic times. It then invites us into what is emerging as one of the most urgent and engaging issues of our time: our *ecological* relationship with every other life form that befriends us in our co-habitation of planet Earth.

Ecological sustainability

'Sustainability' denotes an interplay between the various elements of creation in such a way that each is accorded due recognition, for what it is in itself, and for what it contributes to the good of the whole. (Its *political* significance I explore in Chapter 11.) It marks a shift in emphasis away from the priority of some forms over others (e.g. the human over the animal or plant life) to that of the interdependence whereby every form *co-exists* for the mutual enrichment of each other and of the greater whole. Ruether (1983, p. 67) depicts with great clarity the type of conversion this new vision requires:

> Conversion means that we recognize the interconnectedness of all parts of the community of creation so that no part can long flourish if the other parts are being injured or destroyed. In a system of interdependence, no part is intrinsically 'higher' or 'lower'. Plants are not lower than humans because they don't think or move. Rather, their photosynthesis is the vital process that underlies the very existence of the animal and human world. We could not exist without them, whereas they could exist very well without us. Who then is more 'important'?
>
> . . . We must start thinking of reality as the connecting links of a dance in which each part is equally vital to the whole, rather than the linear competitive model in which the above prospers by defeating and suppressing what is below.

In many of her writings, Ruether advocates an unmasking of the 'domination and deceit' that is so endemic in our Western culture and its replacement with an ethic of 'critique and compassion'. A great deal of contemporary feminist and ecological writing focuses on the 'domination and deceit', as do earlier chapters of this book. The challenge for the future is to envision political and spiritual strategies that will activate in a more dynamic way an 'ethic of critique and compassion'.

Patriarchal culture tends to confuse 'critique' and 'criticism'. Any sentiment or statement that questions the prevailing view of the *status quo* tends to elicit defensive reaction. A subtle assumption underpins most, if not all, patriarchal systems that they have unquestioned access to truth, and any questioning of that truth is perceived as a form of attack. If the truth is considered to be 'of God', then all disagreement is considered to be 'criticism' with varying degrees of disrespect and disobedience.

In such a system there is no room for challenge or constructive criticism. And the one who criticises is quickly labelled (rebel, heretic, etc.), censured, disempowered to make any further 'attacks', and finally excluded or expelled from the system. The strategy of taking the focus off the issue and placing it on the *culprit*, thus personalising the problem, is a powerful way of disowning the criticism and making the system impervious to further challenge or change.

Parallels with the dysfunctional behaviour of family life are often noted. Instead of mature adult relationships, which can listen and respond to criticism in a responsible and mature way, the dynamics of co-dependency are played out in childish behaviour wherein power and powerlessness are dualistically split, and survival requires collusive and abusive behaviours to negotiate a climate of tolerance and acceptance. It is a high price (and a highly destructive one) to pay for 'freedom'.

A creative critique requires a climate of dialogue in an open and trusting engagement. Of its very nature such a critique also veers towards a holistic approach; in other words, problems are analysed and addressed in the largest possible context. The notion of sustainability requires a large canvas, one which seeks to uncover truth, not merely from within the system itself (whether it be a person, a relationship, an ecosystem, a planet), but in terms of the larger 'holon' within which that system operates.

Every living system has an ecological niche, an ambience that promotes growth and development. And no single niche can be fully explained in terms of its 'governing body'. Patriarchy claims that the Earth is an objective reality over which humans are the masters, a perception that is extensively challenged today within an ethical and ecological critique. To follow the patriarchal view – validated to varying degrees by most of the major religions – paves the way for ultimate catastrophe, for humans and for the creation around us, a fact that has been extensively documented in recent decades.

But an ethical, holistic critique goes a great deal further, to what may be the major contention of the present chapter. The ecological sustainability of life – whether personal or planetary – is itself not merely the foundation, but the very scaffolding of a meaningful spirituality for our time. Unless, and until, we rediscover and reclaim the co-creativity of God at the heart of creation, all our God-images and concepts will fall well short of an authentic divine–human relationship.

For those on the way home from exile, the earth upon which we walk is holy ground. The cosmos within which our home planet is held and embraced is the creative vacuum filled with divine life. The journey home from exile is truly a return to the centre, where the sacredness of *all* reality becomes our primary concern and our richest resource.

A radically new way of engaging with the major ecological questions of our day is a prerequisite for rediscovering the power of God in our lives and in our world. The old spirituality which sought to save us from the world is in radical reversal as once more the world comes to our rescue to save us from the destructive power of the religiosity of exile. Sustainability is not merely a form of ecological sensitivity and economic prudence; it is above all else a central aspect of God's own wisdom and grace.

Our reconciliation with God and with life requires, above all else, a new way of relating with creation around us. Therein we, too, like the astronauts in outer space, obtain the bigger and more penetrating picture of divine revelation. This is the basis of all our relationships, the cosmological context which alone will satisfy our cosmic yearnings. And in the light of this enlarged engagement, we'll come to see ourselves, and our personal identity, in a new light; that is the topic we explore in the next chapter.

— 9 —

Reconnecting with our Relational Selves

A Self is a node in the network of world, and in each self is an Eros ensouling the world. The world has heart – where we embrace the Universe as condensed, personified, particularized, in those metaphors of the sacred that inspire us. If we meet God in ourselves, we meet her at the molten course of our heart's desire, ever again energising our courage and our quest.

Catherine Keller

WHEN IT COMES TO HUMAN nature and what essentially it means to be human, religion is enmeshed in a complex neurosis. We encounter several largely disconnected elements which have contributed to our sense of exile: an internal dualism between soul and spirit on the one hand, between mind and body on the other; a being-in-the-world but somehow not of it; worthy of God's love and salvation, yet forever striving to prove one's worthiness; endowed with a 'higher' nature forever trying to transcend the pull of the 'lower' self; called to follow a God who represents the fullness of life, but a fullness that is only attainable in a life hereafter.

Many a devout follower of one or other religion spends an entire lifetime struggling to make sense of it all; not surprisingly, many people on the way home from exile wonder if it's worth all the anguish and soul-searching that they have had to endure. In fact, the struggle is not about the *religion* itself, but rather about *me, the human person* caught in the web of life's search for meaning.

In the more academic climate of the West, the identity question is often projected onto the religious system itself. We blame it when things go wrong; we exalt it when it reinforces our wishes and desires; we use it to scapegoat those with whom we disagree.

And scholars of all religious persuasions get tremendous satis-faction, and at times substantial financial gain, from unravelling the eternal mysteries, but not always to the benefit of the average believer.

Religion thrives or fails, not on some divine fortune, but on its ability to provide humans with reasons for living. As already stated, we consider religion to be a *human* invention, created to forge links of meaning and purpose to substantiate our daily lives. Inherent to that task is the discovery and rediscovery of our identity as individual and collective beings.

Religion has made an enormous contribution to this search for identity, sometimes fruitful, sometimes highly problematic. This chapter attempts to unravel the dynamics at work in the search for meaning and identity, and the implications for the future as we strive to develop a spiritual vision to guide and sustain us on the homeward journey.

Who am I?

Religion provides several answers to the identity question. Basically it states that I am a child of God, unique in myself and destined for eternal fulfilment in the future. Throughout my earthly life, I am invited to share my faith journey with other people, family, friends, but specifically fellow-worshippers. That communal structure is also intended to enhance my personal identity; whether or not it does is a frequently debated question.

One of the major flaws in religious belief and practice – and this seems to go right across the religions – is the confusion of the *personal* and the *individual*. Persons are considered to be autonomous, independent creatures, each unique in his/her own right. This perception takes on more explicit significance in the monotheistic religions. The argument goes like this: God is one, unique and indivisible; so are human beings. To become like God we must cherish and cultivate the individuality that makes each one of us unique and special. At the end of our lives we will be called to render an account to God for what we have done *individually* with our lives and with our talents.

This very individualistic orientation is an aspect of mainstream religion that is rarely questioned and is vehemently safeguarded, especially in the monotheistic faiths. It is a cornerstone to the entire system on which religion is constructed and thrives, yet itself is the product of something much more fundamental and basic.

The *individualising of the personal* is itself a central tenet of the patriarchal will-to-power. It is difficult to 'divide and conquer' when you are dealing with a relational matrix. When the emphasis is on the *connectedness* of all the elements, a policy of fragmentation just does not make sense. Consequently, you seek to undermine the connectedness, which can be done very effectively when you seek to validate it by emphasising the *sacred uniqueness* of each individual element. The overt desire to divide and conquer has been deviously subverted into a covert conglomerate of unique atoms. That still leaves the option for co-operation or competition, but in a climate fuelled by the desire to 'divide and conquer', competition always triumphs over co-operation.

Although religion claims to cherish and protect the individual person – and all the religions adopt a strong rhetoric in favour of the poor and disenfranchised – it is the strong, robust, heroic individual who is favoured at the end of the day. Every religion cherishes above all others its heroes, ascetics, martyrs and warriors; it canonises them and exalts them as the models that the rest of us, everyday ordinary humans, should emulate, a spiritual strategy that has bred its fair share of neurotic and even psychotic behaviour. The ideal follower of the religion must aim to be like the Great God himself: the one who has conquered even the unconquerable.

It will come therefore as little surprise to find that the language of the mainstream religions is predominantly that of warfare and contest, of rulers and victors, of power *over* rather than power *with*. In the sacred texts themselves, the language is frequently that of love and covenant, of healing and forgiveness, of mercy and compassion. Although these qualities continue to be the focus for the preaching and the teaching, they often become subverted within the more virulent patriarchal myth of the conquering hero, because ultimately that is what religion sets out to foster and maintain.

Religion therefore foments an identity of individualised personalism, the uniqueness of which is measured not in terms of how I relate to self or others, but how I relate to the individualised God at the top of the patriarchal ladder. And that relationship – with the patriarchal God – is the model for all other modes of relating, namely one of *dominance* and *subservience*. There is no equality in this relationship and there never could be. One is either dominating or being dominated, ruling or being ruled. Freedom becomes quite ambiguous and often quite manipulative.

The identity of individualised personalism is the breeding ground for many forms of oppression. In this culture it is all too easy to become the victim of *internalised oppression* whereby I no longer question, or even notice, the victimisation that is taking place. I learn to keep my place, and I am often richly rewarded for doing so. And usually, somewhere along the line, there are fringe benefits, for example young women in many Islamic households have little or no say in what happens within the home, but when they become grandparents they will exert on the incoming daughter-in-law a power and dominion far beyond that which the menfolk enjoy. The oppressed themselves become the primary oppressors.

In the Western world today, individualised personalism tends to be translated into *robust individualism*. This has many manifestations, but the most widely witnessed is that of the seditious competition whereby I seek to make it to the top irrespective of whom I 'eliminate' along the way, or how I eliminate them. We encounter it primarily in the world of big business, in the sphere of black marketeering (e.g. drug trade) and in the politics that viciously exploits the poor of our Earth and even the Earth itself. But it occurs with equal voraciousness right underneath our eyes, in the class-rooms of our schools and educational systems where children are brainwashed into being competitors from a very young age. The message is all too clear: 'Anything worth having is worth fighting for, and you fight to win; if you don't win, you're not worth much.'

Consequently, people spend many years evaluating themselves, measuring themselves against the standards of others, living out of somebody else's shadow and never attaining a meaningful or authentic *interdependent* sense of self. This is the basis for so much jealousy, resentment, self-doubt and even self-hate which reaps havoc on self-image, on the capacity to relate, and on inter-personal relationships.

The sum of my relationships

At several times in the history of human evolution, and specifically in the last quarter of the twentieth century, we humans have sought to reclaim a different sense of authentic selfhood. This is often a subconscious movement, one spurred, perhaps, by the very alienation that excessive individualism creates in our world.

It is often stated quite simply: each of us is the sum of his/her relationships. Were it not for the mutual attraction and psycho-sexual engagement of two other people – normally referred to as my parents – I would not even exist. My very existence is dependent on a pre-existing relationship. And no matter how I change through-out the span of my lifetime, I will always embody – especially at a psychic and emotional level – characteristics of my parents.

Most significantly, my own capacity to relate is heavily influenced by the early modelling of parents and/or guardians. The quality of love, trust and security provided for me as an infant – even prenatally – will heavily influence my later growth and develop-ment as a human being.

Other relational influences are also internalised. How I relate to other siblings will significantly influence how I handle conflict in later life. Early school influences are important not just intel-lectually but in terms of the adversarial and competitive attitudes that are subtly but powerfully exerted. Long before I reach adolescence, many patterns and attitudes are set and may remain largely unchanged for an entire lifetime.

It is fashionable these days to think of the human lifespan in terms of its potential for change and for new growth. Indeed, many of us can cite examples of people even in old age making quite dramatic changes in personality and life-style. What tends to be less obvious is the *relational matrix* within which such dramatic changes take place, and without which people are much more likely to remain rigid and resistant to change. The quality – and at times quantity – of our relationships powerfully influences our capacity for change and renewed growth.

Thus far, I highlight the role of relationships in forming and re-forming my growth and identity as a human being. My identity is never complete; in fact, is non-existent, without the 'significant others' who exert a distinctive developmental influence in my life. At all times I am and I become 'the sum of my relationships'.

Traditional religion will wish to add the God dimension to the relational landscape of my life and existence. Indeed, for many people, religion has been and continues to be highly formative in their growing and changing sense of self. Now with the rediscovery of spirituality a whole new set of relationships is claiming our attention.

In evolutionary terms, we humans need all the other creatures on the planet for both our survival and growth. In our evolutionary unfolding we are indisputably *interdependent* beings. The foliage of the trees, the fishes in the seas, the birds of the air and the animals all contribute to the evolutionary ambience within which humanity comes into being. And all the other creatures of creation create that matrix of meaning without which our lives simply would not be meaningful.

It is not just a question of needing other creatures in order to survive. Humans can live quite healthily without ever consuming meat or fish. But we would not be able to survive on a planet completely denuded of the animal, bird and aquatic species. These creatures provide us with a quality of presence, a quality of befriending, without which we cannot reach our full human potential. Our ability to inter-relate mutually with these other creatures also has enormous consequences on how we relate among ourselves.

Not merely does closeness to nature soften and sensitise us as humans, but it can radically change our attitudes and behaviours, not merely to other species but to our own kind. On the one hand, it helps to keep us *humble* (from *humus* meaning 'earth'), more attuned to nature and to the natural world. And strangely it can reconcile us to being able to live more comfortably with paradox, with the strange and often disturbing contradictions of how other species treat and even exploit their environment. Our relationship with other creatures is one of dialogue and mutuality; the very texture of our language depends on this interaction (cf. Abram, 1996, esp. pp. 73–92).

Beyond the realm of other species, the challenge to engage relationally takes on planetary and even cosmic significance. This is very much a (re)discovery of the past few decades. For instance, many of the drug substances used by the medical profession are based on extracts from various plants and trees – a substantial number of which are threatened as tropical forests are stripped away at an alarming rate. This fact alone reminds us that we belong to a planet that is capable of nourishing us in our health and well-being. Conversely, it may well be our alienation from our planetary womb that is the basis of so much sickness and psychological disturbance in our world today (cf. Roszak *et al.*, 1995).

This is not a trivial sentimental notion. Its implications are substantial, challenging and disturbing. There is good reason to believe that creation itself – in terms of its external planetary resources and the internal (inter)personal resources of each one of us – has all the potential that could enable us to live healthy and wholesome lives. Were we really in tune with the healing potential that surrounds us – within and without – we could largely, maybe totally, dispose of the medical profession!

We don't need to hand our lives over to medical specialists to live healthily; there is another way to do it, but it is only possible when we choose to reconnect with the life-giving sources, when we choose to relate in whole new ways.

The relational matrix in crisis

Patriarchal culture is wary of relationships. They generate a creativity and interaction that is not easily controlled. When people relate well, they tend to be much more creative, in both imagination and action. Behaviour becomes unpredictable. Those in charge are not sure where they stand!

To counter the unpredictability, patriarchal culture (and, true to expectation, formal religion also) has evolved quite specific institutions to contain our relational desires. Foremost among these are the institutions of marriage and the family. All the mainstream religions exalt the virtues of each; indeed, they are largely united in the conviction that they have been begotten by God himself!

The institution of monogamous marriage is a relatively recent development, with minimal legal status before the seventeenth century. Bigamous relationships, allowing a man to have several wives, is older and more extensive. The shift from bigamous unions to monogamous ones is very much a Western development and coincides with the rising mechanistic culture of the sixteenth and seventeenth centuries. A more orderly and streamlined model was considered appropriate, and better suited the mechanistic view of human sexuality which also surfaced at that time. The pairing of male and female revealed an obvious biological complementarity for the procreation of the species, and a stable, lifelong relationship guaranteed the greatest security and stability for the growth and development of children.

To readers of a religious background, these ideas will sound shallow and even offensive. We exalt and sanctify marriage and the family to a degree that makes a deeper critique difficult to achieve. Religionists often allude to marriage and the family being 'under attack'. There is a huge cultural investment in protecting these institutions from radical appraisal. This stubborn desire to protect, more than anything else, contributes to the malaise and disintegration which are all too prevalent in the contemporary world.

Marriage, whether bigamous or monogamous, has always been construed to favour the male members of the species. The woman was the object of desire and pleasure, the one who begot the children for the man, who ran the household, adopting the subjugated role. Not surprisingly, as women attain greater self-autonomy, their commitment to marriage becomes more problematic. It is not the *women* who are the problem; rather it is the unexamined assumptions on which the institution of marriage has thrived for the past few hundred years.

Marriage as we have known it – culturally and religiously – is very much a closed system. All needs are to be met within the relationship, especially those of intimacy and sexual desire. We assume that this is a moral and cultural prerogative intended by God and cherished by humans. For well over 90 per cent of our time on Earth this has *not* been the case, and all indications are that it is unlikely to be the norm as we move out of the cultural exile of the mechanistic age.

The monotheistic religions consider the family to be an institution of divine origin, God's own prescription to control the unruly power of human sexuality and the primary locus for the loving and nurturing care of the rising generations. Few would quibble with this ideal, but rarely is the ideal lived out in its full realisation. In many parts of the world, the loving nurturing care is bestowed upon male offspring, but not upon females; they are often aborted or left to die after birth. And in a wide range of cultural situations, family life imposes upon the woman severe burdens, which if not fulfilled leave her at the mercy of oppressive and reckless males. On a global scale, family life has been badly scarred by the desire for patriarchal control.

The religious collusion is both disturbing and frightening. In the Christian tradition, the holy family of Nazareth is often hailed as the model for all family life. Yet the more reliable Gospel evidence portrays Jesus harshly condemning family life and inviting his followers to a radically different and more inclusive sense of family (cf. Mark 3:31–35; Matt. 10:34–36; Luke 11:27–28; 12:51–53). Was Jesus denouncing the family institution because he perceived it to be a harbinger of patriarchal power? The evidence points in that direction; but Christian tradition has rarely acknowledged its duplicity in this regard.

The cherished institutions of marriage and the family are currently in disarray. The religions continue promoting the ideals of former times, knowing full well that they face overwhelming odds. We are quick to blame the secular and hedonistic culture of our time. It is doubtful if that is an adequate explanation. We are encountering something much more complex and profound which includes the breakdown of an old model, the disintegration of a closed system and the evolutionary invitation to more open and creative ways of connecting and inter-relating as a human species.

It is premature to expect clear-cut alternative models. We need to learn how best to befriend the chaos, and support each other in this often difficult and bewildering transition. Going back to something more stable and exclusive is unlikely to resolve our dilemma. On the way back from exile, this topic is frequently explored, but often in muted tone and with a sideward glance. We are scared of offending; perhaps even more frightened of incurring the wrath of the 'moral majority'. In this climate, real dialogue can never take place; somehow we need to break out of the dysfunctional silence and find forums where we can share our stories, and our struggles, and thus move toward a more integrated and wholesome way to model new relational structures for the future.

A world of lonely tyrants

Herbert Marcuse is attributed with creating the term 'one-dimensional man'. It describes the growing influence of technology on human beings (especially men) throughout the course of the twentieth century. More accurately, it refers to the 'mechanised' enculturation whereby men in particular structured their entire lives around the workplace, taking satisfaction and identity, not so much from their achievements but from the money earned, the reward for their sweat and toil.

Even in the southern hemisphere, many parts of which are only now entering the 'Industrial Age', this Western concept of the technologically competent male, who can exert power and influence politically, and especially financially, is widely assumed to be normative, desirable and divinely ordained. The robust individual, referred to earlier in this chapter, is the cherished brainchild of Western capitalism. He is projected to be the best for achievement, dominance, competition, elimination (of every adversarial force), endowed with a 'divine' right to conquer and control the whole of creation.

Only a relatively small percentage of humanity actually attain this status (certainly less than 10 per cent); yet this heroic myth exerts widespread and horrendous influence. What is particularly disturbing is the ease and naivety with which we accept it, not to mention the sheer powerlessness many people feel to do anything about its highly destructive influence.

While it is encouraging to realise that the system created by 'one-dimensional man' is breaking down, and already well frayed at the edges, it still commands a quality of cultural supremacy (validated in many cases by formal religion) that distracts from the need to dream alternative ways of relating and living that are so urgently needed in our time. What I wish to highlight in this book is that the seeds of destruction and reconstruction are already bearing fruit and to suggest that those among us committed to a new and more creative way of being, need to place our energy and resources where the new life has the best chances of flowering and flourishing.

Even to acknowledge the 'sinful' relational base of the culture of 'one-dimensional man' is a significant starting point. Any system of human culture that seeks to make invisible, and oppress so disgracefully, one half of humanity, namely women, surely cannot meet with the approval of those wishing to create a better world. Nor should we give consent or approval to the culture of competition which, as already mentioned, is ingrained in the fabric of our Western educational system. We also need to be wary of the subtle power of religion to undermine our resolve to outgrow and even abandon those belief systems and practices which validate patriarchal ordering in the name of a supreme patriarchal God (e.g. the exclusively male priesthood of Catholicism and its counterparts in other religions).

Those ways of relating characterised by power from the top down, by dualistic divisions, by the philosophy of conquer and control, by atomising people and everything else in nature (i.e. splitting us into independent, autonomous units), by instituting relationships based on competition rather than co-operation, create a sense of personal identity which is profoundly alienating. It alienates us from ourselves, from others, from nature and from God. It turns us into not just 'one-dimensional' people, but more accurately into *non-dimensional* objects.

If we are to redeem ourselves from the catastrophe that looms over our very survival as a species – and it is up to us to consider such redemption and not wait for some magical, divine figure to do it for us – we can at least begin to address the destructive ways in which we relate to one another. Acting like belligerent adolescents, playing highly destructive war games, whether in boardrooms or on battlefields, addicted to power-mongering to prove our little worth, deluding ourselves into thinking that we are still masters of creation, is a pointless and futile exercise. It just piles on pain and suffering, especially on those already at the base of the crumbling patriarchal edifice.

We urgently need some different networks for those who no longer want to live in the world of the lonely tyrants, for those who want to relate in new and inclusive ways beyond all the artificial barriers created in the name of race, religion or cultural superiority. In our essential nature, and apparently for much (perhaps most?) of our evolutionary history, we humans have lived as relational creatures, relying interdependently on one another and on the supportive environment. Now, more than ever, we need to reclaim that lost heritage and make it once more the central project for our future as human, planetary and cosmic creatures.

Reappropriating our Christian identity

Christianity, like the other major religions, is a progeny of a predominantly patriarchal culture, with growing evidence that its central belief and vision has been grossly distorted to serve the dominant culture of its day. At the centre of the Christian vision is the person of Jesus, whose identity was the subject of intense debate in early Christian times, particularly at the Councils of Nicea and Chalcedon.

Ever since then we describe Jesus as a *person*, both divine and human, and in the spiritual literature Christians are encouraged to

foster a *personal* relationship with Jesus Christ. This rather innocent and intimate invitation carries in its trail a long, oppressive
and idolatrous history.

The personal relationship with Jesus Christ effectively reduces
Jesus to a person like ourselves, embodying human personhood as
we understand it at any one moment in human evolution. Jesus is
set up as a human being like one of ourselves, but he is primarily
a divine being, thus effectively negating the uniqueness of what it
means to be human. Because Jesus is perceived to be primarily
divine, the only humanity he can exhibit is an idealistic one, one
in which the instincts, the darkness and the shadow are split off
and renounced for ever.

We are dealing with a form of humanistic reductionism, with
many potential pitfalls, inspiring a call to holiness which undoubtedly has produced saints and sages but also a substantial range of
religious bigots, fanatics and petrified human beings.

For much of Christian history, this unique mode of Christian
relating has been the prerogative of another ideal patriarch: the
spiritual father, known in later centuries as the Spiritual Director.
In other religions, we call this person the spiritual guru – in the
vast majority of cases, a male to which the disciple must give
unquestioned allegiance. The modelling is unmistakable: the
perfect patriarchal God on high requires total and unquestioned
submission from the human being at the base, mediated by a unique
male, himself totally subservient to the ruling God but totally
powerful in terms of the disciple entrusted to his care.

Spiritual Directors today are well aware of the flaws I outline,
and strive to reframe the approach in terms of co-discovery of
God's will in a process of spiritual accompaniment. The 'personal
relationship with Jesus' however still remains largely unexamined.
Resituating Jesus in the context of the Basileia (cf. Chapter 7), and
exploring the fresh understanding of personhood required by this
more biblically-rooted model, is a task for spirituality which has
scarcely begun (more on this topic in Ó Murchu, 1997b). It is not
just a question of adopting the new psychology of personhood;
more importantly, it is about reclaiming the true face of the
biblical Jesus.

The Jesus of traditional Christian devotion and the Jesus of the
Basileia turn out to be very different persons (see pp. 121–4
above). The former is the one in whose name millions have been

encouraged to flee the world to ensure the salvation of the individual soul in another world; it tends to breed a disembodied spirituality. The latter requires us to become incarnationally embodied at the heart of creation, reborn as if it were within the womb of the Earth itself, to be missioned forth as embodied people, to set aright the relationships that make all forms of embodiment truly incarnational. This vocation is personal and interpersonal, but also planetary and cosmic. The New Reign of God knows no human boundaries and its horizons can only be explored in a planetary–cosmic ambience.

As embodied creatures in an embodied universe, we incarcerate ourselves when we submit to a spirituality that decries both our materiality and earthiness. Traditional spirituality cherishes *transcendence* as a core value. There is a transcendence that engages us with life and one that encourages us to escape it; the latter is the one we tend to find in formal religion. Even Christianity, despite its unique incarnational flavour, succumbed to this alien influence.

A spirituality at the service of a more authentic humanisation – of self and others – must reclaim both our earthiness and embodiment as essential elements of an authentic self. We cannot relate as whole creatures without including our bodies, the flesh, blood and bone we uniquely inhabit, but also the earthly body (the Earth) from which we all originate. Because we have been exiled from the earth-body, we have also been estranged from our own bodies. We have been told that our bodies are sources of sin and temptation; that they inhabit dangerous instincts; that they end with death, whereas the immortal soul survives. Although we have also been told that our bodies are temples of the Holy Spirit, somehow that never carried as much weight as our bodily limitations. Little wonder that we yearn for healing and wholeness; we have been the victims of so much fragmentation!

These reflections require us to revisit the notion of *embodiment*. Whether it be the body of the Earth or the human, it is heavily blemished by the scars of disembodiment. Of all the aspects requiring rehabilitation on the journey home from exile, this is a perennial concern. We explore its significance in the next chapter.

— 10 —

Re-membering the Dismembered Body

We become inordinately absorbed in that which we neglect, and we display outlandishly what we do not deeply possess. This inversion of values, full of paradox, is a pattern that makes sense of our extreme interest in things and our tendency at the same time to treat things badly

Thomas Moore

Patriarchal religion is built on many millennia of repressed fear of the power of female bodily processes. Any effort to admit the female in her explicit femaleness as one who menstruates, gestates and lactates, will create psychic time-bombs that may explode with incalculable force. One can expect cries of witchcraft, blasphemy, sacrilege and idolatry to be directed at those who seek to resacralize the female body.

Rosemary Radford Ruether

To THE DOCTOR, it is an object to be kept in as good a shape as possible; to the clothing manufacturer, it is a subject of consumerist fascination; to sensationalised journalism it provides material for titillation; to the long-distance runner, it is the testing ground for endurance and stamina; to the ballet dancer it is a beautiful resource for elegance and exuberance, and for the ordinary folks, who comprise at least 90 per cent of humankind, life just has too many urgent demands to be worried or concerned with what we do with *the body*!

In one sense, the body is the most intimate and familiar dimension of our existence as human beings, and yet very few people think of their bodies in intimate or familiar ways. Estrangement from the human body is a universal experience, augmented in large measure by the influence of formal religion itself. Disconnection from the body, more than anything else, characterises our cultural experience as a species in exile.

We tend to think of the body *in isolation*. We emphasise the uniqueness of each person's embodied self. And although many species have bodies, the humanisation of the body seems to dictate the fundamental understanding we have of all other embodied forms. Our very attempt to highlight the uniqueness of the *human* body, over against other forms of embodied existence, is in itself a major source of our human alienation.

Despite the fact that all the religions highlight the spiritual nature of the body, and its ultimate destiny to endure beyond death, religious devotees more than anybody else seem to be precisely the ones for whom embodied existence is both precarious and problematic. The religious context is largely responsible for the *dualistic bind* in which people view and treat the human body – and this in turn impacts substantially on how we relate with other embodied forms, especially the Earth we inhabit.

One of the most serious consequences of the dualistic bind is the degree to which we have estranged the human body from its own primary and natural source, namely the Earth itself. Not until we *re-member* this broken relationship can we hope to reclaim the body in its true context as a process (and not merely a product) that links humans into the divine cosmic connection, without which our embodied selves are seriously depraved and deprived of real meaning.

What do we mean by embodiment?

Embodiment is first and foremost a process of relating. My body is not an object I inhabit, an arrangement of flesh, bone, fluids and biochemical processes that gives me my individual identity. I am, in my essential nature, a great deal more than my body. My body is a vehicle through which I become my fuller self.

Throughout the aeons of human history, we seem to have adopted several different understandings of the body, yet for much of that time, the body seems to have been largely taken for granted. Despite the increasing positive evidence suggesting that our ancestors in paleolithic times related creatively to the body of the Earth, how they perceived their own bodies is far from clear. The dismembered figures we have obtained from paleolithic art, while apparently focusing on human fertility (especially of the female body) do not indicate a very easy or wholesome relationship with the body. And the assumption hitherto made that men were predominantly hunters and women horticulturalists – one that is now seriously questioned – obviously affects how people would have perceived their embodied identity.

The sacredness of the body in ancient times is evidenced in burial customs which have been conducted in a 'religious' fashion for at least 70,000 years. We also know of customs among hunting groups whereby the shaman (the sacred personage of many ancient cultures) had to be present before animals could be killed. This, along with many of the depictions of Ice Age art, suggests that animals were perceived as being somehow sacred. In fact, we seem to have accumulated more evidence for the sacredness of animal embodiment than we have for human embodiment.

Tentative though it is, the emerging evidence seems to suggest that we did not have any major problem with the human body until formal religion began to evolve. Divisions between the sacred and the secular, the earthly realm and the one beyond it, contributed to the 'splitting' of good and bad in the human body. The instinctual and unruly elements, which do not seem to have been a problem in prehistoric times, became the focus for religious speculation and concern. And with the evolution of the monotheistic religions, the idea of full embodiment only in an afterlife laid the foundations for many of the prevailing dualisms of our time.

Many feminist writers claim that the problem with the body is mainly the result of the patriarchal will-to-power which sought to undermine the cultural power of female fertility. The culture of masculine supremacy could not tolerate the wild creative potential of the feminine (embodied primarily in women and in nature) and consciously sought to control it by undermining its power. The validation of religion was a key factor in this process, with most of the God images being male and imperialistic. Consequently, it was female bodily processes, such as menstruation, procreation and birth that became particularly problematic.

The shift from pre-patriarchal to patriarchal times certainly involved a diminution of the sacredness, the mystery, the fascination of the human body. It was replaced by objectifying the body as a mechanism to be mastered and controlled. Long before the development of the mechanistic world-view promoted by classical science in the seventeenth and eighteenth centuries, and long before the pornographic exploitation of recent times, the seeds of disembodiment were sown, perhaps as far back as 10,000 years ago. Reclaiming a more wholesome sense of the body requires the unveiling and discarding of millennia of oppression.

In fact many of the so-called 'heretical' and even pornographic movements of the recent and distant past may now be understood as subconscious movements to save us from our own alienation. Witchcraft has had long links with sexual and embodied expression; even to this day many coven rituals require the participants to be unclothed. Many of the major religions include stories of temple prostitution, often justified for the initiation of priests and priestesses. The rise of materialism in the nineteenth century is sometimes described as an antidote to prevailing disconnectedness from our earthiness. Nature has its own ways to meet our depraved needs!

The body in Christianity

Brown (1990) provides a comprehensive analysis of how the body was regarded in early Christian and Roman times. Much of his attention is on the distrust of bodily processes and the consequent need for an asceticism to hold at bay the destructive impact of bodily unruliness. Sex, more than anything else, was seen as the real problem. It would seem it was particularly a problem for men; but, in fact, women were always blamed for it.

Valuable though Brown's analysis is, it leaves unexplored the long millennia of evolution and how we, humans, related with our bodies throughout that time. The disregard for the body is not merely the product of Christianity, nor of monotheistic religion. However one interprets it, Christianity, like the other major religions, has inherited a culture of Goddess worship in which the body plays a central role, and Christianity seems to be in collusion with the prevailing patriarchal culture, desperately trying to erode this 'pagan' influence.

Secondly, an *individualisation* of the human body has been flourishing for at least the previous 5,000 years. The body has progressively been disconnected from the body of the Earth and thus juxtaposed to all other embodied forms. This is where the process of dismemberment actually originated. Thenceforth, our perception of the human body is functional and isolationist. And we assume that the embodiment of divine figureheads, e.g. Jesus or the Buddha, is modelled on what we consider to be the standard patriarchal prototype. And that is only one of several misconceptions on which formal religions are construed.

The disparity between the pre-patriarchal understanding of the human body and what subsequently transpired under the aegis of formal religion is paradoxically displayed in the Catholic understanding of the Blessed Virgin Mary. Non-Catholic adherents of Christianity tend to dismiss the virginity of Mary as a myth of early Christian times with no foundation in reality, biblically or biologically. In fact, those who exalt Mary to a pseudo-divine status on the one hand, and those who shun such an attribution on the other, both fall foul of the same shortsightedness. Most scholars fail to attend to the underlying archetypal meaning without which we can never hope to engage the deeper truth.

Marina Warner (1990, pp. 267ff) explores various historical parallels between the figure of Mary in Christianity and the many female goddesses of the ancient Middle East (e.g. Isis, Hathor, Neith and Nut, four of the most prominent Goddesses of early Egypt; Inanna (Ishtar in Sumerian) of ancient Mesopotamia; Anat of ancient Israel, often identified with the Old Testament references to the Queen of Heaven; Hebe of ancient Greece, sometimes identified with Eve in the book of Genesis). Her suggestion that we reappropriate Mary's significance within this context has always met with strong opposition. Many of those Goddess figures are depicted as exercising divine power and influencing people in significant spiritual ways. But many are also portrayed as robustly embodied people, often exhibiting exuberant sexual desire and highly erotic behaviour.

Leeming and Page (1994) suggest that the several female goddesses that populate the ancient cultures of Sumer, Egypt, Greece and Rome exhibit one or more characteristics of the Great Mother Goddess of paleolithic times, but none provides the holistic view or comprehensive insight into the larger cultural and global significance of this ancient goddess. Boelen (1984, p. 21) makes a similar claim:

> . . . the Great Mother Goddess became fragmented into many lesser goddesses, each receiving attributes that once belonged to her: Hera got the ritual of the sacred marriage, Demeter her mysteries, Athena her snakes, Aphrodite her doves, and Artemis her function as Lady of the Wild (wildlife).

Like most things, in the reign of patriarchy, even the Great Goddess was segmented; no aspect of life – even the realm of divinity itself – has escaped the erosion that resulted from the insatiable desire to *divide and conquer!* The dismemberment of the human body begins with the patriarchal desire to dismember the power of the Great Goddess (whether understood factually or symbolically – see Appendix 1). Not surprisingly, therefore, women in particular feel, and often exhibit, the rage and pain that belongs to that ruthless fragmentation.

We have briefly touched on what was dismembered and why it happened. What, therefore does the *re-membering* entail? The Great Mother Goddess is often portrayed as a woman unashamedly grounded in the body, passionately attuned to the body's eroticism and its unbounded fertility and, consequently, forever consorting (often in quite explicit sexual ways) with all who can facilitate the body's capacity to relate and connect across the breadth and depth of the creative universe. The re-membering is unambiguously relational, sexual, erotic and creative. Those very dimensions of our embodied state, long subverted by religious moralism, are precisely the aspects that need to be reclaimed and cherished anew.

Eisler (1995) suggests that it was specifically the Goddess's amorphous sexual appeal and her prodigious fertility that formed the nexus of her power as a spiritual and cultural influence. The divine radiance was reflected in human life precisely through the body, and primarily through its erotic and creative potentials. With these insights, we can begin to reclaim the ancient *archetypal* significance of realities that have become so crudely debased under the aegis of patriarchal control. Perhaps one of the most poignant, yet disturbing examples is what the Christian Churches (and particularly the Catholic Church) have done with the archetypal concept of *virginity*. According to Wilshire (1994, pp. 99ff):

> In its primal sense the word 'virgin' describes a maiden, a very young woman who is leaving girlhood, just beginning to explore and taste her grown-up self. She is in bud – full of potential, unfinished, entering the unknown in a state of joyous uncertainty. Such a one is full of wonder and becoming, curious about all the possibilities in herself and the world – open to the mysteries and dangers that lie ahead.
>
> Clarity does not apply to her, for she is in process, in-between. Anticipation, freedom and spontaneity do describe her. She is highly susceptible to falling in love – with the dawn, with the

changing seasons, with any and all creatures in their miraculous diversity, with people, their eyes and their stories. For whatever the risks, the virgin experiences nature as full of good things, full of gifts, full of possibility.

This powerfully creative archetype became quite distorted in the institutionalisation of femininity which the Catholic Church created around the body of Mary. Catholic doctrine effectively depersonalises Mary, by taking away the heart and soul of what constitutes authentic womanhood – what allegedly was also the most dynamic feature of the Great Earth Mother – namely, the power to co-create. This, for every woman, across time and culture, is what uniquely constitutes womanhood.

According to Catholic doctrine, Mary is reduced to a ghost-like biological mechanism, with all her creative faculties suspended as she becomes totally absorbed by the divine male to whom allegedly she gives birth. Surely, it makes more theological sense that God in Jesus would enter the world through a woman radiant with potential creativity (which is what the word 'virgin' denotes in its archetypal meaning) rather than through one almost totally emptied out of her womanly uniqueness? One suspects of course that there is a hidden agenda here in which Catholicism is hoping to erode for ever the power of the Great Earth Mother. It has largely succeeded for the past 2,000 years; fortunately, the tide of truth is beginning to turn.

With Mary reduced to a biological organism – and a dysfunctional one at that – it was all too easy to highlight the unique divine integrity of malehood. Jesus was a man, and his maleness more than anything else is what made him divine. All this was reinforced by the culture of his day in which women were effectively *non-persons*, despised and belittled by the cruel oppression of patriarchal power.

Although Jesus never colluded with that culture – and, in fact, vociferously opposed it in word and action – Christians continued to build a Christian Church with the oppression and invisibility of women as a key ingredient. It was only a few centuries until Jesus was also co-opted as an oppressor of women.

The oppression of women is not just a female issue, neither does it merely concern the role of women in Church or in society. It even goes beyond issues of gender, and ends up being all about the body; and, as many feminists rightly note, not just the human body but the planetary one as well. More specifically what is under attack is the body's innate and flamboyant capacity for creativity, fertility, erotic passion and visionary imagination. These are the 'forces' that pose the ultimate threat to patriarchy's cherished values of reason, rationality, control and power. Ultimately, the body needs to be regarded as an *object*, subject at all times to the patriarchal need to dominate and control.

Although Hinduism, the oldest of the known religions, retains many features inspired by ancient archetypes – exhibiting several voluptuous images of erotic embrace and expression – the embodied significance of these images has not been well integrated into the lived experience of that faith. Although the public images of Indian gods and goddesses suggest that sexuality itself is a primary medium for accessing the power of the divine, Indian sexual behaviour tends to be based on the same fear, guilt and shame we often encounter in the West.

All the formal religions – and not merely the monotheistic ones – exhibit an irrational fear around the power of the body. In the pre-religious culture the body is often perceived as inhabited by a divine spirit, whose creative energy often awakens in wild, untamed erotic expression. As indicated previously, feminist theorists, in particular, hold the view that the body of the Great Earth Mother Goddess was perceived in ancient times as being synonymous with the body of the Earth itself. The dualistic divisions of sacred v. secular, body v. spirit, which we take so much for granted today, were probably unknown in paleolithic times.

Along come the mainstream religions, and many of those ancient beliefs were quickly denounced as pagan perceptions of a deluded, sinful species. The patriarchs could not control the body – not until we invented science and medicine – therefore the only option was to marginalise it, and no better way to do that than demonize it. And it was not just humans who were victimized; so was the embodied Earth and even the cosmos at large. The impact was far-reaching.

The degradation of the body by formal religion has seeped into every realm of human and earthly life. Enormous repression has ensued, the nature of which we comprehend today in the irrational back-lash that is now taking place across our world. The body is back in business and reclaiming its rightful place with a reckless vengeance. A great deal of confusion prevails on what is, and what is not, personally and ethically appropriate in our treatment of the body. For those on the journey home from exile, this is a central issue of concern requiring profound reflection and discernment.

Sexuality as embodied eroticism

Sexuality leaves us all spellbound, but often frightened and confused. The long history of human sexuality (cf. Foucault, 1980; Eisler, 1995; Mann and Lyle, 1995; Taylor, 1997) exhibits extraordinary freedom and creativity of expression, interspersed with inflated sexual exploits and a substantial measure of moral repression. According to Foucault's analysis, the repression belongs predominantly to the past 300 years in which issues of power and sex become confusedly intertwined.[1] In fact, the repression has much more ancient roots belonging to the various purity taboos that have long been associated with the human body (cf. Douglas, 1966).

Of all contemporary researchers, Eisler (1995) is the one who seeks to forge deep and ancient connections. Her focus is the culture of the Great Earth Mother Goddess of paleolithic times, dating down to about 5000 BCE. She suggests that for much of that time sexuality was perceived to be a divine energy, embodied in the whole of creation and not merely in the human body; that sexuality was a power for *creativity* and for *spirituality*; that connection and interaction with the divine was facilitated through erotic, sexual behaviour; that sexuality was an embodied psychic energy of which procreation was one dominant outcome.

How this sensuous and erotic understanding of sexuality was translated into the sexual behaviours, cultural expectations and religious customs of more recent times – the Egyptian, Greek, Chinese, Indian and Roman cultures – is vividly explored by Mann and Lyle (1995). Right down to the dawn of Judaeo–Christian times, we detect little semblance of the moralism, disembodiment and prudishness that has characterised sexuality ever since then. Undoubtedly, shadow elements surfaced and relational exploitation occurred, but the overall ambience carries a very different set of feelings and values from those we associate today with the development and articulation of human sexuality.

The Hebrew Scriptures begin to articulate a distinctive distrust of the human body, attributing varying degrees of impurity to bodily processes. Ironically, the dimensions considered to be most impure – and requiring the most stringent purification laws and rituals – all have to do with the *female* body: menstruation, lactation, birthing, etc. And the remnants of these ancient taboos have prevailed in the West until recent times, for example the Churching of mothers after giving birth.[2]

It is this female focus on issues of ritual cleanliness and purity that alarms many contemporary feminist and womanist writers. Why are these emerging cultures so determined to undermine the power of the feminine? For Eisler (1995) the answer is obvious: to eradicate for once and for all the power of the Great Mother Goddess, especially her flamboyant eroticism and prodigious fertility which posed such huge threats to the emerging patriarchal desire to dominate and control the whole of creation.

Obviously, scholars do, and will, differ about Eisler's interpretation. What I find attractive about it for the purposes of this book, and especially for the present chapter, is the challenge and urgent need to, first, relocate our understanding of human sexuality in an embodied context, with personal and planetary dimensions duly acknowledged; and, second, to address questions of sexuality from an *archetypal* rather than from a *mechanistic* foundation.

What do I mean by archetypal? Ever since the seventeenth century – which Foucault rightly highlights as the beginning of an erroneous approach – sex came to be seen as everything else was viewed at that time: a *mechanical* process. Put rather crudely, males and females used their respective sexual equipment in an industrial process to produce an object called a child. The Church tried to redeem the crudity by naming it 'sex for procreation'. Catholics will be aware of the fact that up until 1962 this was perceived to be the *sole* purpose of Christian marriage; after 1962, Christian marriage was described as having a dual purpose: first, to promote the love and intimacy of the couple within the marital relationship; second, to propagate the human species.

Although humans have never adhered strictly to a mechanistic understanding of human sexuality, nonetheless it has heavily influenced our cultural, political, social and religious attempts to inculturate sexual behaviour and to formulate sexual laws and guidelines. More than anything else, the mechanistic approach seriously undermines the powerful spiritual and psychic forces at work in our sexual lives. These I refer to as 'archetypal energies'.

In psychological terms, an archetype refers to those instinctual driving forces that underpin the will-to-live and the will-to-meaning in human life. These are primitive energies that surface in myths and images of great age. And their impact on our lives has both individual and collective dimensions to it.

Sexuality is one of the most potent, ancient and complex of all the archetypes, and only scholars with a profound appreciation of anthropology, psychology and spirituality are likely to unravel its deep mysteries; I refer the reader to the erudite exposition of Thomas Moore (1998). When we begin to make archetypal connections, in terms of our personal experience and our intellectual research, we will begin to comprehend the frightening destruction caused by the mechanistic, reductionistic approach.

As Moore (1998, p. xiii) boldly asserts, what we need in our world today is *more* rather than *less* sex. Our compulsive preoccupation with lurid pornography and hedonistic exploitation arises because we have been so exiled from our sexual bodies. For most of the time, in our relationships and in our marriages, we live in sexual estrangement. Our desperate yearning for sex arises from the fact that we have been seriously deprived of real embodied connectedness. Correspondingly, we have also been starved of real spiritual connectedness.

The home-coming involves some momentous challenges! Conceptually, we need to overcome the long-held conviction that the sexual realm has to be one of competitive combat. Apes and chimpanzees may vie for sex, but bonobos do not (cf. de Waal, 1989; Kano, 1990). This recent discovery, where sex is used liberally for play, mutual interaction and the resolution of conflict, may require us to radically assess the conceptual paradigms we have been using to analyse and understand human sexuality.

In a similar vein we may need to re-visit the famous research of Margaret Mead among the Samoan people (Mead, 1929), in which she attributes the lack of overt violence to the ease and comfort with which people engaged sexually; I am aware of the fact that her thesis has been challenged and counter-challenged on several occasions. Mead's insights are particularly pertinent within the growing body of evidence which shows such a strong and alarming correlation between male sexual exploitation and the culture of warfare (cf. Morgan, 1989). So much violence in our world may be directly caused by the lack of loving, erotic touch.

And there are the several questions that surface regularly about the institutionalisation of sexual behaviour in the monogamous heterosexual relationship, still widely perceived as belonging to the institution of marriage, although millions the world over pursue a sexual life outside that formal context. The guardians of orthodoxy – and in this regard I suggest there is a powerful and subtle collusion between political and ecclesiastical realms – become quite defensive when the family and the institution of marriage are under scrutiny, often suggesting that this is what exacerbates the promiscuity and recklessness in today's world. With respect, I suggest it is the refusal, or unwillingness, to examine the archetypal undergirdings that has plunged us into the moral and cultural morass in which we now find ourselves. Our relational estrangement has deeper roots, requiring a much more thorough and perceptive critique.

Sexuality, as a primordial, creative energy, impacts upon every sphere of embodied action, with complex personal and planetary consequences. How we learn to relate to our own bodies will influence greatly how we relate with the body of the Earth itself. Paradoxically, it is in coming home to the sacredness and virility of the earth-body, that we begin to reclaim a revitalised sense of what our own bodies also signify. Befriending the body – on this long journey home – will require enormous trust and love, with a willingness to acknowledge that many of us are deeply wounded, but it is precisely in our embodied selves we can become wounded healers for one another.

The body and beguiled spirituality

What seems like a strangely apologetic rhetoric begins to unfold in the Christian Scriptures when the Church is described as the Body of Christ. One suspects that it is another device to augment ecclesiastical control. In faith, through Baptism, all Christians are incorporated into the life of Christ, but, apparently, can only remain affiliated by being incorporated into the body of the Church. A strange type of displacement seems to be at work. The role of the human body is further diminished – even the human body of Jesus becomes somewhat overshadowed as the body called the Church takes precedence. Little wonder that women found it so difficult – and still do – to belong to this strange corporeal entity.

That an incarnational faith like Christianity could have become so disembodied is tragic evidence of the disabling forces at work for much of the Christian era. Couching the developing Christian faith in Greek culture did little to help; adopting Greek dualisms was particularly destructive. Embodiment was portrayed as dangerous, sinful, wicked and transitory. Disembodiment (often described by words like 'spirit' or 'soul') was deemed a necessary precondition for union with the divine.

The divine itself was perceived to inhabit the ethereal, non-earthly, heavenly realm populated only by souls, not by bodies. And God himself was perceived above all else to be pure spirit. At best, the body was the necessary, but unfortunate instrument that one needed for one's sojourn on Earth; real existence belonged to the post-earthly stage of eternal life.

Rites of Passage, or what Christians call Sacraments, became the means whereby we could rectify the redemption of the sinful body. In many religious traditions, this required the sacrifice of an innocent victim (a scapegoat), prototypically the Christ-figure in Christianity, but in several ancient religious cultures an animal, a bird and, occasionally, another human being. The convoluted treatment of the body permeates all formal religion, and through the religions has seeped into many rituals of tribal and indigenous peoples.

In fact, the major flaw in this entire scenario is not anthropological but cosmological. It is the alienation from our world – the patriarchal drive to conquer and control universal life – that is at the root of all religious oppression. We have it radically wrong on how we construe the human body precisely because we have so crudely misconstrued the *earthly* and *cosmic* bodies. Not until we sort out our confused and confusing cosmology, can we hope to get right both our anthropology and our theology.

This is where our evolutionary story becomes our saving grace. Long before humans ever evolved, God was co-creating within the body of the universe itself, and for thousands of years before the evolution of formal religion, humans connected and interacted with this divine creativity. Intimations that our ancient ancestors considered the Earth itself to be the embodied presence of the divine – especially in paleolithic times – is a conviction that needs to be salvaged from the jaws of that brash intellectualism that undermines and demolishes every creative hunch! Somehow, we need to learn to include rather than disregard many of those archetypal intuitions that belong to our ancient past.

The condemnation of the body – on which so much formal religion thrives – ensues in the condemnation of the religions themselves. When it comes to the body, religion descends into the realms of unmitigated blasphemy. It desacralises the sacredness of the human body, but much more seriously, seeks to undermine the sacredness of the earth-body as God's primary revelation to us, humans, and to the other creatures who inhabit God's creation. Religion is unambiguously at the service of the patriarchal God, a human projection of post-Agricultural times, a God image which is alien to humans because it simply does not resonate with most of our experience as an evolutionary and planetary species.

Coming home to our embodied selves

Spirituality, as distinct from religion, does not have a problem with the body – and neither should theology (cf. Spalding, 1998). The power of spirit has always been embedded in creation and does not belong to some esoteric realm outside the created order. We are an *en-souled* species, not in the sense that we possess a soul, without which we are not even alive (the traditional understanding) but rather that we are possessed by soul, the enveloping sacredness that impregnates everything in the extraordinary ordinariness of our daily existence (cf. Moore, 1992, 1994, 1998).

As a human species, we are the victims of a crippling amnesia whereby we have been forced to forget our long spiritual connected-ness with creation. We have been fragmented and dismembered. And tragically, we now project our internal oppression on to our own species through the growing levels of violence in our world. It appears that our disconnectedness is coming home to roost and haunting us in our alienation. Perhaps something as drastic as this has to happen to awaken in us the acute and urgent need to start *re-membering*, putting back together again the dismembered parts of our fragmented humanity and our desacrated Earth. Re-membering is very much what the journey home from exile is all about.

In order to come home to ourselves as embodied people, we need to reclaim the hearth of that embodiment, namely the created world itself. In our interdependent world, all forms of embodiment mirror the primal and primordial image, and a great deal of our alienation is caused precisely because we are so out of tune with how the global–cosmic body operates.

In our essential nature, we are cosmic–planetary creatures. We are the progeny of the prodigious womb of cosmic–planetary life. We belong to a reality larger than ourselves, from which we draw nurturance for body, mind and spirit. We are participatory creatures in a participatory universe.

The state of exile which engulfs us, from which we are forever trying to escape, is not caused because of our distance from God, but because of our distance from the creation that surrounds us. We need to reconnect with the womb that birthed us and with the Earth Mother that forever sustains us. We must learn afresh to treat the *living* planet with love and reverence. It is only by re-appropriating our belonging to this greater organism that we begin anew to come home to our true selves.

Those of us obliged to live in spiralling urban concrete jungles need to reconnect with nature; we need to visit parks and ponds more frequently. We need to be befriended by animals and birds; we need to touch the *en-souled* soil from which we are begotten and breathe afresh the air of the creative vacuum, the well-spring of everything that comes into being.

These are small but significant gestures of re-engagement if we are to transcend the disengaging alienation to which we have been subjected throughout the past 10,000 years of patriarchy. We need to experience 'moments of awakening' which hopefully will challenge and inspire us to take more radical steps to re-member our nurturing Earth and learn to affiliate and bond anew with the womb that nurtures and sustains us.

We also need to revamp our allegiance to the communal body of humanity. Long before the fragmentation of patriarchy, whereby we humans became identified as Europeans, Americans or Asians, Christians or Muslims, rich or poor, developed and underdeveloped, we shared planet Earth as *one* people. Our essential unity and partnership has been ruptured by our national, religious and ethnic divisions. Such distinctions do not enhance our identity or uniqueness; in fact, they seriously undermine our primary call to be co-creators with our co-creative God in building together a unified human family.

Only after we have reclaimed our partnership with the earth–body and with the body of our shared humanity can we appropriately reclaim an individual sense of embodiment. It is no longer appropriate (in fact, never was) to begin with the individual person and move outwards (the linear approach). Our starting point is the larger reality to which we all belong – the cosmic planetary context – from which initially we receive our identity. Only when we have learned to embrace that enveloping horizon can we truly claim to have come back home!

— 11 —

Political Responsibility for the Homeward Bound

For the State to function the way that it does there must be between male
and female, or adult and child, quite specific relations of domination.

Michel Foucault

The world does not depend upon us, and the world is not available to
us. The world is out beyond us in God's wisdom. It mocks our pitiful
efforts at control, mastery and domination.

Walter Brueggemann

POLITICS IS THE BIRTHCHILD of classical Greece and its
attempts to organise life in the city-state known as the *polis*.
Central to such organisation were the dual notions of justice and
obedience.

For Plato (according to his classical work, *Republic*), justice is
secured when every member of the *polis* is doing what s(he) is best
suited to do, and the best suited to do the ruling are the
philosophers, the lovers of wisdom. And a just society, therefore,
requires that some are to be guided and directed by others, to
whom we owe allegiance and obedience.

How the justice and obedience were exercised in Greek times is
considerably different from how we envisage it today. Because of
the relatively small size of the central political entity, namely the
polis, deliberations often took place and decisions were frequently
made in face-to-face discussions involving all the citizens.

With the publication of Aristotle's *Politics*, such egalitarian
democracy became more structured and institutionalised. The
interdependent relationship of the family unit, the village community and the larger *polis* became more differentiated. And the

hierarchical element came much more to the fore with the tripartite division of the upper-class aristocrats, the middle-ranking 'substantial men', mainly merchants, craftsmen and farmers; and the lower classes of labourers and peasants. Aristotle had the wisdom to anticipate the antagonisms that would ensue, and proposed that politics would include among its essential elements the skills for defining and resolving conflict.

It is often suggested that the concept of the *polis* ended with the death of Aristotle himself (c. 322 BCE), while the Roman Stoics evolved a much more universal concept of the natural law governing all human beings. This new vision justified the Romans in extending their political domination far beyond the local *polis* – indeed right across the known world of the time. Although the political locus had changed, the underlying values of justice and obedience still prevailed.

Meanwhile the notion of the *polis* assumed a more religious connotation as in St Augustine's treatise *The City of God*, the religious and political influence of which is still detectable in many of the townships of the high middle ages.

St Thomas Aquinas in the thirteenth century formulated the theological basis of all law and governance. His starting point was *divine revelation*, God's disclosed plan for the whole of humanity. Aquinas did not emphasise the later dualistic distinction between sacred and secular, although echoes of it are detectable in his writings. Natural law is essentially holistic and spiritual and governs every legal and political system that humans develop.

For much of the Middle Ages, Catholicism dictated the ultimate political values of the European world, just as Hinduism did in India, Confucianism in China, and Islam in much of Northern Africa. It is only in the late sixteenth century and thereafter, as the culture of classical science and its accompanying rationalism began to gain ascendancy, that natural law was differentiated from Christian revelation. Influenced by great thinkers (with the emphasis on 'thinking') such as Niccolo Machiavelli, Thomas Hobbes, John Locke, Charles de Montesquieu, David Hume, Benedict Spinoza, Jean Jacques Rousseau, politics became solidly established as a *secular* reality, and the strong oppositional dualism with the spiritual sphere continues to our own time.

Finally, the work and influence of Karl Marx has rightly been regarded as unique in political history. More than anybody else

Marx highlighted the *economic* element as the over-riding issue in political activity, creating deep and destructive divisions in society between those who exercise economic clout (the bourgeoisie) and those almost totally deprived of economic power (the proletariat). Marx's ideas continue to be hugely influential precisely because they are so blatantly obvious in the contemporary world.

Principles of contemporary government

This patchy historical backdrop will suffice to remind us where key elements of contemporary political practice have come from. In the fifth century BCE, Socrates identified politics with the art of rhetoric and persuasion. The ability to argue one's case persuasively still underpins a great deal of private and public political discourse, with the notable difference that what was envisaged by the Greeks as being the fruit of philosophical wisdom, is often these days the outcome of empty verbiage fuelled by monetarist and manipulative intent – deviously construed to keep us in a state of exile!

The social context also merits our attention. The relationship of the individual to the collective continues to dictate a great deal of political strategy, but the gap between the individual and the 'collectivities' of today's world is now so vast as to be virtually inconceivable, not merely by people, but also by many politicians. Hence the credibility chasm, whereby growing numbers of people do not understand, nor do they care about, the political activity that governs and controls their daily lives.

Although the Greek concept of the *polis* had a distinctive egalitarian feel to it, we need to remember that it belongs to a world-order characterised predominantly by *patriarchy* and *kingship* (dimensions that are inadvertently reinforced by all the major religions). The conquering warrior king, in whom ultimately all earthly power is invested (validated by the kingly God of the sky) pre-dates the ideas of Socrates, Plato and Aristotle by at least 3,000 years. It is that same insatiable will-to-power that dominates political activity today, whether in the so-called democracies of the North or in the several autocracies that prevail elsewhere.

All nation states – even Islamic ones – consider free-market capitalism to be the normative political strategy employed by humans in dealing with their world and with one another. The basic underlying principles are those of European classical science and the rational philosophy that dominated European thought throughout the seventeenth and eighteenth centuries. These principles include:

1. Everything in life operates like a machine and you get the best results by managing reality in a mechanical way. According to Robertson (1998, p. 89), 'The dominant forms of politics and governments throughout the world today are based on mass political parties and centralised bureaucracies. They reflect the factory mentality of the industrial age.'
2. The Earth itself is dead inert matter – there for humankind to exploit, manipulate and use to the advantage of the human species.
3. Humans are in charge of the world; it is up to us to devise whatever means *we* deem appropriate to dominate and manage nature.
4. One section of humanity – namely Euro-Americans – have succeeded in developing the 'divide and conquer' strategy to a more sophisticated level. They consider themselves to be masters at this task; they set themselves up as models (for example, the G7, The World Bank, The International Monetary Fund, World Trade Organisation). They expect everybody else to adopt the blueprint they have devised; everybody else seems to agree that it is wise and prudent to emulate what 'the West' has achieved.
5. Throughout the industrial era, nobody, since Karl Marx, seems to have questioned the governing principle that *competition* is better than *co-operation*. Consequently, the rich North sees nothing wrong in exploiting the mineral resources of several southern nations, even though it creates degrading poverty and crippling financial debts.
6. The nation–state is an ideal institution for capitalist competition. Contrary to popular perception, it does not provide autonomy and uniqueness, but rather the preconditions for rivalry, warfare and the unlimited exercise of the right to power. The nation–state is an archaic, oppressive, immoral institution:

> Increasingly we see the denouément of the nation–state as a viable unit of governance, becoming too big for the small problems of its own local populations and at the same time

too small for the big problems of global relations and ecosystems. (Henderson, 1988, p. 361)

7. Currently, 'economic progress' (or what one theorist calls 'growthmania') is the measuring rod for *all* progress. Essentially this means developing industry-intensive, high-consuming, high-polluting nation–states. In the two-thirds world, the target is to develop post-agricultural industries using engineering and production skills we in the West associate more with the Industrial era.

In the West, we are aiming more at a hyper-industrial culture (Kahn, 1976). In either case, we view people as units of production, remunerated financially for their (slave) labour. Those who don't, or can't, participate in the 'jobs-for-money' rat-race, those who belong to the informal economy (housewives, voluntary workers, etc.), are deemed to be a type of second-class citizenship whose most valuable contribution is that of bolstering up those who really matter.

Little wonder that politics – which is meant to oversee and protect the principles outlined above – is in such a confused state of disarray, with politicians themselves often embroiled in sleaze and corruption. In fact, the majority of nation–state governments in the contemporary world are held in place by the corruption of power and money. And they are adept at keeping up appearances and at feeding their people with *mis*information. Consequently, our governments ensure that we do not develop educational systems in which people are encouraged to think critically and creatively, because then the charade would become visible and the people would begin to disown it.

Meanwhile, the political system painfully grinds to a halt – because fundamentally it still belongs to the exilic culture of alienation. Robertson (1998, pp. 5–8) suggests four main reasons for the eventual collapse of our political infrastructure, a process that may be already impacting internationally by the middle of the twenty-first century:

1. *Social scarcity*: There is a compulsive drive within market-based economies to produce more and more. But the more we produce of any one item, the less valuable that object becomes, for example the more automobiles we produce, the more we

create traffic congestion, depleting the social benefits of using a car. Things pile up to a degree that people, along with their genuine social, personal and spiritual needs, become buried in the 'rubble'. The culture of mass production is a blueprint for social anarchy.

2. *Psychological remoteness:* As more and more people in the industrialized world become dependent on the institutionalized economy, rather than on the household and local community, their sense of co-dependency and alienation grows greater. Impetuously, they start making heavier demands for jobs, for pay, for services, thus paving the way for saturation and breakdown, as the economy's resources become depleted and log-jammed. To an accelerating degree the system disappoints. Ultimately, the rat-race can guarantee no winners; we all end up being losers!

3. *Institutional congestion:* In a world of depleting natural resources, heavy investment in security and litigation, disgruntled and unhappy workers, it requires little imagination to realise that life and vitality are being sniffed out in the industrial sphere. The scenario depicted by Handy (1994) leaves one with the impression of the ultimate apocalyptic nightmare: machines doing all the work and managers competing like hell to get the machines to produce more and more. Presumably, the machines themselves will, at some stage, crumble beneath the pressure.

4. *Conceptual disarray:* The whole strategy is based on unreflective instinct rather than on creative and reflective thought. Everybody is desperately trying to 'keep the ship afloat' but there is no comprehensive policy, neither is there any contemplative vision. People are treated as economic units, the Earth is perceived as an object to be conquered; the procedures of government itself are rational, legalistic and based on party rivalries. Consumerist economics is the chief driving force; indeed, politicians spend most of their time talking about money and the people tend to judge their performance by the financial allurements they offer to their gullible consumers.

The combination of politics–economics–industrialisation thrives on banalities that deprive all creation, people included, of any type of long-term hope for the future. Banished from political wisdom are the key elements of wholeness and sanity: spirituality, relation-ality and interdependence. Until we humans choose to reclaim these elements – and there is little to indicate that it can be done within the prevailing political paradigms – then not merely is our political future in jeopardy, but so is our survival as a human species.

Our primal political legacy

While contemporary politics, theoretically and practically, traces its origins to the developments of classical Greece, the real story of what politics is about is a great deal more ancient. This is yet another example of anthropocentric shortsightedness, a recurring theme in this book. We take seriously, and deem to be normative, that which has unfolded in 'civilised' times, but it is civilisation defined according to our patriarchal, anthropocentric norms. I suggest it is notoriously shortsighted and consequently grossly deceptive.

Our political legacy, like our spiritual one, pre-dates classical Greece by thousands of years. If we take politics to denote forms of social organisation to facilitate co-operative and just use of resources, and if we genuinely seek a comprehensive overview of how we went about that task as a human species, then we need to search much more deeply into our ancient past.

Our search is obviously limited. With the best tools of investiga-tion currently at our disposal, anthropologists and archaeologists will only unearth limited evidence. In recent years, however, this evidence has been significant for what it disconfirms rather than for what it confirms. Our human tendency to project our destructive attitudes and behaviours onto primitive savages in our distant past no longer holds up to serious scrutiny. The barbarity we would like to project elsewhere is *our* barbarity and belongs to *our* times. It is the result of how we behave, and there is growing evidence to suggest that it is the political systems themselves that generate such destructive behaviour.

By contrast, our ancient ancestors often lived and behaved in a more convivial way, close to nature and connected with the *spiritual* meaning of life as a universal process. The ideals of modern democ-racy may indeed be very ancient. They are also a great deal more inclusive – to an extent that even Plato and Aristotle never envisaged.

While not being able to decipher the forms of social or political organisation that prevailed in ancient times, we can glean underlying values which would have been strongly influential. Central to such values is the three-way relationship between *planet*, *people* and *oikonomia*.

Oikonomia, from which derives the English word 'economy', consists of two Greek words: *oikos*, meaning 'house'; and *nomos*, meaning 'law, order', etc. 'Economy' is intended to be about the ordering of the household. 'Ecology' derives from the same root, the science that provides the *logos*, the ultimate wisdom that governs the running of the household.

Oikonomia has a very ancient meaning. It describes the prehistoric experience of being at home in the universe, specifically as experienced through our connectedness with the home planet, the Earth. For well over 90 per cent of our time on Earth, we humans knew no boundaries of nation, religion or ethnic distinction. We roamed wherever we wished, with unhindered and unlimited access to the whole planet. Earth was home – not an object to conquer and control, but something akin to a living organism to which we belonged; and, moreover, the focus of connectedness that helped to make sense out of all other forms of belonging.

Indications are that economics preceded politics in these ancient times, just as they do today. But of course they meant something quite different. *Oikonomia* had to do with the ordering of nature's resources within the realm of belonging. The primordial 'womb' that nurtured and sustained had to be protected. Devoid of 'higher authorities', people seem to have adopted a communal consensus that facilitated what seems to have been an altruistic relationship with the surrounding environment.

As far back as two million years ago, we know of *Homo Erectus* being quite adept at tool-making, requiring not merely a skill of hand, but a quality of intelligence and a potential for expressive creativity. Life involved a great deal more than merely 'the battle to survive'. Even the acquisition of food may have been governed by an altruistic set of values.

The long-established view that our ancient ancestors were hunters who foraged for, and killed, everything they could find, is an assumption that no longer commands scholarly agreement (see the extensive review of Fedigan, 1982). Contemporary evidence points more towards a horticultural rather than a hunting basis for the provision of food. James Campbell also provides some evidence to suggest that the shaman (the sacred personage of ancient times) had a central role in the killing of the animals for meat, and ensured that the bones were properly buried afterwards – possibly indicating a coherent spiritual view of life long before formal religions came to be known.

The best evidence we can glean for ancient forms of worship suggests a keen awareness of nature's cycles and an interdependent relationship with the natural processes of the surrounding world. There is no echo in this ancient *oikonomia* of the exploitative competition, nor the horrific injustices, that characterise our world today. Economics more than anything else meant harmony and co-operation, not merely among people, but with every aspect of life, for the good of the *whole household*. And on that foundation, prehistoric politics unfolded.

Without little doubt it was first and foremost a politics of relationships, it was about the organisation and facilitation of living out the sense of connectedness that governed the consciousness and behaviour of people at that time. How exactly they went about it we don't know, but there are strong indications that *co-operation* and not *competition* was an over-riding principle. Devoid of current national distinctions, many issues had to be faced and resolved locally. Global issues were not a problem, because the popular perception seems to have been one of planet Earth as the great nourishing mother; even if we consider this to be a grand and exaggerated idealisation, it carries a greater potential for meaning than the current view of the Earth as dead, inert matter.

And finally the third element in the tripartite structure, *people*. Humans perceived themselves as part of a greater whole, not its masters, not its controllers, not its enemies! While the relationship with the greater whole would have meant many different things at different stages of human evolution, for the greater part it seems to have been a benevolent and interdependent sense of awareness. Despite the harshness and unpredictability, the Earth was a benevolent 'creature' and for humans it was to their advantage to be in a harmonious relationship with the Earth. The Earth was also perceived to be the primary context of belonging, and it would have seemed crazy to do anything that would rupture the womb from which all life emanated.

The notion that humans were a superior species, a dominant race set apart to conquer and control to its own advantage, is unknown for most of our evolutionary history. This is a perception, a self-understanding of very recent origin, probably no more than 10,000 years old.[1] Progressively we are becoming much more aware of what happened within the past 10,000 years, but since that is such a limited and limiting aspect of our entire story (certainly no more than 5 per cent), we cannot hope to reclaim any meaningful sense of what it means to be human until we reclaim the other 95 per cent that in our anthropocentric ignorance we have split off and tried to disown.

When we choose to reconnect with our own story, we begin to realise that the *oikonomia*, politics and people are interconnected dimensions of a unified reality. In our essential nature we are political creatures, and our politics is not just about people *in isolation* (the great anthropocentric misnomer of recent millennia) but about life in all its dimensions within the one Earth we inhabit and within the one universe that enlivens everything that exists.

Mithen (1996) is among several contemporary scholars who suggest that it may have been the unpredictability of climate change more than anything else that led to the growing anthropocentrism whereby humans began to set themselves up in adversarial relationship to nature and to the Earth. An emerging gender stratification between male and female, with the male perceiving itself as the superior form, seems to have underpinned the first phase of this new development. A deliberate and conscious attempt ensued to undermine the female understanding of nature and the Earth, a process that seems to culminate in the major religions with the male gods claiming unquestioned ascendancy over all of life and seeking to deprive the female form of all generative power (e.g. the virginity of Mary in Christianity, see pp. 160–1 above).

Contemporary ecologists often decry the objectification of nature, but in fact the *de-sacralisation* of nature is a much deeper and more sinister move and long pre-dates the objectification. We only began to treat nature as an object, and the Earth as dead inert matter, in the late sixteenth and early seventeenth centuries; this latter development is merely the icing on the cake for a much longer, more insidious and pernicious drive of the raw masculine will-to-power.

Transcending political dualisms

I now wish to outline my central concern for the present chapter. We in the West largely take for granted the distinction between Church and State. It is a powerful dualistic assumption that goes largely unquestioned.

Dualisms can be unbelievably deceptive. On the surface they attempt to set things apart, and keep them separate, but in fact what they often create is not separation but *collusion*. The dualism between Church and State is one of the most sinister and dangerous collusions of our contemporary world. Two powerful institutions have agreed to keep splitting reality apart because it enhances their own patriarchal compulsion to 'divide and conquer'. And both seem equally committed to the exclusion of the Earth and its several creatures apart from human beings. Politics is primarily about people; so is religion. Politics is about the impact of law; so is religion. Politics fosters patriarchal and hierarchical values; so does religion.

Over the past 5,000 years (the age of 'civilisation'), religion has had the ascendancy in exerting political influence. In the 2,000 years of Christianity, the Church has had major influence up to the seventeenth century. Today, the rift between politics and religion has widened as economics dictate the ultimate values for each. In fact, there is a three-way split between religion, politics and economics; and of all three, politics is the greatest loser. Ultimately, that leaves humans as planetary creatures in an extremely vulnerable situation.

That vulnerability is nowhere more apparent than in our dealing with multinational corporations. The multinationals are the ultimate dictators of today's values and the greatest threat to political sustainability; in the words of Comblin (1998, p. 122):

The multinational industrial and service companies transfer funds from one country to another and no nation can monitor what is happening. The companies constantly seek these countries that offer them incentives and where taxes are lower – or can be evaded. They seek refuge in tax havens. Multinationals thereby avoid contributing to the nation as they ought. A great deal of the activity of these companies is removed from oversight by nations.

Indeed, multinationals make demands and claim privileges for setting up their factories. Because they provide employment, they ask for compensations and obtain exorbitant conditions. Nations cave in to their arrogance.

It is this inability – of the political sphere to exert social and financial accountability, and of the religious sphere to awaken complementary moral and altruistic values – that leaves increasing numbers of people disillusioned and cynical. Unfortunately, as the governing structures of the contemporary world become functionally exhausted, the people, too, seem unable to muster the enthusiasm to challenge the haunting dysfunctionality.

Yes, the people are dubious and cynical, but confused on where to turn next. We have given up on religion, and wish we could give up on politics, too. But since most of us are in the grip of economic co-dependency and at the mercy of consumerist multinational gods, we can't afford to do what spiritual integrity requires us to do: stand up in massive protest, cease colluding and bring the whole edifice to its feet – which we could do in many 'democratic' countries if we, in block, refused to vote at major elections!

To many readers this suggestion may feel preposterous and even downright irresponsible. But when, I ask, are we going to take off the blinkers and step out of our political myopia? In the past three presidential elections of the USA, 50 per cent of the electorate did not vote; the pattern is common in most Western democracies, with huge proportions of young people never bothering to cast a vote. The people have already lost faith in the political system. They want something different, something radically different.

To get in touch with our own deeper needs, we need to reclaim the fuller story of who and what we are as a human species. Already unknown to themselves, millions all over our world are doing that. People have grown weary of the patriarchal power games of both Church and State. There is a deep yearning for something that feels radically new and for that reason feels to many as if it is totally beyond our reach. When we choose to connect with our deeper evolutionary story, then, I suggest, we can make greater sense of what is going on deep within.

Our political reality, our very identity as political beings, is incomprehensible without the spiritual context, and this we can access most authentically by engaging with the evolutionary story itself. If we choose to enter through the medium of religion we are immediately thrown into disparity and confusion. The dualism between religion and politics has left us intellectually strained and spiritually fragmented. Politically and religiously we are a species without meaningful, life-giving anchorage.

Beyond the politics of patriarchy

Even the politicians themselves acknowledge that corruption is rife in the political arena. In the West, consumerism dictates all our values, with politicians often at the mercy of economists, themselves assimilated into the greed and aggrandisement of multinational corporations. In South America, clientelism – powerful élites with private interests (see Comblin, 1998, p. 127) – frequently dictate political strategies while in much of Africa tribal rivalries perpetuate often bitter and debilitating feuds. Few will acknowledge that the underlying malaise is within the political system itself, variously manifesting the dysfunctionality in different cultural contexts around the world.

Deep problems require in-depth solutions. The political *problematique* is global in nature and will require globally based revisioning. And the roots percolate deep into our past as a human species, thus requiring a historical and cultural critique before we can hope to revision a different future.

Without a radically revamped political vision, humanity stands little chance of surviving the twenty-first century. Many of our major problems – economic, social, ecological – are global in nature and can only be addressed through global, political strategies (as outlined by writers like Kung, 1997). Current political entities, such as the nation–state, national economies and party-political systems, are obsolete, unworkable and a threat to a more sustainable future for humanity and for planet Earth.

Thanks to the insights of the new cosmology, we know that our world – as cosmos and home-planet – works as an interdependent whole. Fragmenting the Earth into political entities called states and regions is no longer tenable. In fact, the nation–state never made either cosmic or planetary sense; it is an invention of the past few thousand years perpetuated by patriarchal overlords committed to their own power and self-aggrandisement.

In the patriarchal culture of 'divide and conquer', the nation–state is a functional requirement, entitling us to subdivide and break down into ever smaller and manageable units. In a world of growing interdependence, this approach is alien and counter-productive. As Henderson (1988) and Ohmae (1995) highlight, strategies based on mutual interaction and international co-operation offer a much greater guarantee of a sustainable and productive future.

The United Nations, and attempts at regionalisation elsewhere in the world (for example, the European Union, the East African Partnership, the Pacific Ring), are already evidence of a growing desire within the people of our world to move towards something akin to a world government. Such a structure, however, only becomes another oppressive monolith without a new vision of global networking around issues of major concern to humanity and the guarantee of a sustainable future for the planet we inhabit.

The politics of connectedness

Three words encapsulate a new way of being political as we strive to come home to ourselves as a planetary, cosmic and spiritual species: *interdependence, sustainability* and *justice*. In recent decades, we witness a growing awareness of how everything is inter-connected and interdependent. But that awareness has scarcely begun to seep into the consciousness of the political arena.

The universe that sustains our existence and the planet that nurtures our relational well-being require political strategies and structures that will both honour and enhance that relational interdependence. And this applies not merely to people but to all creatures inhabiting creation, as well as to the various ecosystems that sustain and nurture our mutual co-existence. In fact, other life forms innately veer in this direction. It is we humans, as vociferous consumers, who threaten the ecological equilibrium.

In biological and ecological terms, 'equilibrium' describes a state of creative interaction, with often unpredictable outcomes. It does not mean a state of complete harmony, with everything in perfect balance; such would be a prescription for stagnation and anarchy.

Nowadays, we often use the word 'sustainability' to describe this state of creative equilibrium. The word denotes a set of behaviours and attitudes whereby we acknowledge that all resources have limits, requiring a constrained and creative use, and that the well-being of future generations (of humans and other creatures) depends on how we use creation's resources today.

Sustainability is a profoundly spiritual notion. It seeks to challenge our anthropocentric arrogance over other creatures and over the resources of our planet. It denounces the male mastery of the Judaeo–Christian tradition that justifies humans in 'lording it over' other life forms and, inadvertently, justifies the 'powerful' in usurping Earth's resources, thus forcing over half the human race to live in squalor and debilitating poverty.

More significantly, sustainability reminds us, humans, that we belong to a covenant of solidarity with the rest of creation. We were never destined to become a 'superior' species ruling the world under the aegis of a powerful God, who in reality is a projection and caricature of our self-imposed exilic alienation.

Once again, we need to return to the context of our unfolding evolutionary story, the anchor point where we reconnect with the truth of who and what we are. We are the progeny of a greater life-force, planet Earth, itself sustained by a greater organism, the web of universal life. Excessive production, consumption, toxication and reckless reproduction all contribute to rupturing the womb that sustains and nourishes us. We can only sustain a meaningful human existence within the context of a meaningful planetary and cosmic co-existence. It is to our detriment and ultimate destruction that we forget the larger organism that gave us birth, and over which we never can and never should claim total control. To do so, only destroys the very meaning of our existence.

The political and economic implications of these principles have been explored by several theorists, notably Daly and Cobb (1989), Daly (1991), Nash (1991), Robertson (1998) and Ruether (1974, 1992). According to Robertson (1998, p. 90), the shift to a more sustainable political policy will involve:

> . . . a shift of emphasis away from means towards ends; away from economic growth towards human development; away from quantitative towards qualitative values and goals; away from the impersonal and organizational towards the personal and interpersonal; and away from the earning and spending of money towards the meeting of real human needs and aspirations. A

culture that has been masculine, aggressive and domineering in its outlook, will give place to one that is more feminine, co-operative and supportive. A culture that has exalted the uniformally European will give place to one which values the multi-cultural richness and diversity of human experience. An anthropocentric worldview that has licensed the human species to exploit the rest of nature as if from above and outside it, will give place to an ecological worldview. We shall recognise that survival and self-realisation alike require us to act as what we really are – integral parts of an ecosystem much larger, more complex, and more powerful than ourselves.

Sustainability, as explained above, requires us to rehabilitate moral and ethical values; in a word, policies and systems that promote *justice* as a core value.

Western governments – notably in USA and Britain – subscribe to a rhetoric of social justice and even set up committees to work on it. According to Forrester (1997), such efforts are frequently inspired by the theories of Jurgen Habermas (cf. White, 1988), John Rawls (1971) or F. A. Hayek (1982). These theorists – of whom Rawls, in academic circles, is considered to be the greatest contemporary proponent of social justice in the West – all theorize from within the cultural context of Western imperialism and patriarchal individualism. Little or no attempt is made to relate justice to the larger cultural, ecological and economic domains. Politicians are deviously selective in their choice of moral theorists. And they use the theories quite unashamedly to bolster their often blatantly oppressive regimes.

Forrester (1997, p. 198) describes the ambivalence with measured scholarly caution:

> Indeed, the modern public forum seems inhospitable to serious moral discourse. Questions of the common good, the nature of community and its goals, of what it means for human beings to flourish together in relationship are rarely entertained. Moral choices are commonly regarded as private matters, and there is a pervasive scepticism about the possibilities of determining ends and norms for a society.

For Rawls, and other contemporary moral philosophers, *fairness* is the essence of justice. This quickly translates into giving everyone what (s)he is due. Humans choose to put themselves at the centre; everything revolves around us, and around our rights. Implicitly, everything is there for *our* use and benefit, to be used as *we* determine from our perspective as the *dominant* species. Our anthropocentric perception of reality is a conceptual nightmare, totally incapable of generating any sense of fairness, and so unjust in its basic design that one wonders how we could ever have taken it seriously.

At the beginning of the present chapter we noted that Plato considered justice to be a central element of political activity. For Plato justice is secured when every member of the *polis* is doing what he or she is best suited to do, yet slaves, women and workers are totally excluded from all his considerations. In other words, justice is for those who rule and hold power, and they alone have a voice in its development and implementation. With good reason, at least 50 per cent of today's six billion people would add: 'And things have not changed much since the time of Plato.'

Currently, the rhetoric about justice is largely the reserve of philosophical debate and legal diatribe. The real voices of real people in the real world are rarely heard and scarcely never acknowledged. Both the debate and its several outcomes are shrouded in a clinical respectability that belongs to the rich and powerful. Quite rightly liberation and feminist theologians emphasise that for the multitudes of people today *injustice* and not justice is the substance of their daily experience. Not surprisingly, this makes the victims of injustice excited and angry.

And herein lies a vital clue to an authentic *praxis* of justice, whether within the political or religious realm. True justice begins with an empathetic solidarity with those condemned to experience life as *non-persons*; the justice-seeker (and the justice-promoter) needs to be able to stand inside the skin of the other and know, at a gut level, what it's like to be condemned to such a meaningless existence. Then, and only then, will we truly hear the excitement and anger that cries out for justice.

Solidarity of this nature tends to awaken the fires of one's own anger and passion. It is only when our passion is evoked that we generate the energy and enthusiasm to 'go the extra mile' that is at the core of justice work. Christianity, and many of the great religions, has been cursed with a debilitating spiritualism in which *apatheia* ('without passion') was a cherished value. Justice demands tough love that requires all the passion we can mobilise to sustain and motivate us as we struggle to bring about desired change.

And once that passion is awakened, it flows into action. Sometimes the action may be little more than doling out food to starving children, trying to maintain some semblance of dignity and sanity in awful conditions. But justice that is fuelled by passion and prophetic outrage will never stop short at emergency charity. Not all the charity on Earth can bring about the liberation of people and creation that the Christian Gospel calls for.

Prophetic outrage is the third step in the work for justice. This is where we go beyond the charitable handout and the verbal denunciation, and embark upon political engagement, lobbying politicians, protesting publicly, and challenging the structural sin that causes such unjust divisions (for example, between rich and poor) in the first place.

The ultimate goal of justice work is the establishment of right relationships wherein mutual interdependence is a core value. At this level, justice moves beyond the mere concerns of humans, to include the socio-economic and political systems within which people live and operate. A great deal of injustice is structural rather than personal in nature. For that very reason, we can never obtain justice for humans until we also review the injustice built into how we treat other creatures, our environment and the planet we inhabit.

In fact, no dialogue on justice is complete or comprehensive while we exclude ecological and global factors (see Boff, 1997). *Eco-justice* or *geo-justice* (Conlon, 1990) is the call of our time. And any political regime that fails to make this an issue of central concern does not merit the support of its electorate.

Being political in a new way

Many people have given up on mainstream politics, and from a theological viewpoint to opt *out* rather than *in* may, in fact, be quite a creative Christian response. We need to withdraw power from what is essentially a corrupt and corrupting system, and then proceed to explore alternative ways in which to reclaim our political will-to-power, which is essentially a will-to-justice.

How can we do this? Fortunately, we have some embryonic models. The closing decades of the twentieth century witnessed a world-wide upsurge of NGOs (non-governmental organisations), many attempting to address current political and social issues in a new way. Sadly, many of these efforts have been co-opted by the mainstream governments (who sensed their potential threat). However, they do provide seminal models for the alternative mobilisation of political creativity.

We have also witnessed the rise (or more accurately, the re-discovery) of the social network, the many movements of people-power addressing local needs and issues. Feminists have invented some very creative networks to counter the oppressive power of patriarchal modelling. Social-political networks such as Greenpeace, Amnesty International, Worldwatch, Campaign for Nuclear Disarmament, Friends of the Earth, exert profound influence on social and political policy and champion the call to eco-justice in creatively disturbing ways.

The principles that underpin trade unionism are precisely those that can help to engender an alternative political consciousness. Unfortunately, trade union power has largely been subverted in today's world, largely because unions themselves became too closely aligned with the patriarchal will-to-power which they were seeking to transform. An important lesson from this experience suggests that alternative structures can achieve little without a new vision of how reality works. The real conversion confronting humanity today is a transformation of consciousness rather than mechanistic changes in human or social behaviour.

I am consciously advocating a subversive strategy for future political engagement. Current models of political activity are largely beyond reform. We need to withhold our support and redirect our imagination and energy into different, more egalitarian, ecological and sustainable ways of relating to creation and to other people.

The economist Hazel Henderson (1988, p. 5) gives forceful expression to what she calls the politics of reconceptualization:

Together we must demystify today's counterfeit priesthood of 'puppet' leaders, and map and align our own energies with these larger-field forces and the energies that, in reality, drive our planet: the daily solar flux, which in turn drives our planetary weather system; the cycles of oxygen, of nitrogen, and of hydrogen, and the plant photosynthesis that is our *primary economic system*. Only if all the 'little people', the laity, the growing numbers of planetary citizens, can align themselves in a correspondingly powerful 'force field' of growing human awareness of these realities can we join together and surround the narrow logic and rationalising of today's puppet leaders, trapped in their institutional and conceptual bunkers and enmeshed in the intellectual baroque of the old order. We can see ourselves and our diverse social-change activities as part of a living orchestration, generating larger patterns, out of which grow new paradigms of knowledge, policy and personal behaviour. This for me is the politics of reconceptualization.

Far-fetched though such an ideal may seem, it is very much a feature of daily conversation as people make the journey home from exile. Pilgrims who are homeward bound see the homeland in a whole new light. The old thread-bare models don't make sense any more. We need new ways of looking after the household, a new *oikonomia*! Playing patriarchal games that bolster the fortunes of the powerful, and plunge the powerless (80 per cent of the human species) deeper into the alienation of exile is a cruel game we don't want to play any more.

Politically, as well as personally, we want to learn to live and relate in a whole new way. There are few blueprints, but there are some experimental models. What we have in abundance is imagination and creativity and these are our richest resources as we seek to walk afresh the pathways of today's political landscape.

— 12 —

Rediscovering Spirituality on the Homeward Journey

Spirituality is an effort by people without a name in history to go back to their past and to draw from their spiritual heritage, which has been so distorted or even erased by dominant power groups.

Aruna Gnanadason

I believe that the only effective resistance to the corrosive individualism of the age is the renewal of authentic contemplation linked to political commitment. This will involve the formation of networks of communities committed to politics and to prayer.

Kenneth Leech

FOR THOSE ON THE journey home from exile, formal religion has not played a major role. Some suspect – and rightly we think – that religion contributed significantly to their alienated state in the first place. Others, having sought refuge or hope in religion, felt misunderstood or were simply unable to match religious guidelines to their particular struggles. For significant numbers, religion lost them, rather than they losing it; it just became irrelevant! And the irrelevance became even more pronounced in the place of exile. The people still cried out to God, but the God of stark silence felt more credible than the empty rhetoric of the god(s) of formal religion.

Spirituality entered the vocabulary of the alienated. Some don't like it because it still smacks of religion. But it does express something of that relentless search for meaning and for hope that endures even in our darkest nights. And it does encapsulate a sense of belonging to that higher life-force, who even in the midst of our darkness is never far away, and lures us through and beyond the scorching heat of the noon-day sun!

We have long known that the dark night creates a paradoxical readiness to anticipate the dawn. It's when we are down in the gutters, in the classical Job-like crisis, that spiritual forces – some reassuring and some frightening – erupt from primal spaces. We talk about these things on the way home from exile. Occasionally, we connect with the 'specialists' to help us make sense of our experience. Most of the time, they don't seem to know what we're talking about!

So, we continue talking, exploring, discerning! We learn to connect with wisdom from our ancient past, and as we do so we tend to trust our own intuitions a bit more. Sometimes the exploration is exciting; other times, it is deadly lonely. Light and shadow are always around!

Religion and spirituality

In this concluding chapter, I wish to revisit briefly some of the central convictions upon which this book is based. At the very outset, I drew attention to the distinction between religion and spirituality. Having explored the central thesis of exile and homecoming, I now wish to highlight the enveloping spiritual vision that accompanies that transition, and to indicate the more modest role for formal religion that ensues from that pilgrim experience.

That one can have a spirituality without a religion, or that Christianity could be about the abolition of religion, are ideas that believers do not easily entertain. It is frightening to think that the foundations on which we have built so much meaning and hope can no longer sustain or nourish us. Prior to such a conclusion, however, is the vast spectrum of conditioning and confusion – in the name of religion – which is what really blurs the horizons of truth and creates so much of the make-belief and superficial religiosity we encounter in the world today.

Spirituality can embrace a sense of inclusiveness that feels quite alien to formal religion. Spirituality deals with a larger landscape which includes many people who have never followed a formal religion, and growing numbers who one time did but no longer do so now. Spirituality is concerned with that deeper, inner hunger for meaning and connectedness which characterises all humans, and, as argued in previous chapters, is also innate to creation itself.

However, religion still carries the potential to awaken and enrich our spiritual growth, or to hinder and confuse its unfolding. We note, for example, that parliamentarians the world over, many of whom are not overtly religious and some avowedly atheistic, tend to follow a universal sense of diplomacy, whereby one does not interfere in religious protocol and, whenever possible, respects religious custom.

There also exists a widespread perception, usually expressed and acknowledged with great ambiguity, that questions of moral import are the primary concern of religion (or of the Church) and these considerations must not be mingled with political deliberations. These archaic and destructive dualistic perceptions do little to enhance a healthy view of religion, and they are extremely corrosive of growth in spiritual maturity.

Two urgent considerations arise here. First, there is the need for those who govern to *integrate* and not *relegate* moral and ethical values. Second, and much more controversial, governments have a civic duty to protect people against religious bigotry, sectarianism, oppression and exploitation. The religions of humankind seem to be accountable to nobody other than to their own closed patriarchal leaderships, and in the interest of a more humane and spiritual world order, this is neither adequate nor acceptable. The dualism between the sacred and secular needs to be bridged and that is a *joint* responsibility for politicians and religionists alike.

A similar blindness characterises the social consciousness of our time. Social scientists evaluate trends and movements within religious belief or practice, but rarely do these findings offer a more enlightened or comprehensive view of what is really going on. Not infrequently, these days, agnostics and atheists can offer more enlightened and informed judgements on religious matters than devoted religionists can. Spiritual insight, and an appreciation of spiritual value, does not require commitment to a particular faith system; in fact, sometimes such allegiance can distort and confuse the central issues.

The events of Jonestown, Guyana in 1978 and of Waco, USA in 1993, when large numbers of religious devotees committed mass suicide, are not as extreme as they initially appear. Religious fanaticism can easily take hold of people's lives, especially in those conditions of exile that thrive on dualistic thinking, where people tend to be searching for spiritual meaning from without rather than from within. Like all patriarchally-maintained institutions, the mainstream religions do not take kindly to self-criticism. The conviction that all we do, and stand for, is approved by the all-powerful God, often has lethal consequences for people and cultures alike.

With religion so much centre-stage – even by people who conceptually and politically may not be religious at all – spirituality has something of an uphill struggle to regain legitimate recognition. Of its very nature spirituality is not, and never can be, a system where all the ends are neatly wrapped up; consequently, it will always be held suspect by formal institutions, religious and political alike.

But the fundamental problem is deeper and more complex, and at the risk of repeating what has been said several times in previous chapters, it requires re-statement at this juncture. The culture of formal religion is officially a culture of exile; religion triumphs on exile. Religion uses exile as the central notion around which the whole religious system is construed. Religion cannot survive if people outgrow the feelings of exile (or alienation).

Religion declares the state of exile to be God's creation and destiny for humankind on this Earth: humans are innately incomplete, prone to suffering and to sin; even the natural biological process of death is construed as the inevitable outcome of our exilic condition. Moreover, the world in which God has placed us is also considered to be an alien place. For religion, the only way to resolve the alienation is to escape from this 'valley of tears' to the joy and fulfilment of heaven (perceived to be beyond and outside this world).

As already indicated, I believe it is *patriarchy* rather than *religion* that has generated this set of beliefs. Religion upholds and promotes them precisely because it remains trapped in the stranglehold of the patriarchal world-view.

Spirituality, on the other hand, long pre-dates the development of that culture of patriarchy which belongs to the post-Agricultural era of the past 10,000 years. Apart from its depth in time, it is also the name we give to the 'depth of spirit' that animates and sustains the whole of creation. To rephrase the words of St Paul in the letter to the Romans, there is *no law* that can counteract the creative, unifying and fulfilling power of that spirit. And ultimately no force, patriarchal or otherwise, that can fragment and dismember it perpetually.

Our spiritualised universe

The journey home from exile is, more than anything else, an attempt at getting our priorities right. We are first and foremost a spiritual species – because we belong to a spiritualised universe. The fact that some have become religious is, in fact, quite secondary, although for them it may feel quite important. The retrieval of the spiritual *raison d'être* of personal and planetary existence is the single greatest challenge of this unique historical moment in our evolution as a human species.

To sustain us on our journey home from exile, we need to reclaim our spiritualised story. It enlivens our hope, but also helps to put in context the questions and yearnings that arise in our conversations. Fragmented and dismembered though our history may be, we can *re-member* – sometimes from recorded historical experiences, but also from the depth of the psyche, individually and collectively.

In the early part of the twentieth century, the Jesuit palaeontologist, Teilhard de Chardin, met with ridicule from the scientific community and a virtual black-out from the religious world for suggesting a spiritual significance to the course of evolution itself. For Teilhard, a divine intelligence permeates the entire unfolding of cosmogenesis, culminating in the fulfilment pre-empted by the Christ of Christianity. Despite the opposition and misunderstanding, and the wish to desist from the explicit Christian focus adopted by Teilhard, his ideas have engendered a substantial following among scientists, cosmologists and theologians. The last decades of the twentieth century have witnessed a rebirth of cosmology with a renewed conviction that the course of evolution is a value-laden process, fuelled by a will-to-meaning imprinted in the very fabric of life itself (cf. Laszlo, 1996, 1998).

Thus we witness some radical changes in perception and understanding. It is no longer esoteric to talk about an *intelligent* universe, an *alive* Earth, matter impregnated with *consciousness*. While many mainstream scientists quibble with these ideas, and some consider them extremely bizarre, growing numbers of people detect a deeper sense of truth and meaning for which these are key articulations.

Concepts such as field influence, the creative vacuum and the self-organising potential of life processes, all augment the notion of a highly creative and meaningful universe. And perhaps, most important of all, the discovery that interdependence and inter-relatedness underpins the causal connections of the biochemical and physical world is what pushes the human imagination to raise questions of a distinctly spiritual nature.

That evolution itself embodies a spiritual driving force, with a highly creative will-to-meaning, is what has instigated us – in the pages of this book – to consider the flourishing of spirituality over billions of years before humans ever evolved. In the words of one contemporary writer:

> The earth is much more sacred than we have supposed, much holier than we have treated it . . . It is not only the human being that has Spirit. There has been Spirit hovering over all the world since the beginning of creation. (Donovan, 1989, pp. 121, 123)

Spirituality is not something that pertains to humans alone; it long pre-dates the existence of humanity. In fact, all indications are that we are endowed with a spiritual capacity precisely because the greater life-force that begot us is itself fundamentally spiritual. Born into a spiritualised world, we could not be other than spiritualized creatures.

While these observations evoke a whole new set of questions on the meaning and agelessness of spirituality (cf. Ó Murchu, 1997b), my concern in this chapter is to review and highlight the dynamics at work in those undergoing the spiritual transformation that characterises the homeward journey.

As people become more educated and liberated from the 'delusion of civilisation', and begin to name the culture of imposed exile for what it really is, they tend to become more reflective and critical of self and others. They begin to ask questions, frequently under the disapproval of 'elders', which can be anybody from parents, to teachers, to politicians, to clergy. If they have the self-confidence and integrity to keep asking the questions, they will eventually face the challenging and at times daunting task of having to discern truth from falsehood, freedom from slavery, reality from unreality, and faith from superstition. Because increasing numbers of people across our world are 'coming of age' and out-growing the hypnotism of patriarchal hood-winking, the culture of formal religion is being seen for what it often is: a facade for religious infantalism and not a means to Gospel liberation.

Not surprisingly, then, people in their droves are walking away from religion, and one can safely predict that same process will begin to happen in what is still the fastest growing of the religions, Islam; give it another ten to twenty years and the trend is likely to reverse, quite dramatically! Although people are walking away in droves, they are not parting company completely; on the journey home from exile, some get cold feet and end up in one or other of the several sects and cults which populate the confusing waste-land of outdated religiosity.

The big problem for those disillusioned with formal religion is where to turn next. The brain-washing always told them that ultimate truth resides within the system and not outside it. Some people discover that the ultimate truth resides within their own hearts, and this for many marks the first step to reclaiming a genuine spirituality. But millions in today's world are deprived even of that holistic sense of self – religion has often eroded that, too – and so the spiritual search culminates in the dead-end of a life half-lived. The culture of exile is not just about a place without; it can also eat deeply to the recesses of our inner beings.

What does it mean in practice?

In a previous work (Ó Murchu, 1997b), I delineated what may be considered to be some of the contours of this new spiritual landscape, along with some of the personal, social and ritual engagements that help to make sense out of this virgin territory. In Chapter 5, following the seminal insights of the sociologist, Pitrim Sorokin (1950), I suggested that it is 'the restless middle classes' who provide the ferment in which people struggle with issues of exile and home-coming as explored in this book. Although the following observations are rather general, hopefully they will alert and attune us to the evolving nature of this new spiritual ferment. They highlight some of the contextual situations that call for a new quality of discerning vigilance.

1. Connection

Often the awakening takes place by meeting others struggling or engaging with questions of meaning. In my own travels of Europe, USA, Africa and Asia, it seems to me that the desire to connect in new ways is quite a universal aspiration of our time. People take risks – to disclose, to be vulnerable, to speak! Sometimes, the words are hard to come by; frequently, it is the supportive word of the significant other that fills the awkward lull when we can't find words. At some indefinable moment, heart meets heart; nothing romantic or dramatic like an intense courtship, but undoubtedly something of that small inner voice, the power of connection, the power of God's creative Spirit. After that moment, or usually after several such moments, seeds of new possibility are likely to start sprouting.

2. Conversation

The need to talk things out is the pastoral context where possibilities begin to unfold. This nearly always involves a process of unloading – all that baggage we have carried for years, long or short. Perhaps, feelings of never being good enough; the hurts accumulated, and sometimes imposed, that have left emotional and spiritual scars; the expectations to live up to certain standards or beliefs without ever being able to understand why; the toxic secrets, never shared, and the beautiful ones too. On the journey home from exile, people often are heard saying: 'I have believed that for years (for example, the closeness of God through nature) but it didn't feel safe to talk about it.' Dialogue is what breaks down the crippling edifice of fear and unworthiness.

And we need to honour respectfully the cynicism which says: 'What's the point in talking when no one will listen?' This phrase often expresses the deep anguish of our sisters and brothers in the two-thirds world who often feel – and with good reason – that we, in the West, simply don't care. We have promised so much, but have not delivered. Or worse still, we promised to give, but what we gave with one hand we took back with two – and we were caught in the dirty tricks of Western consumerism. After that type of hurt, it takes a long time to trust again and resume a meaningful dialogue!

3. Exploration

True dialogue has a wonderful power to liberate the imagination. And people are at their best when they begin to dream. When we dream together, and especially when we see openings for the realisation of our dreams, then something truly revelatory irrupts from the human soul. It is this innate capacity for creativity that has been severely corroded, and corrupted, by mainstream education.

The bitter-sweet moment of spiritual exploration comes with the realisation that so much we thought was the exclusive reserve of specialists (e.g., tasks reserved to male clerics in the monotheistic religions, or, in the two-thirds world, the expertise we thought belonged exclusively to the white man) was intended by God to be shared among all believers. As creative adult people, we don't need a holy Iman to lead us in prayer on every solemn occasion; God's creative Spirit awakens the gift of prayer in all our hearts – male and female alike.

Furthermore, we realise that all of us are endowed with a need and a capacity for *ritual*. We (re)discover that Sacraments are not a unique invention of a Church or a formal religion; sacramental experience is born out of our desire and wish to beseech and glorify our co-creative God. Saturated in a tradition of Rites of Passage, African people are probably the world's experts in the creation of sacred rituals. In their hearts they have known the deep meaning of sacramentality long before European missionaries ever disembarked upon their shores.

4. Interiority

The pain of our imposed exile, and the frightening but exciting desire to come home once more, requires tender and gentle nurturing in the sanctuary of inner space. In the face of profound mystery, which we all encounter more frequently than formal religion would allow us to acknowledge, we spontaneously turn inward; this is how God's creative Spirit works in our hearts. The call to contemplation is one we, humans, have known for millennia. Without it, we would never have flowered into creative beings formed in the image and likeness of our co-creative God.

But the culture of exile tried to reduce us to one-dimensional entities; it sought to infiltrate our minds, strangle our imaginations; undermine our intuitive vision and subvert our passion for contemplative justice. Instinctively, we know all about the need for inner space and centring; we don't need to resort to special manuals to learn it for the first time. Some of the ancient wisdom may be useful to help us rediscover what was so barbarically torn away from us. But relearn it we will, because our shared wisdom informs us that it is an essential resource for the journey ahead.

5. Proaction

The spiritual awakening delineated in these pages, rarely results in an outburst of religious fervour. The creativity moves in another direction – often after a lot of hesitancy. Life-style changes are often an indication that a deeper type of transformation is also under way.

In our Western culture, these changes can result in an option for long-term therapy; a change of job or career; the development of some long neglected personal talent; a move out of an unfulfilling relationship. Less conspicuous, although more courageous, are those who opt into projects related to alternative health care, or alternative technology; those who shift energy and resources to work within or alongside agencies like Greenpeace, Friends of the Earth, Amnesty International, Peace Corps, or a wide range of women's liberation movements active today in all the main continents.

A type of quantum leap has taken place as people negotiate this new spiritual awakening: the dualistic distinction between the sacred and secular has completely broken down. People are not that interested any more about the great philosophical or theological questions of life. They rarely talk about God, yet they know they are co-creating with a life-force greater than them-selves. Can we venture to suggest that what Jesus called the Kingdom of God (the Basileia) has caught up with these people?

6. Leadership

People often ask: Where is the spiritual leadership in this movement? I suggest it has two main elements to it: first, people trust their own intuitions much more deeply than in former times; and secondly, people tend to look for wisdom *within* their circle of friends, or in some grassroot movements rather than looking to leaders of a hierarchical system.

A sense of distrust of hierarchical leadership certainly prevails in the new spirituality. It is not an antagonistic feeling; people are not interested in venting their angry denunciations. That day is over. Intuitively, they are beginning to sense that the major institutions are a spent force and, consequently, it is much more responsible to withhold and withdraw power from them. That then liberates people to place their power elsewhere. While the alternative options are often far from clear, the desire for such alternatives is a growing demand from increasing numbers of people in all spheres of contemporary society.

Many look askance at this new development, and see it as extremely narcissistic, a type of cult of self-indulgence. People with this critical view tend to be those who have little or no experience of the phenomenon itself. They tend to be those who judge from a distance, and may never even have spoken to anybody undergoing this type of journey. Of course, there are risks of escapism and self-delusion here, as there can be even in formal religion itself. And there certainly is an urgent need for both *discernment* and *support* for the growing millions who are veering into this largely unexplored territory.

Is home-coming possible?

I conclude by returning to the sub-title of this work. This may puzzle and even confuse the reader. In Part One, I outline the prevalent religious context of today's world, suggesting that the very structure of mainstream religion, with the central focus on *place* and *word*, is designed to maintain a culture of exile. The estrangement is rooted in the antagonistic relationship between person and planet, the dualistic opposition between humans and creation, culminating in the promise of fulfilment in an 'outside-of-the-world' afterlife rather than in the midst of God's creation.

I suggest that this antagonistic relationship is a relatively recent development in our human story. There is growing evidence to suggest that, prior to the Agricultural Revolution of some 10,000 years ago – in other words for well over 95 per cent of the time we have inhabited the home planet – we, humans, lived out of a different human, earthly and spiritual vision. What today we consider normal and normative may in fact be a great deviation belonging to the dark age of 'civilisation' within which the monotheistic religions are the jewel in the crown.

In evolutionary terms, there is no going back, nor do I in any way wish to suggest a one-time 'golden age' that we can re-invent once more. The dark age of 'civilisation' is also part of our story, as important and significant as any other chapter of our long evolutionary history. But it is only *one* chapter, and with that chapter now largely written, we need to retrieve the rest of our sacred story.

We need to reclaim, particularly, those dimensions of our co-evolution that have been seriously undermined, and in some cases virtually eroded, by the destructive forces of 'civilisation': our affiliation with the cosmos and the home planet, our essential nature as a relational species; our feminine intuition; our erotic creativity; our faith in the co-creative power of God.

Many things feed into the culture of exile and alienation, particularly the dysfunctional institutions of politics, economics and religion. Throughout this book, I have dealt mainly with the third element, religion. While many politicians and economists may look favourably upon religion, although they often don't practise it themselves, I adopt a less favourable stance. It seems to me that religion has been used very effectively by the patriarchal culture of the past 5,000 years to maintain a veneer of stability and sanity in the midst of a dysfunctional world-view of exile and alienation. But instead of making transparent the root causes of the estrangement, the patriarchal powers kept addressing the symptoms. They kept throwing light on dark pathways, but never asked why they are dark in the first place.

All the religions, therefore, evolve strategies and structures which short-circuit the real issues. The great Eastern religions invent a re-incarnational recycling of hope and new life in some distant future that ably distracts from doing something proactive about conditions in the here and now. Christianity invents a mystique of suffering, creating the powerful scapegoat of Calvary so that the violent-prone patriarchs are justified in continuing to fight 'just' wars (see Ellis, 1997). And all the religions exonerate and glorify the institution of the family, not because it is the most constructive and creative way to contain sexual drive and provide the best guarantee of responsible child-rearing, but because it is a powerful arrangement to guarantee the continuity of the masculine will-to-power.

Formal religion is an invention of the age of patriarchy. Its primary purpose is not about revealing God's design for humanity, but about validating the masculine will-to-power, in its insatiable desire to conquer and control the whole of creation. Undoubtedly, good came out of religion, but in the form of validating a man-made *status quo*, rather than in unravelling ultimate meaning. Now that the rule of the patriarchs is itself in jeopardy, with growing numbers turning their backs on the patriarchal value-system of power and domination, religion itself is under threat as more and more people begin to suspect that its foundations have been spurious even from the beginning.

When, therefore, I address the notion of the *journey home from exile* (in Part Two), I am alluding to that rather amorphous and globally diffuse group of people whose hearts are no longer in the religious systems. Some have never been attached, and yet are often disturbed by religious feelings; some are still clinging on, and often not sure why; others have walked out because they were not being nourished in ways that enabled them to engage more meaningfully with the world of our time. These are the people I have in mind when I describe that state of mind (spirit) meta-phorically named as 'the journey home from exile'.

What characterises many of these people is a new spiritual hunger, often described as a search for meaning. What they are searching for, however, is not just another form of psychological fulfilment or some type of far-fetched utopian ideal. Seeking to outgrow the isolation and competitiveness of robust individualism; seeking to relate afresh – with every life form, planet Earth included – is a recurring theme in the stories that characterise the homeward bound. And there is a real hunger for a different way of being than that upheld by the prevailing culture, although people are not quite sure what that will eventually look like.

Do these people believe in God? I guess the most authentic response to that question is: 'Join the experience and somewhere in there you're likely to encounter the face of the living God.' There certainly is a reluctance to use the word 'God', and this may arise from the fact that many of the homeward bound have ceased trying to play God. They no longer trust those who for so long have 'played God', whether in the political, economic or religious spheres.

With a Buddhist-like directness, those heading for the homeland want to make the homeland a more hospitable place to live in, one where all peoples can be included, cared for, clothed, fed and loved. Many suspect that when we truly care for our sisters and brothers, and for the planet that is the source of all our nurtu-rance, then the God-question will not be a problem any more. The God of heady philosophical debate will have outgrown his usefulness, and the incarnational spirit of God will find room in the inn once more.

Lest the reader be deluded, let me make clear that not everything on the homeward journey is neat and clear. The new befriending space allows many awkward issues to be talked about and explored, and with a transparency and trust not commonly found where patriarchal control prevails. Refugees try to regain some dignity and self-worth; unemployed people share their stories of insecurity, knowing in their hearts that they can never return to 'the workplace' again; people speak of anxieties about failed relationships and what it takes to make partnerships more life-giving in this new place. How we turn breakdown into breakthrough is what many agonise about on the journey home from exile.

What all have in common, however, is the search for a new spirituality; a search for meaning that embraces a 'beyondness'; a sense of being embraced and held by a larger life-force, at one time very earthly, and yet inclusive of everything that belongs to the life-spectrum of past–present–future.

How this new spirituality relates with God as traditionally understood, or how it might be incorporated into the mainstream religions, is of no real interest to those who are homeward bound. There is an unspoken sense that the age of religion is over, that religion is a kind of barrier that gets in the way, that the baggage of religion is not worth the hassle. Above all, there is a strong consensus, sometimes articulated most strongly by people who have never had much to do with religion, that the 'divine' belongs to the whole of creation, and can never be confined to either one, or to all, the religions put together.

Revolution rather than revision is what the journey home is about. But it's not a revolution that seeks to topple all before it. Rather it is a passionate commitment to a new future, in the process of which things can be left behind, and left to die a timely death. To the outsider, it often seems like a reckless abandonment; but to those on the journey, it is all about the choices that need to be made in response to the call of this new moment.

The old securities don't feel secure any more. They are too confined and confining. They limit our options to connect and relate, when so many voices of our time claim that the way to truth is in making as many connections as possible and relating as inclusively as we can. These are the important landmarks of the homeward journey. However tentative or nebulous they may seem, they carry within them a reality that embodies a deeper truth, a truth that can liberate us all from the shackles of exile and alienation.

— Appendix 1 —

The Great Mother Goddess: Fact or Fiction?

The Goddess's power can now come out of hiding. (Now) it is needed more than ever before, as established religions lose their hold and the world, in its near-suicidal state and dire need for peace and colla-boration, is in crisis.

Alex Pirani

The monolithic Goddess whose biology is her destiny may be to a large extent an illusion, a creation of modern need, but in acknowledging greater diversity in religious expression we allow for the possibility of finding new patterns in a rich and fascinating body of evidence.

Lucy Goodison and Christine Morris

THROUGHOUT THIS BOOK, I make several allusions to the Great Earth Mother Goddess. I employ the concept to draw attention to very ancient perceptions on the meaning of the divine power in human life but also something quite contemporary, especially in women's experience. There are also ecological and planetary dimensions to which I make frequent reference.

In contemporary research, the notion of the Great Mother Goddess is employed in at least three different contexts, each of which I will briefly review.

Historical evidence

Was there a time when humans believed in, and worshipped, God as a woman? Scholarly opinion is divided between those who respond with a resounding 'Yes' and those who warm to the idea but feel the evidence is not sufficiently convincing for a categorical affirmation.

Foremost among the proponents is the Lithuanian archaeologist, Marija Gimbutas, who emigrated to the USA after the second world war and held many reputable academic posts. Her particular interest was in pre-history and the culture of South-East Europe. Her first major work, *Gods and Goddesses of Old Europe* (1974) won her wide international acclaim, but when the book was re-issued, eight years later, with the changed title, *Goddesses and Gods of Old Europe* (1982), she began to lose favour among her academic peers who feared she was drifting into esoteric and nebulous speculation and betraying the precision and objectivity of true science.

In the early 1980s, Gimbutas developed cancer and was dogged with ill health until her death in 1994. Some scholars suggest that her illness engendered a type of crusade-like enthusiasm to foster and promote her conviction that we humans are the beneficiaries of a long sacred history, focused largely on the Goddess Creatix, an egalitarian and highly creative force that dominated human civilisation for much of the paleolithic era. Her conviction that people over widely diffuse geographical places believed in, and worshipped, the Goddess, and regarded her body to be that of the Earth itself, is elucidated most vividly in her two final works *The Language of the Goddess* (1989) and *The Civilisation of the Goddess* (1991).

The anthropologist-cum-lawyer, Riane Eisler (1987, 1995) is probably the most widely read exponent of Gimbutas' ideas. A range of feminist writers, including art historian and sculptor, Merlin Stone (*When God was a Woman*, 1976), Naomi Goldenberg (*Changing of the Gods*, 1979), Carol Christ and Judith Plaskow (*Womanspirit Rising*, 1979), Charlene Spretnak (*The Politics of Women's Spirituality*, 1982) and Elinor Gadon (*The Once and Future Goddess*, 1989) strongly endorse and affirm Gimbutas' theories – see the *Journal of Feminist Studies in Religion*, Vol. 12/2 (1996), where many of those named above join in paying tribute to her life and work.

Gimbutas tends to give unquestioned credence to facts for which we have very little real evidence. She draws on archaeological field work to substantiate her personal intuitions, but critics claim she takes unprofessional liberties in her interpretation of that material. Ice Age art is the primary resource for the claims she makes about the extensive existence and influence of the Goddess, and that art form is, and has been for some time now, the subject of several interpretations.

As we move more into Neolithic times (after 10000 BCE), Gimbutas draws more heavily on the research of Alexander Marshack (*The Roots of Civilisation*, 1991) and more specifically on that of James Mellaart, the main excavator of the ancient Turkish site of Catal Huyuk (the actual title of his main work published in 1967). Here she is dealing with more reliable evidence (despite a recently conflicting interpretation by the British archae-ologist, Ian Hodder) on the basis of which she goes on to raise the question if the several female goddesses of Neolithic cultures in Crete, Egypt, Mesopotamia, etc. are not, in fact, fragmented images of a one-time Great Goddess. It is, indeed, a valid and timely question, but the question in itself cannot be used to posit the actual existence of the Goddess in the first place.

As already indicated, the work of Gimbutas has encountered several negative and some highly dismissive reviews, for example Brian Morris ('Matriliny and Mother Goddess Religion', *Journal of Contemporary Religion*, 13 (1998), pp. 91–102). A range of contem-porary female archaeologists are exploring afresh her views and insights, and while they continue to criticise her methodology, one detects a fresh receptivity to her conviction that a form of divine engagement prevailed in ancient cultures which merits serious scholarly attention and may have huge cultural, spiritual and theological implications for the present time and for the future of human civilisation.

Among such reviews I note those of Margaret Conkey and Ruth Tringham, 'Archaeology and the Goddess: Exploring the Contours of Feminist Archaeology' in D. C. Stanton and A. J. Stewart (eds), *Feminisms in the Academy: Rethinking the Disciplines* (1995, pp. 199–247); Asphodel Long, 'The One and the Many: The Great Goddess Revisited', *Feminist Theology*, No. 15 (May 1997), pp. 11–29; and most comprehensive of all, Lucy Goodison and Christine Morris (eds), *Ancient Goddesses*, 1998.

We also record the controversy of the 1970s and early 1980s between Carol Christ (and others) who warmed to the historical evidence, and Rosemary Radford Ruether who strongly dismissed it, accusing her opponents of bigotry and being misguided in their allegiance to the Goddess (1980, pp. 842–7). The details of this controversy are reviewed by Mary Jo Weaver in 'Who is the Goddess and Where Does She Get Us?' in *Journal of Feminist Studies in Religion* 5/1 (1989), pp. 49–64.

To this day, Ruether is an ardent advocate of reformation from within a faith tradition (Christian or otherwise) rather than looking for a 'revolution' from outside. Although she deals exclusively with the Christian tradition, we note that Hinduism, the oldest of the world religions, is richly embellished with female deities, and to this day many Hindus in their own homes erect altars, pray to and worship female deities.

It is women's reaction to the historical claims for the Goddess that makes the evidence compelling. It seems to mirror and reawaken something very profound in women's experience, and so potently real that many proceed to consider it real – both for now and for the ancient past. I offer a brief overview of that experiential material.

The experiential evidence

The notion of the Great Goddess seems to generate a kind of 'fire in the belly' for numerous women of our time. It awakens within the deep soul – of many women and some men – something far more sacred and profoundly more enriching than the beliefs and doctrines of monotheistic religion. The recipients begin to realise that 'The Dark Age of Monotheism' (Asia Shepsut) has deprived or robbed them of an inner, feminine 'resource', the reclaiming of which is long overdue, and the reappropriation of which becomes a primary preoccupation for many women today.

Already in 1955, M. Esther Harding (*Women's Mysteries Ancient and Modern*) described this experiential reawakening in these words:

> In the image of the Mother Goddess – ancient and powerful – women of olden times found the reflection of their own deepest feminine nature. Today, the ancient feminine principle is reasserting its power. Men and women are turning once again to the Moon Mother, not however, through a religious cult . . . but through a change in psychological attitude. For the principle, which in ancient and more naive days was projected into the form of a goddess, is no longer seen in the guise of a religious tenet, but is now sensed as a psychological force arising from the unconscious . . . having power to mold the destinies of mankind. (p. 241)

Closer to our own time, Starhawk (in Spretnak, 1982, p. 51) writes in a similar vein:

The image of the Goddess inspires women to see ourselves as divine, our bodies as sacred, the changing phases of our life as holy, our aggression as healthy, our anger as purifying, and our power to nurture and create, but also to limit and destroy when necessary, as the very force that sustains all life.

We note that Starhawk, unlike Harding, does not describe this as a *psychological* state, in that way side-stepping the possible accusation that this is nothing more than an introspective self-delusory fantasy fuelled by an anti-male polemic. She suggests that something much more subliminal, and distinctly spiritual, is at work. Mary Daly, in her book, *Pure Lust* (1984, p. 26) offers the following description of this inner experience: 'When I choose to use such words as *Goddess*, it is to point metaphorically to the Powers of Be-ing, the Active Verb in whose potency all biophilic reality participates.'

Here, we move from something purely internal to a quality that belongs to universal life, one which Daly develops with some powerful, and often baffling, metaphors and symbols of a literary and mythic nature. For Daly, the spirituality of what she calls the Sado-Society is unambiguously *necrophilic* – it highlights suffering, sacrifice, scapegoating and guilt, and leaves behind it a world (planet Earth) emaciated with torture and pain. The spirituality of the Goddess, on the other hand, she envisages as a *biophic* force, the *womb-force* which is unique to women, but also the generative principle working from within the womb of planet Earth itself. In the words of Raphael (1996, p. 77), 'The Goddess, the earth, the female body are unified and charged with sacral powers for the transmutation of matter, for shape-shifting and for the production of cosmogonic effluvia: blood, milk and water.'

This 'sacredness within' has led several feminist theorists to develop a spiritual–theological vision with the following as key elements:

1. *Relationality:* The Goddess is a power-towards-connectedness, a propensity for relationship, not just for people but for the whole of creation. This theme is extensively covered in feminist literature with several titles similar to that of Carol Robb and Beverly Harrison, *Making the Connections: Essays in Feminist Social Ethics* (1985). The ecological dimension is explored in works such as: Carolyn Merchant (*Radical*

Ecology, 1992); Anne Primavesi (*From Apocalypse to Genesis*, 1991); Rosemary Radford Ruether (*Gaia and God*, 1992).

Richard Grigg (*When God Becomes Goddess*, 1995) represents a small group of male writers with an interest in Goddess spirituality. Grigg maintains that the God of conventional religion has left the stage of history and has been absorbed into a private, functional relationship with the individual believer. He envisages faith in the Goddess as a process of 'enacting the divine' in self, others and the cosmos at large, in which all three aspects need to be activated interdependently.

2. *Transcending dualisms:* The Goddess symbolises relationship, connection, unity and the healing of the dismemberment and fragmentation caused to the female body (and to the Earth itself) at the hands of patriarchy over many millennia. All forms of dualistic division are considered alien to the divinity within. In the words of Ursula King (*Women and Spirituality*, 1989, p. 27), 'The battle is with dualism in all its forms.' The philosophy of 'divide and conquer', so central to patriarchy and to the monotheistic religions, is perceived to be antithetical to all that the Goddess stands for.

   Dualistic splitting has an uncanny power to make invisible that which we seek to denigrate. Whereas several goddess figures of the ancient Near East were initially treated as consorts of male Gods, they were consequently demonised for being consorts; the Hochma of cosmic wisdom was reduced to a quality of the Torah; Sophia (Wisdom) became a dimension of the male Trinity; and, perhaps most destructive of all, the parthenogenic heroin of Hebrew times became the degenerative, a-sexual Mary of Christianity, emptied of all that uniquely constitutes womanhood.

3. *Embodiment:* Retrieving the sacredness of the human body (and particularly the female body), in both its personal and planetary dimensions, is another major concern of those wishing to reappropriate a spirituality of the Goddess. Once again several references come to mind, notably Gloria Ornstein, *The Reflowering of the Goddess* (1990) and Melissa Raphael, *Thealogy and Embodiment* (1996).

4. *Sexuality:* What evokes fear, suspicion and reaction among many critics – male and female – is the radical affirmation of human sexuality advocated by proponents of the Goddess

revival. This is not just a reaction to the violence of sexual repression from which women have suffered for so long (as illustrated in the disturbing account by B. Ehrenreich and D. English in *Complaints and Disorders: The Sexual Politics of Sickness* (1972). Primarily, it is the conviction that our sexuality is a dimension of the divine eroticism itself, poised for creativity at every realm of life, a theme that surfaces in virtually every page of Mary Daly's main works, and is elaborately developed in Raine Eisler's *Sacred Pleasure* (1995).

5. *Ecofeminism:* Although few contemporary feminist theologians concur with the claim that in ancient times people understood the Earth itself to be the body of the Great Mother, there is a wide consensus that the Earth's ecosystem is basic to all life and growth, that it has in itself a spiritual and theological significance, that the patriarchal engagement with creation is both exploitative and immoral, and that an authentic re-appropriation of the human body is impossible without coming home to ourselves as earthly and cosmic creatures.

    This is not just about the need to include ecological concerns in feminist scholarship. It has a substantial *justice* dimension, more accurately an *eco-justice* (what Conlon, 1990, calls Geo-justice) dimension. It seeks to recognise that the prevalent distorted relationships with the Earth result from unequal power relations wherein women, the poor and the weak tend to be losers. God's embodiment in the creation is the catalyst calling us, humans, to revise radically our understanding of the creation itself and our embodied presence within it. Ruether (1992), McFague (1993) and Johnson (1993) are among the leading proponents of ecofeminism.

6. *Ritual:* Because women have been excluded for so long from the realms of liturgy and sacramental celebration, and motivated by the desire to outgrow all dualisms, Goddess-worshippers tend to be spontaneous, Earth-centred, creative and highly imaginative in the use of symbol and ritual. They tend to be keenly aware of the terrible and destructive depri-vation of ritual that permeates our world today.

    In some circles this has led to a re-discovery of wicca-wisdom, often dismissed as pagan witchcraft. These groups consciously evoke the power of the Goddess using the four elements of wind, water, earth and fire, with storytelling, music, dance and chants used as media to articulate gratitude and intercession, all combined under the rubric of magic. Starhawk (*Dreaming the Dark*, 1982; *Truth or Dare*, 1988) is probably the best known and scholarly-informed source for this practice, the contemporary significance of which is documented by Lynne Hume (1998, pp. 309–19).

Feminists, devoted to the Goddess, are sometimes accused of being idiosyncratic, morally apathetic and politically indifferent (cf. Dorothy A. Lee, 1999, pp. 19–28), so immersed in a fantasy world that the real world continually eludes them. To this allegation, Ornstein (*The Reflowering of the Goddess*, 1990, p. 15) gives the response with which many feminists would concur:

> In a contemporary feminist matristic world woman will not be expelled from the garden by her female creator; she will, on the contrary, be called upon to cultivate the garden, to revive the wasteland that the garden has become today . . . Now in the late 1980s the Goddess has come to signify a fusion of ethics, aesthetics and politics in a global ecological vision of survival both for humankind and for all non-human life on earth.

The archetypal evidence

The notion of *archetypes* is popularly associated with Jungian psychology in which they refer to patterns of psychic energy which seem to exist in time–space and manifest in human consciousness as dominant images and values. When ordinary objects such as water, candle–light, oil, bread, take on religious significance across time and culture, then it is suggested that they serve to give expression to our archetypal longings and desires. In the case of the Goddess, we note the long association with the symbol of the *serpent* (cf. Viki Nobel, *Uncoiling the Snake*, 1993), to denote healing and wisdom, as two of the dominant qualities of the Goddess.

In the great mythologies of humankind we also encounter archetypal personages such as the Wise Old Man, the Puer Natus (the eternal child), the tripartite figures of the Virgin (Maiden), the Mother and the Crone. These are time-honoured images that often

occur in dreams and engage our creative imaginations in reconnecting us with the search for meaning that forever preoccupies the
human soul.

The Great Goddess may also be considered to be one of these
archetypal images, whose appeal and presence seems to endure
across the aeons. Some suggest that her appeal is particularly
strong in our time, because patriarchal culture – and particularly
monotheistic religion – has seriously suppressed the nurturing,
liberating power of motherhood (see Alex Pirani, *The Absent Mother*,
1991). At the level of the unconscious – whether understood
individually or collectively – we yearn to reconnect with, and be
empowered by, the womb that begets and sustains all life.

Contemporary research into the nature of *consciousness* – from
both psychological and scientific sources – confirms complex and
subliminal dynamics for which we employ the concept *archetypes*.
In plain language, something is going on deep within the human
personality, and deep within the creation around us, which hugely
impacts upon our feelings, perceptions, values and especially upon
our capacity to relate. By invoking and befriending the Goddess,
women particularly know that they are reconnecting with something
very ancient, deep and sacred. They know they are engaging with
ultimacy and with something that relates to the very essence of
God-life itself. This field of research they name 'Thealogy'.

It seems to me that Christian scholars are to the fore in
unearthing the archetypal significance of the Goddess consciousness, particularly in re-discovering the mythic-value of *wisdom*. I
allude specifically to the research work of Susan Cady, Marian
Ronan and Hal Taussig whose work *Sophia: The Future of
Feminist Theology*, was published in 1986. This pioneering vision
was subsequently taken up by Elizabeth Schussler Fiorenza and
Elizabeth Johnson, each of whom focuses on the Wisdom archetype
and its potential to reframe and reclaim new and enriched insights
for our understanding of God/ess.

Both draw on the Wisdom (*sophia*) tradition of the Hebrew
Scriptures, with the Wisdom Woman as the primary charac-
terisation of God. The Scripture scholar, Kathleen M. O'Connor
(*The Wisdom Literature*, 1988, p. 59) offers us a cryptic description:

At the centre of the Wisdom Literature stands a beautiful
and alluring woman. She is Lady Wisdom, or as I prefer to

call her, the Wisdom Woman. The primary mode of being of the Wisdom Woman is relational. In all the texts, where she appears, the most important aspect of her existence is her relationships. Her connections extend to every part of reality. She is closely joined to the created world; she is an intimate friend of God; she delights in the company of human beings. No aspect of reality is closed off from her. She exists in it as if it were a tapestry of connected threads, patterned into an intricate whole of which she is the centre.

In a sense, this quotation forms a resumé of everything explored thus far in this overview of the Great Mother Goddess. We begin to glimpse an ancient faith tradition, centred around a female God-image, deeply embedded within creation and appropriated by people at both individual and relational levels. For reasons that seem complex and unclear, that tradition faded substantially – nearly all scholars agree that it was deliberately subverted and suppressed by a rising patriarchal power which sought to substitute the Earth-based egalitarian Goddess with a warrior, conquering sky-God.

At the present time, we seem to be experiencing a revival, which in the work of scholars like O'Connor, Schussler-Firoenza and Johnson seems to be coming full circle in the discovery that the Christian Jesus – and presumably God-figures of the other religions too – can be revisioned anew within this ancient Wisdom tradition.

Both Schussler-Firoenza (*In Memory of Her*, 1983 and *Jesus, Miriam's Child, Sophia's Prophet*, 1994) and Johnson (*She Who Is*, 1992) set out to relocate Jesus not within the power-structure that belongs to the culture of patriarchy, but within the relational, egalitarian, values-driven culture epitomised in the Wisdom Literature. They proceed to unearth the subverted dimensions of this ancient tradition from within the Christian Scriptures themselves, reclaiming a much more feminine and inclusive understanding of both the person of Jesus and of Christian discipleship, an approach which mainstream scholarship seems very reluctant to acknowledge or adopt. Consequently, it is encouraging to see that male theologians like Peter C. Hodgson (*Winds of the Spirit*, 1994) and Denis Edwards, *Jesus the Wisdom of God: An Ecological Theology*, 1995) also embrace this new approach.

While I wish to highlight the contributions of Schussler-Fiorenza and Johnson, the reappropriation of an archetypal quality like wisdom is a great deal more manageable than some of the other volatile challenges thrown up by archetypal images from the ancient past. Linking wisdom with the male figure of Jesus, and in that way helping to create a more inclusive Christology, will appeal even to a lot of male scholars. But what happens when we suggest that perhaps the Blessed Virgin Mary also belongs to that tradition and should be viewed as an embodiment of the Great Goddess – as suggested by E. Ann Matter 'The Virgin Mary: A Goddess?' (1985). (In fact, it is difficult to avoid that challenge without being downright evasive, particularly when we acknowledge the highly-charged role of the Black Madonna in so many cultures, past and present (cf. Begg, 1985).)

Archetypes rarely come in neat, manageable packages, especially when they represent energies and values that have been subverted for so long. Consequently, some of the growing archetypal awareness around sexuality and eroticism – of the type explored by Carter Heyward in *Touching our Strength*, 1989; Mary E. Hunt in *Fierce Tenderness*, 1991; or the ground-breaking Christology of Rita Nakashima Brock, *Journeys by Heart*, 1992 – is likely to prove provocative and threatening to the academic world of mainstream theology and spirituality.

The ecological link is also loaded with archetypal intent, often to the extent of evoking total abhorrence on what patriarchal religion has done to creation, and sometimes evoking a reaction to abandon formal religion completely, as in the case of people like Mary Daly, Carol Christ, Naomi Goldenberg and Daphne Hampson. (Personally, I see this 'abandonment of faith' as something more akin to 'outgrowing the need for it'). As we move into the new millennium, the ecological aspects of the Goddess revival may well prove to be the most controversial – yet, the most engaging – features of the new spiritual vision I have been outlining in this overview.

Fact or fiction?

Once again, we are in danger of being swamped by a misleading dualism. When it comes to the Great Mother Goddess, we don't know all the facts; truthfully, we know very little of a precise, quantifiable, objective nature. If we are to wait until we have more substantial information, the chances are that the information will be totally irrelevant by the time we establish its veracity. In this realm, as in many others in contemporary research, trying to tie up all the loose ends, and obtain scientific certitude, is not likely to be very productive.

Those who dismiss the whole thing as a fictitious fantasy are unlikely to be convinced by any counter-arguments, scientific or otherwise. It also feels both unjust and dangerously arrogant to dismiss all the people named above as people who base their convictions on fictitious fantasy. These are scholars of distinction and vision, and all the better equipped for the exploration under consideration, precisely because they are also people of great feeling and imagination.

I guess the main area of contention is well named by Carol Christ, writing in 1996: 'We know our scholarship is passionate, is interested, is aimed at transforming the world we have inherited. There our first task as scholars must be to deconstruct the myth of objectivity and to provide alternatives to it.'

Undoubtedly, the revival of the Goddess is an alternative to the sacred dogmas of the God of patriarchal religion. I am not convinced that she will totally demolish that God. She'll certainly undermine a lot of his power; she'll help to recreate a God-image that will be a great deal more humane and incarnational, and above all she'll empower us to reclaim the gift of the divine, not in some far-off heavenly realm, but right here within the womb of the Earth itself. To me, at least, all that feels like an attractive proposition, and something deep within me also suggests that it is exactly what the Jesus of Christianity also wanted to achieve.

Addendum

As this book goes to press, my attention has been drawn to a piece of critically acclaimed research by Leonard Shlain (*The Alphabet Versus the Goddess: The Conflict between Word and Image*, London and New York: Penguin Books) claiming that the demise of the Great Goddess did not result from the physical onslaught of external assailants, but rather from the undermining influence of literacy with its heavy emphasis on linear, left-brain development and the subsequent culture of rationality, an overload of masculine value, and a corrosive imbalance in gender relations. Incidentally, the same book offers a much more comprehensive analysis of the material I explore in Chapter 3.

— Appendix 2 —

Being a Theologian as People Come Home from Exile

If my understanding of theology, as ultimately rooted in the common language and in general human experience, is correct, it has a general cultural significance; and there is no reason for it to be restricted to the parochial confines of the church or to be regarded as an esoteric or subrational discipline. Whether the church as an institution lives or dies, theology has an important role to play.

Gordon Kaufman

If creative change comes from the outer edges of systems, that is why thealogy is, in all senses, always on the edge of chaos.

Melissa Raphael

THE CULTURE OF EXILE is densely populated by experts, people considered to be wiser, holier and more highly qualified than the majority of ordinary people. We have political experts, scientific geniuses and religious specialists, among whom the theologian holds an honoured position. We consider the theologian to hold a quality of expertise with the aid of which we can comprehend something of the mystery of God and also the mystery of our daily lives. Enlightened with theological wisdom, the mysterious things of life become a little more accessible and meaningful.

In the culture of exile, we look to the theologian to help us unravel something of that ultimate mystery that legitimates exile in the first place. Like Job in the Hebrew Scriptures, we ask many penetrating questions, and sometimes the more questions we ask, the more baffling the mystery becomes.

Perhaps, like Job, we acquiesce, grin and bear it all, hoping in our hearts that God knows what's going on. But that martyr-like attitude carries very little conviction today. Something tells us that life should not be that irrational, and if there is some God behind the irrationality, most of us today are not particularly interested in that God, and are unlikely to go on believing in 'him'. Indeed, Zuckerman (1991) argues, with scholarly erudition, that, properly understood, the Book of Job is a parody protesting against the stereotype of the righteous sufferer, and not an affirmation of humble resignation as it is frequently interpreted.

This is often where the transition begins to unfold from the place of exile to the journey home from exile, and it is also at this critical juncture that the theologian may lose or reclaim credibility. People who have chosen to outgrow the place of exile do not much trust any expert, the theologian included.

While the religions prevail, there will always be a place for the theologian, but who will s(he) be speaking to; and, more critically, on whose behalf will s(he) be speaking? While the Christian theologian seeks to access truth from within the deposit of faith, transmitted through formal religion, the 'faith seeking understanding' among today's people, and particularly for those on the journey home from exile, has long outgrown the limited world of religious belief.

The ultimate questions for which people are seeking theological wisdom are not questions relating to Church or formal religion. Rather they relate to *meaning* and *purpose* in the complex universe of our time. Assuredly, many of them are 'God questions'; God is definitely not dead, nor subsumed in post-modern nihilism. The questioning mind of our time does not have a problem with belief in divinity; it has major problems with how the formal religions construe that belief.

Nurturing the theologian in each one of us

Theology is largely a Christian concept, although the profound questions of the other religions can no longer be excluded from theological discourse and, sometimes, can shed a great deal of light on the issues that concern theologians. As a Christian discipline, theology has largely been the reserve of clerics (priests). Prior to 1960, lay people in the Catholic Church required special permission to study theology; few sought that privilege and of those that did only a mere handful were allowed. Theology tended to be taught by male clerics and solely to male clerical students. And the exclusive focus was strictly that of Scripture and tradition as approved by Church authority; all other sciences were considered secular, inferior and irrelevant to the theologian.

Such was the nurturing ground of the Catholic theologian – and of virtually all Christian theologians – for at least 400 years, from the mid-sixteenth to the mid-twentieth century. Although nobody set out to do so, things began to change in the 1960s, and after 1970 we experienced a virtual avalanche of lay interest in theology. It is now estimated that by the year 2010, 60 per cent of all theologians in the Catholic Church will be lay people, of which three-quarters will be women.[1]

This may well be the greatest revolution happening in the Catholic Church today. For many people it is the strongest ray of hope, perhaps the only one that is keeping them in the Church. In fact, the revolution may not have a great impact within the Church, because on closer examination this revolution belongs to the world rather than to the Church.

The fact that one can be a theologian and not belong to the Church may sound strange, but this is increasingly the case among the rising generations of theologians. Church membership is no longer perceived to be essential, and for a growing number of theologians, accountability to the world is considered far more serious and urgent than accountability to the Church. Questions of ultimate concern arising from the world of our time are far more engaging and profound than those which concern the Church. The Church's urgent questions often seem unreal, inward-looking and excessively moralistic. They do not seem to be the urgent questions of our age.

This perceptual shift is largely due to the increase in lay involvement in theology. Lay people bring to the table of dialogue very different questions and issues from those of the cleric. They convey a 'faith seeking understanding' which is about the struggle and challenge to live with greater meaning and integrity in a world battered and bruised by the forces of patriarchy, often under the aegis of formal religion.

The people are also more consciously attuned to the movements of Spirit at work in the world of our time: the growing ecological consciousness, the upsurge of feminism, the pluralistic call to acknowledge diversity and its potential richness, the priority of the relational, co-operative mode over the long-sanctioned (and religiously validated) competitive one. While the formal Church talks about 'the signs of the times', what these really are, and what they mean in practice, is the wisdom with which lay people are best acquainted.

For those who remain close to the earthly condition, we readily discern that the world of our time cries out for theological recognition! Even scientists, immersed in their (ir)rational preoccupation with the world of 'dead inert matter' often find themselves in the realm of mystery. And those who veer into the exploration of modern cosmology find it all the more difficult to evade the beckoning horizon of mystery.

All the scientific discoveries of our time point to a world that is beginning to look quite strange. The more we discover, the more there remains to be discovered, and the landscape has now become so vast, in terms of both space and time, that traditional methods of research are proving not merely inadequate, but profoundly dissatisfying for the scientific imagination.

The strangeness which the scientist encounters is precisely that same strangeness that creates so much estrangement in our world today. We can't come to grips with it all, and the patriarchal modelling of the past still haunts us with the illusion that we should be fully in control. What we need above all else is the wisdom and discernment to befriend the strangeness, so that we discover its paradoxical will-to-life rather than be overwhelmed by the shadow of its debilitating alienation.

This I suggest is virgin soil for the contemporary theologian, opening up unprecedented possibilities for a theological–scientific dialogue unknown to previous generations. It is the task and privilege of the theologian to point us in the direction of ultimacy, to keep us focused on the mystery which permeates reality and to employ a multi-disciplinary hermeneutic so that we can engage with the encompassing mystery in its multi-dimensional nature.

While God is the ultimate source and foundation of this mystery, its mediation touches our lives at many levels. In the past we tended to give priority to the realm of the human intellect regarding humans as superior to every other life form on planet Earth. But as we seek to reclaim the ancient cosmological story, we realise that our anthropology also needs to change radically. The theological subject is no longer simply the human *qua* human, but rather the human as a relational, planetary and cosmic creature.

The new theological subject

Not merely are we dealing with a new theological subject – our fresh understanding on what it means to be human – but that very understanding requires us to begin with the larger life-force (i.e. the cosmos) within which our co-creative God begets humanity in the first place. In other words, the theologian is now called to reverse the order of bygone times in which we began with the human and argued towards the rest of creation (usually highlighting its limitations and sinfulness). We now begin where God in time seems to have begun, with the prodigious unfolding of creation in its cosmic and planetary grandeur. That is the source and well-spring of every life form populating the world today – our own included.

It is the *universe* itself, and not just human perceptions based on the sacred traditions of religions and Churches that, henceforth, will engage the theologian. Our connection with the universe is primarily through our creatureliness within the home planet, our Earth. It is home to all those who seek ultimate meaning in a world of elegant complexity, undulating unceasingly between creation and destruction in the evolutionary process of being and becoming.

It is home to those who know that the search never ends and that its very open-endedness is what offers hope for the future. It is home to those who feel called to engage in something that is bigger and greater than themselves, yet, in some mysterious way also pulsates within them. It is home to those who have lost faith (and hope) in the securities of 'civilisation' (which effectively means the past 5,000 years), and in their hearts long for something new and fresh. It is home to those who hear the clarion call: 'Behold, I make all things new' (Rev. 21:5) and want to respond with an unambiguous 'YES!'

Nobody should be excluded from this adventure, nor does anybody have a right to exclude another in the name of religion, race or ethnicity. Nor does God need protecting from those whom we consider ungodly, or not properly trained for theological discourse, or unworthy of so noble an undertaking.

The God who has nursed and nurtured our universe, in all its ecstacy and chaos, is well able to cope with the limitations of the human condition. As all the religions indicate, one of the persistent features of God is the *invitation* given in radical freedom. Humans respond to this invitation more often than we care to acknowledge; the problem is that the responses do not fit within the categories of formal religion and they undermine the authority of those who believe they have direct access to the mind of God.

When we strive to begin our theology where God begins the co-creative process of evolution, then several perceptions and convictions will require reformulation. The notion of *Incarnation* serves as a timely example. Theologically, we believe that something uniquely new and redemptive happened to our humanity when God was incarnate in Jesus Christ, about 2,000 years ago. Something radically new happened to the God–human relationship, as a result of which things were radically different from there on. In fact, it is often suggested that it is with the coming of God among us in the person and ministry of Jesus that we become truly human for the first time. In mainstream theology, Incarnation (God coming among us in the embodiment of Jesus) marks a totally new beginning.

Many today consider these theological views to be short-sighted, reductionistic and imperialistic. Some even consider them to be idolatrous. They side-step and underestimate the involvement of God in history and in evolution for the billions of years preceding the past 2,000 years. They depict a God-image, reduced to and curtailed by the manageable parameters of patriarchal consciousness. And the outcome is not about humanity in the image of God, but rather God in the image of anthropocentric humanity.

If God has always been involved in history, co-creating within the creative process of evolution – an assumption held across all the religions – then Incarnation in the strict sense began four-and-a-half million years ago when the first fully hominoid creature evolved on Earth. In that original moment of human evolution God was fully present, saying a total 'Yes' to that newly evolving creature. We did not need to wait for Jesus to arrive on Earth – a mere 2,000 years ago – to declare that being to be a creature of God, nor to assert that God is fully present in our sacred humanity. Nor is there anything in the long evolutionary story of humanity to suggest that the original creature was cursed with some type of fundamental flaw that would eventually require a special form of divine intervention to set everything right. No, God was fully at work as God always is, and God knows what s(he) is about!

Theologically, I suggest we stand on much more solid ground, and in a much more creative space, by accepting that Incarnation began 4,400,000 years ago and, perhaps, long before that (if paleontologists find evidence to suggest an earlier dating – which is likely). Where then does that leave our current Christian understanding and the complex theological edifice we have constructed around it?

If we accept that Incarnation began in the dim and distant past of our evolutionary story, then perhaps the Jesus event of 2,000 years ago is best understood as a *celebration* of humanity reaching a threshold of incarnational maturity. Could it mark the type of development that Teilhard de Chardin suggested; that humanity has reached its fullest possible *biological* development, and that evolution is now pushing us towards *psychic* evolutionary growth! Perhaps this is what is meant by the alleged statement of Jesus recorded in John's Gospel (16:7): that Jesus' own departure (in his biological earthly state) was a prerequisite for the coming of the Holy Spirit. Jesus marks and celebrates what our species has achieved in terms of human biological evolution; God as Spirit marks the (formal) initiation of our evolution as creatures of spirit!

This also helps us to comprehend Christ's resurrection with fresh insight and coherence. The Risen Jesus – irrespective of whether there was a post-Easter embodied presence or not – proleptically announces and affirms this newly constituted human creature. Incarnation is poised to reach a new level of divine–human integration.

What then of the Calvary experience, and the long tradition of atonement, redemption and salvation requiring the Cross, passion and death of Jesus? Contemporary theologians and Scripture scholars such as Brock (1992, pp. 50–70) and Crossan (1995, pp. 123–58) suggest that the death of Jesus should be regarded primarily as a *political* event incurred by the strong prophetic stance which Jesus adopted on behalf of humankind. Viewing it in this light, we are challenged to follow Jesus in his prophetic mission, even if we too have to give up our lives. In other words, Calvary is not about something special that Jesus undertook on our behalf, offering himself to be yet another redemptive scapegoat, but rather it is an invitation to that courageous prophetic action that helps us to break the vicious cycle of injustice and violence that creates the need for the scapegoat in the first place. Feminist theologians hold some quite differing views on this topic (see Ross and Hilkert, 1995, pp. 341–6).

We also consider the Calvary experience to be an integral dimension of human evolution in terms of its dual aspects of light and shadow. The incarnation of God in Jesus celebrates the maturation of humanity over some four million years in all that humanity has achieved, but also in all that humanity has damaged through anthropocentric interference. Light and shadow always intermingle in the human heart – individually and collectively – and *both* are held in paradoxical tension within the life and ministry of Jesus.

Implicit in these reflections is the need for a theological vision that is much more grounded in a multi-disciplinary hermeneutic. If theology wishes to continue to be a science that grapples with questions of ultimacy, then we should strive to promote it as a pioneering science in providing a multi-disciplinary synthesis. As evolution pushes us into new realms of consciousness and a cross-disciplinary search for meaning, theologians need to be on the ready to discern and give voice to new questions; more importantly, to the new revelations of God irrupting at this time.

The theologian as pastoral catalyst

The greatest challenge for the contemporary theologian, and some are already doing this in admirable ways, is to shift theology out of the staid and sturdy environment of academic institutions. Theology belongs to the living elements of creation itself. Where God began to fashion life and meaning, there the theologian needs to begin too. The primary revelation of our God is not contained in some set of holy books, but in the unfolding process of the universe itself, an evolutionary story we believe to be several billions of years old. While we cannot access it in *academic* detail, we can begin to contemplate something of its mysterious elegance. Long before the theologian engages with sacred texts, s(he) needs to be saturated in contemplative gaze! The landscape of creation, and not the realm of academic discourse, is where theology begins today!

In connecting with creation's story itself, the theologian will begin to empathise and accompany people in their searching and in their questions. At this juncture the 'pastor' who befriends takes precedence over the mentor who informs. Intellectual information – even on faith matters – should follow and not precede the pastoral connection. The faith tradition from without makes a great deal more sense when we have truly encountered the God who works from within! All theology becomes pastoral theology.

The 'faith seeking understanding' in our time still has many echoes of people struggling with the darkness and pain of exile, but gradually realising that home-coming is once more possible. People are negotiating this new spiritual landscape far beyond the closed worlds of religion and Church allegiance. Some have deliberately abandoned the Churches/religions; some were never there in the first place; and others are consciously acknowledging that they are outgrowing the need for formal Church and religion.

The theologian viewing this new landscape may try to pretend that this new world-order does not exist, or even if it does it is so far removed from God (traditionally understood) that it does not deserve serious theological redress; only those of an evangelical slant are likely to adopt such a stance today. Nor is it appropriate any longer for today's theologian to invoke an older type of scholarly integrity and strive to analyse the emerging world objectively from the scholarly gaze of a university, seminary or theological college. While the intellectual dimension is undoubtedly important, the pastoral ambience (the story-telling, the healings, the table-fellowship of Jesus) is what provides the raw material for a theology that speaks meaningfully to the hungering masses of our time.

This new theological vision stretches beyond all boundaries set by political or ecclesiastical authorities. The search for truth cannot be hemmed in or penned down. To whom, therefore, is the theologian accountable? In short, to the *human community at large*. But because we now realise that humanity cannot live meaningfully without a meaningful planet to inhabit, and a meaningful universe in which to participate, that accountability goes beyond people to the creative energy of life itself. People of religious (spiritual) upbringing will call that creative energy 'God'; others may hesitate to use the name. In either case, *theology* can happen in the creative pursuit of ultimate meaning.

In summary, the following elements are likely to need a new quality of attention and time from the theologian of the future:

1. *Connectivity.* Everything in our universe is interconnected and inter-related. Nothing makes sense in isolation. We cannot engage with ultimacy without a real desire to connect widely and deeply requiring a committed effort to engage with the whole of reality.

2. *Longevity.* There is an agelessness to our world and even to our own species. We have inhabited planet Earth for over four million years (the most recent estimate). And for all that time we have been grappling with ultimacy – subconsciously if not consciously. We have a story to tell that is imbued with universality – which in our barbaric anthropocentrism we have tried to reduce to religious and national sectarianism. There is a great deal in our story to be reclaimed, retrieved and integrated anew in our lives.

3. *Spirituality.* Long before we humans ever evolved, strange and wonderful things were happening in our universe. It is a cosmic miracle that the forces of life have outpaced those of non-life, but they have, and often against tremendous odds. The will-to-survive is itself driven by a will-to-grow (become) which in turn is fuelled by a will-to-meaning, and this is the kernel of that spiritual energy which will fascinate the theologian of the future. No need to invoke an external agent, divine or otherwise! There is more than enough *meaning within* to engage the creative imagination for aeons yet to come.

4. *Interiority.* In the contemporary world, and possibly for the past 10,000 years, we humans tend to gauge value by measurements, quantities, usefulness, productivity, marketability, performance, fulfilment of duties or expectations. These are all *external* criteria and if we try to apply them to some of our most intimate and cherished experiences, we run ourselves into alienation and anomie.

Although religion has long advocated a sense of interiority, it has taken some of the outstanding discoveries of the twentieth century – e.g. science (the quantum theory), psychology (the role of the subconscious), the perceptions of planet Earth viewed from outer space – to alert us to the primacy of the meaning within. The propensity for self-organisation (autopoiesis), while still poorly understood, is more widely accepted as being inherent to all life forms, thus consigning the really real to what is not seen, and requiring a less dogmatic attribution to the importance of external phenomena.

5. *Multi-disciplinary*. Traditionally the theologian was considered versed in the things of God (via the Scriptures and sacred learning) because the things of the world were considered of little or no consequence. Although that simplistic dualism has long outlived its usefulness, it survives (especially in the Churches and the religions) with a type of parasitic virulence. While many contemporary theologians do adopt a wider spectrum of learning and experience, the perceived rootedness of the theological task within official religion, and its primary accountability therein, stultifies and, at times, totally erodes the cosmic and planetary engagement deemed to be primary and essential for the theologian of the future.

The underlying conviction here is one of honesty and realism. The complexity of contemporary life, and the evolutionary unfolding which makes that complexity necessary, requires a broad spectrum of wisdom and understanding to comprehend meaningfully what life is all about. The theologian needs to be the *catalyst* for this new quality of broad and inclusive wisdom. It is not a question of being an expert at everything, a human and intellectual impossibility. It is not about human expertise, but about the readiness to share and explore in the discerning context where the two or three (or more) are gathered in God's name.

6. *Relativity*. Guardians of orthodoxy, including some eminent theologians, consider relativism to be a dangerous and misleading ideology. Relativism evokes a number of fears, but primary among them is the perceived threat to religious dogmatism: that there is only *one* foundational truth to everything in life, one right way of understanding things, one true God. Consequently, all suggestions of diverse or multiple understandings are perceived to be a threat and are construed as undermining the essential truth and nature of reality.

Theologians of the future will cherish relativity as both a pathway to truth and an essential safeguard against self-deception and idolatry. In the pursuit of ultimacy, we are forever probing deeper meaning but never attaining the final answer. The orthodox conviction that God is the final answer is itself a construct of the human mind that we attribute to God. Perhaps the final answer is within the unfolding co-creative process of evolution itself, based on radical freedom and unceasing novelty. The faith-inspired theologian wants to *wait on* God for those deeper meanings that unfold as we engage creatively with the theological process of 'faith seeking understanding', a process that never does, and never should, cease from the call to probe the depths.

7. *Power.* This issue follows closely on the heels of the previous paragraphs. Theology has often been used – within and outside the Churches – as an instrument of patriarchal power and political oppression. And this will-to-power underpins the fear that considers relativism a real threat. It is not a threat to truth, but it is a threat to power.

The theologian of the future will come to the theological engagement as a servant endowed with and forever seeking that wisdom (sophia) which ultimately belongs to God, and not to us. A theologian with final answers is more likely to be promoting ideology rather than theology. The theological task is about *befriending* our co-creative God in the cosmic unfolding of life. The accountability is not just to a higher ecclesiastical or religious authority, but to the whole of the co-creative process in a discernment that will require the wisdom and attention not just of *one* but of *many* disciplines.

8. *World-based.* The wisdom and goodness of God should never have been relegated largely or exclusively to a 'spiritualised' realm called Church or religion. In fact, that dualistic construction of the sacred and secular is very much an invention of the age of religion and one we now need to abandon and discard.

More difficult to dislodge will be the *ideology* in which it is couched, a blind and compulsive set of convictions that states that God and all God's dealings with the world can only be what the formal religious system states they are. And despite some valuable work on religious hermeneutics throughout the twentieth century, the religion of fear still holds an unrelenting grip.

Meanwhile, the theologian of our time strives to be where the new spiritual ferment is struggling to unfold, in the lives of those people who encounter God on the fringes of creative thresholds (see, for example, Davis, 1997). This is a space which is not *post*-religion or *post*-Christian (as many scholars try to convince us) but rather one that seeks to *transcend* the narrow and ideological confines of the religion of power and the religion of fear. The new spiritual space is, in fact, deeply resonant with the liberation of the Christian Gospel and with the creative engagement of the New Reign of God at the heart of our world.

Endnotes

Chapter 1

1. As a theology student, I recall many derogatory comments about psychology and its threat to faith and religion. I have found those statements to be so unfounded I am still puzzled as to why any reasonably intelligent person would make them.

    My perception is that psychology does not stand in judgement over religion, but in helping to clarify our motives, attitudes and perceptions, it can render religion and religious behaviour more transparent and coherent to believers and non-believers alike. Precisely because the psychologist tries to access the inner realm of the psyche, s(he) is often in touch with emerging developments before specialists of other fields can even detect them.

    For instance, Wulff (1997) originally wrote his compendium of the psychology of religion in 1991 beginning with a chapter entitled 'Formal Beginnings', but when he revised the work in the second edition (1997), he added a new introductory chapter entitled 'The Psychology of Religion in a Changing World' (pp. 1–20). One section of that opening chapter is entitled: 'Spirituality: A Contemporary Alternative' (pp. 5–7), outlining sentiments and convictions almost identical with the contents of the present work. Often, it is the psychologist who names the *experiential dimension* of faith and religion with greater clarity, depth and wholeness of vision.

Chapter 2

1. Marshack's thesis is even more compelling in the light of another recent discovery, namely that much of the paleolithic era was one free of great global catastrophes, in which climate was moderate and food would have been available in abundance. For most of the time, it would have been unnecessary to resort to hunting.

Chapter 4

1. In alluding to exile as a Judaeo–Christian concept, writers have in mind the conquest of the Babylonians in 586/587 BCE. In fact, this is only the first of four great conquests of the Jews, the other three being those of the Medians, the Greeks and the Romans. The destruction of the temple in Jerusalem in 70 CE (by the Romans) is often perceived in

Rabbinic literature as a perpetuation of the original conquest of the Babylonians. (For more on this topic see Milikowsky in Scott, 1997, pp. 265–96.)

2. Ever since Mary Daly's denunciation of Christianity as a religion that fosters and promotes necrophilia – a culture of death (e.g. Daly, 1973, 1978) – feminist scholars have been seeking to re-envision the scriptural, theological and symbolic significance of the death and crucifixion of Jesus. Several motives drive this reappropriation, particularly the desire to undermine the tendency to scapegoat Jesus as the one who makes up for all our wrongdoing; also to integrate the death of Jesus into the larger project of Jesus' life and ministry, rather than focusing on the death and suffering in relative isolation.

    One of the emerging differences between *feminist* and *womanist* scholarship is precisely on this point. For womanist scholars (many of whom are black), the ability of being able to identify one's suffering with the crucified Jesus, thus making that suffering more tolerable and spiritually meaningful, is a central conviction many womanist theorists wish to safeguard. (See Emily Townes, 1993). Inevitably, this has consequences for the ensuing Christology.

Chapter 5

1. Contemporary proponents of the new physics, in conjunction with several religious commentators, identify reductionism as the great barrier to a more holistic understanding of reality. While I endorse this view, I am aware of the fact that some scientists consider reductionism to be the very process that helps to uncover ultimate truth. Consider the response of Douglas Hofstader in 'Reductionism and Religion', *Behavioural and Brain Sciences*, 3 (1980), p. 434:

    People have an instinctive horror of any 'explaining away' of the soul. I don't know why certain people have this horror while others, like me, find in reductionism the ultimate religion. Perhaps my lifelong training in physics and science in general has given me a deep awe at seeing how the most substantial and familiar of objects or experiences fades away, as one approaches the infinitesimal scale, into an eerily insubstantial ether, a myriad of ephemeral swirling vortices of nearly incomprehensible mathematical activity. This in me evokes a cosmic awe. To me, reductionism doesn't 'explain away'; rather it adds mystery.

Chapter 7

1. Drumming has an innate and ancient appeal to the human soul because according to O'Donohue (1997, p. 98)

    The first sound that every human hears is the sound of the mother's heartbeat in the dark waters of the womb. This is the reason for our ancient resonance with the drum as a musical instrument. The sound of the drum brings us consolation because it brings us back to that time when we were at one with the mother's heartbeat. That was the time of complete belonging.

2. There are several allusions in this book to *pre-patriarchal* ways of living and relating. In general I allude to the positive evidence, suggesting that the behaviour of our ancient ancestors often exemplified a collaborative and egalitarian set of values. Throughout the text, there are several references underpinning these observations.

    In particular, I want to counteract the widely held assumption, a cherished tenet of patriarchal consciousness, that everything we humans did before the 'age of civilisation' (usually dated as commencing about 3000 BCE) was primitive, barbaric, uncivilised and based on an intelligence that was instinctual and animal-like rather than genuinely human. I wish to suggest that this perception is largely, if not totally, based on a huge cultural projection whereby we humans use our ancient ancestors as scapegoats for those destructive behaviours we find so intolerable in ourselves. Instead of blaming ourselves, and taking more direct responsibility for *our* problem, we find a safe scapegoat to blame, one that exonerates us from having to do anything significant about it.

    While our ancient ancestors were certainly not perfect, and undoubtedly also exhibited destructive and violent behaviours, a growing body of palaeontological, anthropological and even archaeological research indicates that for the greater part we have been a species whose behaviour has been peaceful, creative and constructive for most of our time on Earth. Man, the violent savage, is very much a figment of the patriarchal imagination, one that is affirmed by most of the major religions! Not surprisingly, therefore, it is under the aegis of patriarchy that this conviction is haunting our world as a self-fulfiling prophesy. (More on this topic in Endnote 4, below.)

3. Anthropologists extensively agree that the shaman is the oldest known religious personality. (Because history tends to be written from a male perspective, we know relatively little about shamanesses; they may have been as widespread as shamans.) Shamans are known to have existed as far back as 20000 BCE and their primary mediating role was one of healing and the transformation of consciousness. Occasionally, feminist writers claim that priestesses pre-date priests by thousands of years; I am not aware of any evidence to support this view.

    The evidence to hand suggests that an official priesthood was unknown before 4000 BCE; it evolved around that time to bolster the male conquering campaign, validated by the patriarchal sky-God. Consequently, rituals related to sacrifice uniquely became the prerogative of priests, a precedent that continues to the present day.

    Theologically and spiritually, I suggest that a renewed understanding of priesthood really belongs to the ancient world of shamanism rather than to the patriarchally construed notion of priesthood. *Priesthood-for-power* is precisely what is making priesthood so problematic in contemporary religion.

4. How we interpret the origins and nature of human aggression, and the extensive cultural violence that accompanies it, is a topic extensively debated among scholars (e.g. Konrad Lorenz, Niko Tinbergen, Robert Ardrey, Desmond Morris and Rene Girard), most of whom agree that violence is innate to the human species as a dimension of the

fight/flight syndrome, or because of a competitive rivalry (mimetic desire) innate to the human condition. Currently, many scholars invoke the research of the French theorist Rene Girard, who claims that sacrificial violence is the universal foundation of every social order, in mythology, pagan religion, as well as in modern political order. To maintain some sense of social equilibrium, Girard maintains that humans have evolved a system of scapegoating in which acts of violence are carried out on randomly chosen victims.

Girard then goes on to suggest – and this is his appeal to scholars of religion – that it is only in the Judaeo–Christian religion that the nature and power of this scapegoating is both exposed and subverted, with Jesus serving as the supreme 'redemptive' scapegoat for all humanity (cf. Bailie, 1997 for a comprehensive elucidation).

I have several reservations about Girard's analysis. His understanding of violence is very much based on masculine perception which assumes as normative (and divinely sanctioned) the masculine will-to-power. To exert this power, life is construed as a series of vying forces for which the good v. evil dualism is foundational. In other words, a fundamental sense of conflict is built into life and evolution and, consequently, is innate to human beings. The feminist philosopher, Luce Irigaray, also criticises Girard on this point (cf. *Sexes and Genealogies*, 1993, pp. 73–88).

The philosopher Paul Riceour and theologian Gabriel Daly both make the point that most of the meaningless suffering (evil) in the world today is caused by us, humans. The meaninglessness of suffering, and the barbaric violence often accompanying it, is very much of our making. We widely assume that this has *always* been the case, and apparently Girard makes this assumption. But the more we unearth pre-patriarchal culture (before 10000 BCE), what comes to the fore is a culture of mutual co-operation rather than one of adversarial violence (some of which undoubtedly prevailed).

The evidence that substantiates how humans behaved over the past 10,000 years (less than five per cent of our time on Earth) is taken as normative for the 4.4 million years of our existence. Research from several different sources indicates that this naive, patriarchally validated assumption is no longer tenable. For a more holistic and systemic interpretation, see Wink (1992).

Chapter 10

1. Initially, Foucault envisaged six volumes on his treatment of human sexuality. Only one materialised. In the process of exploring the sexual mores of the ancient Greeks, he found himself drawn to address ethical questions, partly related to sexual matters but to other areas of morality as well. Apart from his introductory volume on human sexuality (Foucault, 1980), some pertinent observations are also made in *The Use of Pleasure*, 1985 and *The Care of the Self*, 1986.

2. In his commentary on Mark's Gospel, Ched Myers (*On Binding the Strong Man*, 1988, p. 75) refers to a purity ranking scale which would

have been widely known and used at the time of Jesus. The list reads as follows:

(1) priests;
(2) Levites;
(3) Isralites;
(4) converts;
(5) freed slaves;
(6) disqualified priests or the illegitimate children of priests;
(7) netins – temple slaves;
(8) mamzers – bastards;
(9) eunuchs;
(10) those with damaged testicles;
(11) those without a penis.

The reader will note that women are considered to be so impure that they don't even feature on the list. Little wonder that women's emancipation movements of all ages tend to denounce religion as a primary agent of oppression. Sadly, the oppression continues, even to our own time, as in the requirement of the Catholic Church that the ordination of women cannot even be *talked about* in official Church circles.

Chapter 11

1. Because of the restricted linear thinking we pursue in our current educational systems, our imaginations are unable to grasp time-spans that extend beyond a few hundred years. This intellectual homicide does untold damage to our progress as a human species and forces us – as a species – to spend most of our time in extreme ignorance. Today, we know that our species in its basic human form has been around for at least four million years; in our upright form (*Homo Erectus*) we have been around for at least two million years; and the 10,000 years we refer to is merely five per cent of that time. Is it not about time we began reclaiming the other 95 per cent (more accurately 99 per cent) of our unique human story?

Appendix 2

1. Evidence for this swing can be gleaned from a brief observation made in *The Tablet*, (21 November 1998, p. 1,539). It reads: 'A sign of the times from Ireland: All Hallows College in Dublin, which for nearly 200 years has sent priests especially to Australia and America, now has not a single clerical student. On the other hand, it has 550 lay people taking theology courses.'

Bibliography

Abraham, Ralph (1994), *Chaos, Gaia, Eros*, San Francisco: Harper-San-Francisco.

Abram, David (1996), *The Spell of the Sensuous*, New York: Vintage Books.

Aldredge-Clanton, Jann (1995), *In Search of the Christ-Sophia: An Inclusive Christology for Liberating Christians*, Mystic, CT: Twenty-Third Publications.

Bailie, Gil (1997), *Violence Unveiled*, New York: Crossroad.

Bales, Kevin (1999), *Disposable People: New Slavery in the Global Economy*, Berkeley and Los Angeles: University of California Press.

Barrow, John D. and Tippler, Frank F. (1986), *The Anthropic Cosmological Principle*, New York: Oxford University Press.

Begg, Ean (1985), *The Cult of the Black Virgin*, London and Boston: Arkana.

Boelen, Jean Shinoda (1984), *Goddess in Everywoman*, San Francisco: Harper and Row.

Boff, Leonardo (1995), *Ecology and Liberation: A New Paradigm*, Maryknoll, New York: Orbis Books.

Boff, Leonardo (1997), *Cry of the Earth, Cry of the Poor*, Maryknoll, New York: Orbis Books.

Boros, Ladislaus (1968), *In Time of Temptation*, London: Burns & Oates.

Brock, Rita Nakashima (1992), *Journeys by Heart: A Christology of Erotic Power*, New York: Crossroad.

Brown, Peter (1990), *The Body and Society: Men, Women and Sexual Renunciation in Early Christianity*, London & Boston: Faber and Faber.

Brown, Raymond (1966), *The Gospel According to John, 1-XII*, Garden City, NY: Doubleday.

Brueggemann, Walter (1993), *The Bible and Postmodern Imagination*, Minn.: Augsburg Fortress; London: SCM Press.

Cady, S., Ronan, M. and Taussig, H. (1986), *Sophia: The Future of Feminist Theology*, San Francisco: Harper and Row.

Capra, Fritjof (1982), *The Turning Point*, London: Fontana/Flamingo.

Ceruti, Mauro (1994), *Constraints and Possibilities: The Evolution of Knowledge and the Knowledge of Evolution*, New York: Gordan & Breach.

Childe, V. Gordan (1958), *The Dawn of European Civilisation*, New York: Knopf.

Christ, C. and Plaskow, J. (1979), *Womanspirit Rising*, San Francisco: Harper and Row.

Colinvaux, Paul (1980), *The Fates of Nations*, New York: Simon & Schuster.

Comblin, Jose (1998), *Called For Freedom: The Changing Context of Liberation Theology*, Maryknoll: Orbis.

Conkey, M. and Tringham, R. (1995), Archaeology and the Goddess: Exploring the Contours of Feminist Archaeology, in D. C. Stanton and A. J. Stewart (eds), *Feminisms in the Academy: Rethinking the Disciplines*, Ann Arbor: University of Michigan Press.

Conlon, James (1990), *Geo-Justice: A Preferential Option for the Earth*, San Jose, CA: Resource Publications Inc.

Corballis, M. C. (1992), On the Evolution of Language and Generativity, *Cognition*, Vol. 44, pp. 197–226.

Crossan, John Dominic (1995), *Jesus: A Revolutionary Biography*, New York: HarperCollins.

Cunningham, David S. (1998), *These Three are One: The Practice of Trinitarian Theology*, Malden, Mass. and Oxford: Blackwell.

Daly, Herman E. (1991), *Steady-State Economics* (2nd edn), Washington, DC: Island Press.

Daly, Herman E. and Cobb, John B. Jr. (1989), *For the Common Good: Redirecting the Economy Toward Community, the Environment, and a Sustainable Future*, Boston: Beacon Press.

Daly, Mary (1973), *Beyond God the Father* (new edn 1985), Boston: Beacon Press.

Daly, Mary (1978), *Gyn/Ecology*, Boston: Beacon Press.

Daly, Mary (1984), *Pure Lust*, Boston: Beacon Press.

Davies, W. D. (1974), *The Gospel and the Land: Early Christianity and Jewish Territorial Doctrine*, Berkeley: University of California Press.

Davis Claire (1997), 'Journey Across the Desert', *The Tablet*, 25 January, pp. 106–7.

Deacon, Terrence (1997), *The Symbolic Species*, London and New York: Allen Lane/Penguin Press.

de Wall, Frans (1989), *Peacemaking Among Primates*, Cambridge, Mass.: Oxford University Press.

Donovan, Vincent J. (1989), *The Church in the Midst of Creation*, Maryknoll: Orbis Books.

Douglas, Mary (1966), *Purity and Danger*, New York: Praeger.

Edwards, Denis (1995), *Jesus the Wisdom of God: An Ecological Theology*, Maryknoll: Orbis Books.

Edwards, James C. (1997), *The Plain Sense of Things: The Fate of Religion in an Age of Normal Nihilism*, University Park, PA: The Pennsylvania State University Press.

Ehrenreich, B. and English, D. (1972), *Complaints and Disorders*, New York: Harcourt Brace Govanovich.

Eisler, Raine (1987), *The Chalice & the Blade*, San Francisco: Harper & Row.

Eisler, Raine (1995), *Sacred Pleasure: Sex, Myth and the Politics of the Body*, New York: HarperCollins.

Eldredge, Niles (1985), *Time Frames: The Rethinking of Darwinian Evolution and the Theory of Punctuated Equilibria*, New York: Simon & Schuster.

Eldredge, Niles (1999), *The Pattern of Evolution*, New York: W. H. Freeman and Co.

Eldredge, Niles and Gould, Stephen J. (1977), Punctuated Equilibria: The Tempo and Mode of Evolution Reconsidered, *Paleobiology*, Vol. 3.

Ellis, Marc H. (1997), *Unholy Alliance: Religion and Atrocity in our Time*, London: SCM Press; Minn.: Augsburg Fortress.

Fedigan, Linda Marie (1982), *Primate Paradigms*, Montreal: Eden Press.

Ferguson, Kitty (1994), *The Fire in the Equations*, New York: Bantam Books.

Foucault, Michel (1980), *The History of Sexuality: An Introduction*, New York: Vantage Books.

Foucault, Michel (1985) *The Use of Pleasure*, New York: Pantheon Books.

Foucault, Michel (1986) *The Care of the Self*, New York: Pantheon Books.

Forrester, Duncan B. (1997), *Christian Justice and Public Policy*, Cambridge, England and New York: Cambridge University Press.

Fuellenbach, John (1995), *The Kingdom of God*, Maryknoll: Orbis Books.

Gadon, Elinor (1989), *The Once and Future Goddess*, San Francisco: Harper and Row.

Gimbutas, Marija (1974), *Gods and Goddesses of Old Europe*, London: Thames and Hudson.

Gimbutas, Marija (1982), *The Goddesses and Gods of Old Europe, 7000–3500 BC*, Berkeley: University of California Press.

Gimbutas, Marija (1989), *The Language of the Goddess*, London: Thames and Hudson.

Gimbutas, Marija (1991), *The Civilisation of the Goddess*, San Francisco: Harper and Row.

Goertzel, Ben (1993), *The Evolving Mind*, New York: Gordan & Breach.

Goldenberg, Naomi (1979), *Changing of the Gods*, Boston: Beacon Press.

Goodenough, Ursula (1998), *The Sacred Depths of Nature*, New York and Oxford: Oxford Univeristy Press.

Goodison, L. and Morris, C. (eds) (1998), *Ancient Goddesses*, London: British Museum Press.

Greenstein, George (1988), *The Symbiotic Universe*, New York: William Morrow & Co.

Grigg, R. (1995), *When God Becomes Goddess*, New York: Continuum.

Handy, Charles (1994), *The Empty Raincoat: Making Sense of the Future*, London: Hutchinson.

Hanegraaff, W. J. (1996), *New Age Religion and Western Culture: Esotericism in the Mirror of Secular Thought*, Leiden and New York: E. J. Brill.

Harding, M. Esther (1955), *Women's Mysteries Ancient and Modern*, London: Michael Joseph.

Harris, Errol (1981), *Cosmos and Anthropos*, London: Humanities Press International.

Hayek, F. A. (1982), *Law, Legislation & Liberty: The Mirage of Social Justice*, London: Routledge & Kegan Paul.

Henderson, Hazel (1988), *The Politics of the Solar Age*, Indianapolis: Knowledge Systems Inc.

Hessel, Dieter T. (1996), *Theology for Earth Community*, Maryknoll: Orbis Books.

Heyward, Carter (1989), *Touching our Strength: The Erotic as Power and the Love of God*, San Francisco: Harper.

Hodgson, Peter C. (1989), *God in History: Shapes of Freedom*, Nashville: Abingdon Press.

Hodgson, Peter C. (1994), *Winds of the Spirit: A Constructive Christian Theology*, London: SCM Press.

Hofstader, Douglas (1980), Reductionism and Religion, *Behavioural and Brain Sciences*, 3, p. 434.

Hume, L. (1998), Creating Sacred Space: Outer Expressions of Inner Worlds in Modern Wicca, *Journal of Contemporary Religion*, 13.

Hunt, Mary E. (1991), *Fierce Tenderness*, New York: Crossroad.

Irigaray, L. (1993), *Sexes and Genealogies*, New York: Columbia University Press.

Jantsch, Erich (1980), *The Self-Organizing Universe*, Oxford: Pergamon Press.

Jantsch, Erich and Waddington, Conrad H. (1976), *Evolution and Consciousness*, Reading, Mass.: Addison-Wesley.

Johnson, Elizabeth (1992), *She Who Is: The Mystery of God in Feminist Theological Discourse*, New York: Crossroad.

Johnson, Elizabeth (1993), *Woman Earth and Creator Spirit*, New York: Paulist.

Kahn, Herman (1976), *The Next Two Thousand Years*, London: Associated Business Programmes.

Kano, Takayoshi (1990), The Bonobos' Peaceable Kingdom, *Natural History*, November, pp. 62–70.

Kaufman, Gordon (1993), *In Face of Mystery: A Constructive Theology*, Cambridge, Mass.: Harvard University Press.

Keen, Sam (1994), *Hymns to an Unknown God: Awakening the Spirit in Everyday Life*, London and New York: Bantam Books.

Keller, Catherine (1986), *From a Broken Web: Separation, Sexism and Self*, Boston: Beacon Press.

King, Ursula (1989), *Women and Spirituality*, London: Macmillan Book Co.

King, Ursula (ed.) (1995), *Religion and Gender*, Oxford (England) and Cambridge (Mass.): Blackwell.

Kung, Hans (1997), *A Global Ethic for Global Politics and Economics*, London: SCM Press.

Lane, Belden C. (1998), *The Solace of Fierce Landscapes: Exploring Desert and Mountain Spirituality*, New York and Oxford: Oxford University Press.

Laszlo, Erwin (1993), *The Creative Cosmos: A Unified Theory of Matter, Life and Mind*, Edinburgh: Floris.

Laszlo, Erwin (1996), *Evolution: The General Theory*, Cresskill, NJ: Hampton Press Inc.

Laszlo, Erwin (1998), *The Whispering Pond: A Personal Guide to the Emerging Vision of Science*, Rockport (Mass.) and Shaftsbury (England): Element Books.

Leakey, Richard E. (1992), *Origins Reconsidered: In Search of What Makes us Human*, London: Abacus Books.

Lee, Dorothy A. (1999), Goddess Religion and Women's Spirituality, *Theology*, Jan.–Feb.

Leech, Kenneth (1997), *The Sky is Red*, London: Longman, Darton & Todd.

Leeming, David and Page, Jack (1994), *Goddess: Myths of the Female Divine*, Oxford: Oxford University Press.

Lemonick, Michael D. (1996), Ghost Hunters: Physicists set out to trap the most elusive particle in the universe, *Time* Magazine, 8 April, pp. 62–3.

Leroi-Gourhan, Andre (1968), The Evolution of Paleolithic Art, *Scientific American*, Vol. 218, pp. 58–70.

Lewis, C. S. (1964), *The Discarded Image*, Cambridge (England) and New York: Cambridge University Press.

Long, Asphodel (1997), The One and the Many: The Great Goddess Revisited, *Feminist Theology*, No. 15, May, pp. 11–29.

Mann, A. T. and Lyle, Jane (1995), *Sacred Sexuality*, Shaftesbury, Dorset and Rockport (Mass.): Element Books.

Marshack, Alexander (1991), *The Roots of Civilisation*, Mount Kisco, New York: Moyer Bell Ltd.

Matter, E. Ann (1985), The Virgin Mary: A Goddess?, in Carl Olsen (ed.), *The Book of the Goddess*, New York: Crossroad.

McFague, Sallie (1993), *The Body of God: An Ecological Theology*, Minn: Fortress.

Mead, Margaret (1929), *Coming of Age in Samoa*, New York: Morrow.

Merchant, C. (1992), *Radical Ecology*, San Francisco: Harper and Row.

Meyer, Ben (1979), *The Aims of Jesus*, London: SCM Press.

Mithen, Steven (1990), *Thoughtful Foragers: A Study of Prehistoric Decision Making*, Cambridge (Mass.): Cambridge University Press.

Mithen, Steven (1996), *The Prehistory of the Mind*, New York and London: Thames & Hudson.

Moore, Thomas (1992), *Care of the Soul*, San Francisco: Harper.

Moore, Thomas (1994), *Soulmates*, San Francisco: Harper.

Moore, Thomas (1998), *The Soul of Sex*, New York: HarperCollins

Morgan, Robin (1989), *The Demon Lover: On the Sexuality of Terrorism*, London: Methuen.

Morris, Brian (1998), Matriliny and Mother Goddess Religion, *Journal of Contemporary Religion*, 13, pp. 91–102.

Murphy, Ronald E. (1990), *The Tree of Life: An Exploration of Biblical Wisdom Literature*, New York and London: Doubleday.

Myers, Ched (1988), *On Binding the Strong Man*, New York: Maryknoll.

Nash, James A. (1991), *Loving Nature: Ecological Integrity and Christian Responsibility*, Nashville: Abingdon Press.

Nobel, V. (1993), *Uncoiling the Snake*, San Francisco: HarperSan Francisco.

Nouwen, Henri (1986), *Reaching Out*, New York: Image Books.

O'Connor, Kathleen M. (1988), *The Wisdom Literature*, Wilmington, Del: Michael Glazier.

O'Donohue, John (1997), *Anam Chara: Spiritual Wisdom from the Celtic World*, New York and London: Bantam Books.

O'Hear, Anthony (1997), *Beyond Evolution*, New York and Oxford: Oxford University Press.

Ó Murchu, Diarmuid (1997a), *Quantum Theology*, New York: Crossroad.

Ó Murchu, Diarmuid (1997b), *Reclaiming Spirituality*, Dublin: Gill & Macmillan; New York: Crossroad.

Ohmae, Kenichi (1995), *The End of the Nation State: The Rise of Regional Economies*, New York: Simon & Schuster.

Ornstein, G. (1990), *The Reflowering of the Goddess*, New York: Pergamon Press.

Panikkar, Raimundo (1973), *Trinity and the Religious Experience of Mankind*, Maryknoll, New York: Orbis.

Panikkar, Raimon (1993), *The Cosmotheandric Experience: Emerging Religious Consciousness*, Maryknoll: Orbis Books.

Pannenberg, Wolfhard (1977), *Theology and the Kingdom of God*, Philadelphia: Westminster Press.

Pirani, Alex (1991), *The Absent Mother: Restoring the Goddess to Judaism and Christianity*, London: HarperCollins.

Primavesi, A. (1991), *From Apocalypse to Genesis*, London: Burns and Oates.

Raphael, Melissa (1996), *Thealogy and Embodiment*, Sheffield: Sheffield Academic Press.

Rawls, John (1971), *A Theory of Justice*, Oxford: Oxford University Press.

Riceour, Paul (1977), *The Rule of Metaphor*, Toronto: University of Toronto Press.

Robb, C. and Harrison, B. (1985), *Making the Connections: Essays in Feminist Social Ethics*, Boston: Beacon Press.

Robertson, James (1998), *Beyond the Dependency Culture: People, Power and Responsibility*, London: Adamantine Press Ltd.

Rolheiser, Ronald (1979), *The Restless Heart*, Denville, NJ: Dimension Books.

Ross, Susan A. and Hilkert, Mary Catherine (1995), Feminist Theology: A Review of Literature, *Theological Studies*, Vol. 56, pp. 327–52.

Roszak, Theodore, Gomes, Mary E. and Kanner, Allen D. (eds) (1995), *Ecopsychology: Restoring the Earth, Healing the Mind*, San Francisco: Sierra Club Books.

Ruether, Rosemary Radford (1974), *New Woman, New Earth: Sexist Ideologies and Human Liberation*, New York: Seabury Press.

Ruether, Rosemary Radford (1980), Goddess and Witches: Liberation and Countercultural Feminism, *The Christian Century*, 97 (September).

Ruether, Rosemary Radford (1983), *To Change the World: Christology and Cultural Criticism*, New York: Crossroad.

Ruether, Rosemary Radford (1992), *Gaia and God: An Ecofeminist Theology of Earth Healing*, San Francisco: HarperSanFrancisco.

Sahtouris, Elisabet (1989), *Gaia: The Human Journey from Chaos to Cosmos*, London and New York: Pocket Books.

Schneiders, Sandra M. (1991), *The Revelatory Text*, San Francisco: HarperSanFrancisco.

Schussler-Firoenza (1983), *In Memory of Her*, New York: Crossroad.

Schussler-Firoenza (1994), *Jesus, Miriam's Child, Sophia's Prophet*, New York: Continuum.

Scott, James M. (1997), *Exile: Old Testament, Jewish and Christian Conceptions*, Leiden and New York: Brill.

Sheehan, Thomas (1986), *The First Coming: How the Kingdom of God Became Christianity*, New York: Random House.

Smolin, Lee (1997), *The Life of the Cosmos*, New York and Oxford: Oxford University Press.

Sorokin, Pitrim (1950), *Modern Historical and Social Philosophies*, New York: Dover Publications.

Spalding, Anne (1998), The Place of Human Bodiliness in Theology, *Feminist Theology*, No. 20, pp. 71–86.

Spretnack, Charlene (1982), *The Politics of Women's Spirituality*, Garden City, New York: Anchor Press.

Sprott, Julian C. (1993), *From Strange Attractors: Creating Patterns in Chaos*, New York: M & T Books.

Stanton, D. C. and Stewart, A. J. (eds) (1995), *Feminisms in the Academy: Rethinking the Disciplines*, Ann Arbor: University of Michigan Press, pp. 199–247.

Starhawk, (1982), *Dreaming the Dark*, Boston: Beacon Press.

Starhawk, (1988), *Truth or Dare*, San Francisco: Harper and Row.

Stone, Merlin (1976), *When God was a Woman*, New York: Dial Press.

Swimme, Brian and Berry, Thomas (1992), *The Universe Story*, San Francisco: Harper.

Taylor, Timothy (1997), *The Prehistory of Sex*, London: Fourth Estate Ltd.

Townes, Emily (1993), *A Troubling in my Soul: Womanist Perspectives on Evil and Suffering*, New York: Maryknoll.

Van Ness, Peter (ed.) (1996), *Spirituality and the Secular Quest*, New York: Crossroad.

Von Baeyer, Christian (1992), *Taming the Atom*, London: Viking.

Warner, Marina (1990), *Alone of All Her Sex: The Myth and Cult of the Virgin Mary*, London and New York: Quartet Books.

Weaver, Mary Jo (1989), Who is the Goddess and Where Does She Get Us?, *Journal of Feminist Studies in Religion*, 5/1, pp. 49–64.

White, Stephen K. (1988), *The Recent Work of Jurgen Habermas: Reason, Justice and Modernity*, Cambridge: Cambridge University Press.

Wilshire, Donna (1994), *Virgin, Mother, Crone: Myths and Mysteries of the Triple Goddess*, Rochester, Vermont: Inner Traditions International Ltd.

Wilson, Edward O. (1992), *The Diversity of Life*, London: Penguin Books.

Wink, Walter (1992), *Engaging the Powers: Discernment and Resistance in a World of Domination*, Minn.: Augsburg Fortress.

Wright, N.T. (1996), *Jesus and the Victory of God*, London: SPCK.

Wulff, David M. (1997), *Psychology of Religion: Classic and Contemporary*, New York: John Wiley & Sons.

Zohar, Danah (1994), *The Quantum Society*, London: Flamingo Books.

Zuckerman, Bruce (1991), *Job the Silent: A Study in Historical Counterpoint*, New York and Oxford: Oxford University Press